D1716318

Portraiture in Prints

Portraiture in Prints

by

Constance Harris

McFarland & Company, Inc., Publishers
Jefferson, North Carolina, and London

Library of Congress Cataloguing-in-Publication Data

Harris, Constance.
Portraiture in prints.

Bibliography: p. 311.
Includes index.
1. Portrait prints—History.   I. Title.
NE218.H37   1987   769′.42′09   85-43579

ISBN 0-89950-207-5 (acid-free natural paper) ∞

Printed in the United States of America.

McFarland   Box 611   Jefferson NC 28640

For Ted,
Marcia, Stephen, Shelley,
and
David

Contents

viii   Contents

Preface

I have assembled many outstanding illustrations for this book, trying to choose those which are most representative of their time and style. Many, but not all of the prints described, are reproduced here. Many of them will be familiar to admirers of prints; others, less significant perhaps, have been included because they either mark a new direction or serve as a pointed contrast to higher quality work. Some are here because I like them a lot.

Since art does not exist in a vacuum, but is a reflection of the various periods in which it flourished, I have included a generous amount of historical background, adding to the quantity with each succeeding century because I think that the times, manners, and styles themselves have increasingly helped to determine artists' goals as well as to influence the expectations of their subjects and the public. I also believe that most readers have a greater interest in affairs of the world closest to their own lives.

On a personal note, I would like to acknowledge the helpfulness of a number of people. Some fifteen years ago Dr. E. Maurice Bloch, then head of the Grunwald Center for the Graphic Arts at the University of California at Los Angeles, permitted me to audit and participate in his graduate seminar on portraiture in prints. Because I could find no single reference work that covered this topic, I began to keep notes for my own use and benefit. This book is an extension of that process of self-education. I have been generously aided by a superb teacher, Professor Ruth Weisberg of the Department of Fine Arts at the University of Southern California; by Orrel P. Reed, Jr., scholar, gentleman, and art dealer; by Ebria Feinblatt, erudite Curator Emeritus of Prints and Drawings at the Los Angeles County Museum of Art; and Dr. Bruce Davis, the very knowledgeable Associate Curator at the same institution. For their willingness to read parts of this manuscript and to share their expertise, I am very grateful. I am also most appreciative for the permission of numerous museums and collectors to reproduce their works of art.

My husband has put his time and love into every page, to say nothing of his editorial skills. His encouragement, as well as that of my mother, children, and friends, has been my particular joy.

"It seems to be a law of nature that no man ever is loth to sit for his portrait. A man may be old, he may be ugly, he may be burdened with grave responsibilities to the nation, and that nation be at a crisis of its history; but none of these considerations, nor all of them together, will deter him from sitting for his portrait."
Sir Max Beerbohm

Introduction

The Portrait, The Print

It is no longer the mark of a cultivated gentleman to hang portraits of prominent noblemen or scholars on the walls of his study, nor is his wife inclined to decorate her boudoir—if indeed she has one—with the likenesses of once famous ladies. Other than those of family or friends, if portraits are displayed at all in homes today, they are likely to be of movie or rock stars tacked up on the doors, ceilings, and walls of teen-agers' rooms. Yet there were periods in history in which both self-esteem and hero-worship reigned and portraiture flourished. At other times, over-riding philosophies or religious principles seemed to be incompatible with human distinctiveness, and portraiture was almost ignored.

A portrait is simply a pictorial representation of how one person has thought about another. It is the artist's opinion of his sitter, sometimes shared by that sitter and his friends, sometimes not. Portraits have fascinated people almost since the beginning of recorded art and have been the most widely used motif of all prints. For our purposes, beginning with the sixteenth century, they will be defined as the delineation of a real person whose identity is known, either drawn from life or transcribed from an original work in another medium, even though the artist may have used the model more as a study exercise than as a description of a specific individual.

What makes a portrait artistically worthy? If it is true that a man's face becomes what the man is, though he may try to mask it, then the great portrait is one which pierces that mask to convey tension, a feeling for per-sonality, a sense of the period, and the mood of the subject. It is helpful for us to know who the sitter is, but not essential, because it is the quality of the portrait's aesthetic and expressive interpretation, its use of har-monious proportions, and its juxtaposition of contrast and form that make it a distinguished work of art. Two eyes, a nose and a mouth can be drawn with the most consummate skill, precise likeness, and the most perfect indications of light and shade, but unless the artist can render a convincing presence, the portrait will not elicit an appreciative response.

Physical beauty alone rarely contributes to a portrait's excellence or significance. Some of the world's most interesting likenesses are of "imperfect" faces, often plain and no longer young. What the artist must convey is a probing interpretation of character and a vitality that evokes a strong response. The artist manipulates or transcribes each feature according to its capacity to establish the subject's feelings. The eyes are acknowledged to be the windows of the soul. They can indicate humor or pain, gentleness or intensity; they can be penetrating or merely observing, trusting or cynical, kind or cruel, friendly or remote. Artists have made countless variations on the theme of eyes, and if they are interested in the psychological aspects of the face, the eyes and the placement of the eyelids are likely to be the primary means of determining the expression. Immediacy and dynamism are expressed when the eyes turn away from the direction of the head; an animated functioning mind is most easily imparted when the sitter faces the viewer. The mouth is likewise a very suggestive feature — compressed or smiling, weak or decisive, grim or relaxed.

The portraitist takes into account the relative sizes, irregularities, and spacing of the features, and makes meaningful use of the bonyness of the nose, the fleshiness of the cheeks and jowls, the undulations and character of the tissues, bones, and skin. When the facial muscles, of which there are over forty, are in repose, very little emotion is registered. As they contract in various combinations, they become another medium through which communication is achieved. Once the artist has discovered the qualities of the various features, he must integrate them through the use of light and shadows into a unity that implies an inner life, something more than a disparate collection of parts within a contour line.

On the other hand, some portraits are not intended to be psychological studies at all, but serve instead as authority figures, commemorative images, fashion plates, or decorative art; in such cases, the hero's clothes, posture, and accoutrements also have a vital role. Suggestive backgrounds, the incorporation of symbols, inscriptions, and characteristic gestures also help to capture the sitter's distinctiveness.

The artist must give serious consideration to the technical means with which he fills the allotted space. The format might be tall, narrow, square, oval, or round. He may choose a balanced or asymmetrical placement, a close-up view or one set far back. He decides whether to use the head and shoulders alone or the full-length figure; he arranges horizontals and verticals, which tend to be weighty, or diagonals, which often suggest vitality and action.

Artists may represent people with likenesses as true as possible to reality or as far as abstraction can take them; now and then they express their own feelings more than those of their subjects. Portraits may be stylized, formal, relaxed, comprehensible or not, depending on the personality of the artist, his sitter, and the nature of the times. Most have been rather straightforward records or historical documents produced in order that one person might know who another was or how he appeared. Occasionally, portraits function as experiments in uncharted areas that are conscious rejections of past styles. In the twentieth century they have often been less recognizable, more difficult to understand, and sometimes too far ahead of public taste, although by now most of us have become accustomed to bare, spare, and obscure contemporary art that reflects the mechanistic computer world or embodies distortion and exaggeration. But regardless of style or period, our judgments are still based on the same criteria: We look for a fusion of those qualities, such as insight, intensity, artistic tastefulness or attractiveness of design, that enhance our spirit or affect our emotions.

The concept of originality carries special connotations in printmaking. Unlike drawings, carvings, or paintings, a print is *not* a unique work of art. By its nature it is capable of multiple impressions. In some cases, many thousands of the design were printed, differing only in minor variations or in the inked quality of their lines; but because each impression is presumed to be the result of the artist's hand and mind, each is considered an original print.

"Original" is also used with another meaning. It refers to designs created by the artist; reproductive prints are copies of those designs, done with more or less exactitude by someone else. Reproductive printmaking, particularly in portraiture, was very common before the nineteenth century, and was clearly regarded as valid on its own merits. Fine copies after fine prototypes have been made from the beginning of printmaking itself, and though they have been frequently denigrated, they should not be. John Buckland-Wright, a twentieth century printmaker and teacher, has described reproductive artists as "interpreters standing in relation to the originals much as musicians stand in relation to works of composers." No one denies that the more personal portrait prints of original artists such as Rembrandt, Van Dyck, or Picasso are rightly held in greater esteem, but each has its legitimate place. One problem that has risen in recent years is that sophisticated photomechanical processes, which permit high-quality replicas, are often improperly identified as originals, even though the designer of the work did not have anything to do with its making—he may in fact be long since dead.

Prints, as well as drawings, often are more personal and original expressions of the artist than are his paintings; his hand is more intimately revealed in his graphic work than in any other. Many of the greatest artists in the world have practiced printmaking; many have included portraits among their most inspired efforts. One reason printed portraits have had a special appeal is that, their size being typically small, their impact is particularly direct and immediate. The basic questions to be asked are, "Am I interested in this portrait?" "Does it evoke a sense of life?" and "Does it avoid the superfluous?" Connoisseurs or professional critics may have universally accepted answers. However, we will hope that the average person who knows nothing about art, but knows what he likes, may find after looking at enough portraits that the best examples will provoke his curiosity and capture his sympathy.

Chapter 1

Beginnings

Since very early times men have believed that they could achieve immortality by commissioning a portrait. Lasting fame often was conferred by artists as they handed down to posterity the face of a friend, a celebrity, or occasionally, themselves. Those less concerned with the remote future enhanced their immediate prestige with a likeness as true or as flattering as skill could produce or conscience allow.

For thousands of years artists have created faces heroic or weak, handsome or ugly, factual or idealized, drawn with contempt or deference, awe or wit. But whatever the purpose of the portrait it is to be expected that the artist have, above all, a lively and thoughtful response to his sitter. If the response is indifferent or lacks insight, then the portrait fails as art, and remains simply a replica, empty of character or vivacity. A. Hyatt Mayor, the late curator of prints at the Metropolitan Museum of Art, in his introduction to the museum's *Portraits and Masks*, said he chose the faces included after asking of each portrait, " 'Have you lived? Can you show us that you have loved, fought, hated, seen God, sneered, whimpered, exulted, plotted, bled?' If the artist had the skill to make his face say *yes*, we took it."

The first people to master this kind of expressive portraiture were the early Egyptians. When an unknown sculptor made a slate carving of King Mycerinus and Queen Kha-merer-Nebty forty-five hundred years ago, it was in the belief that their spirits would endure through eternity if those portraits lived on, and that the statue would be a link between themselves and their descendants. (Fig. 1) The artist concerned himself with their actual likenesses, yet gave them an idealized existence. He clearly understood the obsessive yearning for perpetual life that drove Mycerinus, along with his father and his uncle, to build the great pyramids, which were among the wonders of the ancient world. Although the typical stiff frontal treatment of the figures was intended to convey royal authority and divine power, what will be remembered as long as the stone survives is the appeal of their affectionate pose.

A thousand years later, in a more personal style, an anonymous artist sketched on limestone the profile head of Sen Mut, the Egyptian architect who said of himself, "I was the greatest of the great in the whole land." (Fig. 2) The portraitist was evidently aware that his first effort was lifeless and dull, and improved the overlapping design by adding a bit of a smile and slanting the eye, which, as usual, faces the viewer. Although most profile studies lose something in expression and vitality, this one clearly does not. Side views, outlining the face's most prominent features, have been thought to suggest nobility, capture the clearest resemblance, and provide an opportunity to delineate graceful contours.

Perhaps these are the reasons that the limestone bust of Queen Nefertiti, dating from 1372–1355 B.C., is most frequently photographed in profile. (Fig. 3) This extraordinarily beautiful sculpture, originally painted in flesh-like colors, as was all ancient statuary, was found in an excavated royal studio. The artist evoked an artistocratic appearance by slightly tilting up her head and elongating her neck; in its very simple realism it is a splendid and commanding image. Nefertiti was the wife of Ikhnaton, the king who adopted the worship of a single deity — the sun — thereby almost changing the course of Egyptian religious history. His radical ideas included a toleration of alternate art styles that were truer to nature and more expressionistic than the art of earlier periods. However, this permissiveness lasted only until the brief reign of his son-in-law, the boy-king Tutankhamen, whose priests forcibly reasserted the worship of plural gods and reestablished rigid postures and inflexible geometrical formulas in art.

The Egyptians never seemed to tire of their interest in portraiture; well-preserved likenesses, realistically painted in colored wax on wood, have been found in mummy wrappings dating from the second century A.D. when Egypt was under Roman domination. These faces have a typical Mediterranean appearance, with thick brows and dark eyes heavily outlined and shaded, somewhat similar to paintings found in Pompeii. The *Portrait of a Man* was no doubt drawn from life; the eyes look directly into our own, confronting us with a self-assertive steady gaze. (Fig. 4) The identity of these funerary figures is occasionally known. Their finely modeled features display a startling fidelity to nature, often with the troubled expressions of men who once lived and suffered.

The great classical Greek artists of the fifth and fourth centuries B.C. aimed at something quite different: representing the general and enduring rather than the momentary qualities of their subjects. Greek art precluded authentic portraiture since even when representing mortal beings, it was not based on reality but on ideal or dreamlike standards of physical beauty. The smooth and expressionless marble countenance of Aphrodite, goddess of love, is empty perfection, lacking the kind of human appeal and distinct personality that is found in Egyptian art. (Fig. 5) Not a hint of animation was permitted to suggest emotion or reveal intrinsic character. Both sides of the face were depicted symmetrically since any natural irregularities would have detracted from the dignity, balance, and serenity that were the quintessence of divine form. Yet the subtle half smile and

Left: Fig. 1. Anonymous. *King Mycerinus and Queen Kha-merer-Nebty II.*
Courtesy Museum of Fine Arts, Boston, Harvard University and Museum of Fine
Arts Expedition. *Right*: Fig. 2. Anonymous. *Sen Mut.* Courtesy Metropolitan
Museum of Art, Anonymous Gift, 1931 [31.4.2].

gentle tilt of her head imply a note of uncertainty and lend it validity and
temperament.

But the history of art is the history of change, and in the years after
the Greek Golden Age styles shifted away from abstract models to more
specific types. Whereas the Greeks thought of the head as an integral part
of the whole body, Roman artists after the second century B.C. concentrated more on the psychological aspects of the face, stressing individuality
and variety of expression, those elements which differentiate one man from
another. Realistic sculptures were based on death masks or plaster-casts
of living people, retaining every flaccid muscle and sunken feature as candid evidence of sickness or age. The marble head of the emperor Vespasian, who lived from 9 to 79 A.D., strikes the viewer either as strong or
hard; he was characterized by his enemies as "infamous and odious" and
by his friends as "upright and highly honorable." (Fig. 6) This trend
toward naturalism, often unflattering, continued into the second century
A.D., indicating that, at least in the world of art, Romans did not place
a great emphasis on conventional beauty, although they painted and gilded
their sculptures to make them as lifelike as possible.

After the official beginning of the Christian Church in 313, Second

Fig. 3. Anonymous. *Queen Nefertiti.*
Courtesy Staatliche Museum, Berlin.

Commandment injunctions against graven images prohibited human portraiture. In addition, men were taught to turn away from materialism and to lose themselves in the ideal of religious and spiritual devotion. In early Christian art, therefore, the uniqueness of a particular face or personality, like everything that was clearly mortal, became submerged in the mystery of the universal spirit. Individuality was less important once again, and for a thousand years the portrait all but disappeared. This otherworldly preoccupation continued throughout the Gothic period, although monasteries kept alive devotional and secular book production in which, on rare occasions, an illuminated miniature portrait of a church scholar or emperor was admitted.

Meanwhile, enormous changes were stirring in Europe. The intellectual world found its greatest impulse among Arab and Jewish philosophers, but in those cultures, too, portraiture was strictly avoided. In economic life the onset of capitalism undermined the feudal system as wealth and power shifted from landed estates to growing cities. Marco Polo began the travels that encouraged exploration of new worlds, and new philosophies were examined in the universities that were rising all over the continent. The Black Death destroyed half or more of Europe's population and much of its social and cultural order. Mighty kings as well as insignificant rulers of small principalities flourished at the expense of the weakened Holy Roman Empire, which, as has often been pointed out, was neither holy, Roman, nor an empire, but rather a loose association of Christian states. Lastly, the Church was seriously shaken by the existence of rival popes in France and Italy, and by humanist writers whose independent thinking challenged the corruption that infected the papacy.

Many people believed that the calamities around them were God's punishment for their sins, which they hoped to expiate by commissioning works of religious art and intruding their own figures as suppliants. With a reawakened interest in the individual, the portrait returned to take its place as a separate artistic element, sometimes in terms of the new secularism, as in tomb statues laid out on stone couches, and sometimes in the service of religion, as part of sacred paintings. An anonymous portrait of Richard II of England attended by his patron saints in the *Wilton*

Top: Fig. 4. Anonymous. *Portrait of a Man*. Courtesy British Museum. *Bottom Left*: Fig. 5. Anonymous. *Head of Aphrodite*. Courtesy Museum of Fine Arts, Boston, Francis Bartlett Collection, purchased of E. P. Warren. *Bottom Right*: Fig. 6. Anonymous. *Head of Vespasian*. Courtesy Musei Vaticani, Rome.

Fig. 7. Anonymous. *Wilton Diptych (Richard II with His Patron Saints)*. Courtesy National Gallery, London.

Diptych, c. 1395, represents him kneeling in humble petition to the Madonna and Child. (Fig. 7) Yet he is proudly clothed in gorgeous costume and crown and is further differentiated by being shown in profile; the only other member of the celestial group so pictured is the angel correspondingly placed for balance in the lower right corner of the adjacent panel. Although Richard is painted smaller than Mary, he is about the same size or larger than the rest of the heavenly host, suggesting that he regarded himself as worthy to mingle with holy figures. Savanarola, the fanatical Florentine spiritual reformer, bitterly opposed such displays of self-esteem and never accepted them as marks of devotion.

Nevertheless, as a wealthy class began to emerge in the fifteenth century, its members discovered that by supporting the arts they could flaunt their recently acquired positions in society and at the same time secure themselves a place in history at the hands of the best practitioners of the day. Before long the portrait artist again found himself in great demand, and he took the opportunity of shedding his anonymity, proudly signing his works, and not only painting the faces of the great worthies, but looking into a mirror and depicting his own.

The Renaissance unfolded in an environment of humanism where the importance of men in their relationship with each other, not just in their relationship with God, was recognized as significant. Now man was considered momentous in his own right, and not merely as a part of the Christian cosmos. Observant artists made critical distinctions between saintly faces, which were intended to induce worship, and the earth-born features of their human sitters. Naturalistic portraits, revealing inner thoughts and feelings, once again appeared.

But these were all unique works of art and could not provide for the many requirements of an expanding society. Multiple specimens of written or descriptive matter were necessary, especially for those who could not afford hand-decorated manuscripts or painted pictures. As more people participated in everyday affairs, there was a need for better methods of communicating and disseminating written information, as well as for illustrations in religious, scientific, and travel books. Of course, the possibility of distributing samples of one's likeness to family and friends must also have been an appealing idea. Fortunately, the manufacture of inexpensive paper coincided with ingenious technical breakthroughs. In about 1450 Johann Gutenberg invented movable type, making books far more accessible. He also made them readable by introducing oil-based inks, which provided sharp, clear lines.

But several decades before that, a method of producing multiple identical images had been developed, in which artists cut designs into wood and metal, inked, and pressed them onto paper. The print was born in the Western world, and the portrait soon became its most popular subject.

Chapter 2

The Fifteenth Century

By the first quarter of the fifteenth century inexpensive *reproducible* images were already available; by the last quarter, printed portraits were at the service of those important enough to commission them. Here and there, in those embryonic days of printmaking, even the unimportant occasionally joined their betters, sitting for artists who were just learning their trade. Portraits, however, were not the first kind of prints made, which was just as well, since the earliest woodcuts and engravings were crude and generally undeveloped; good portraiture had to wait for more skillful craftsmen.

Woodcuts, and soon after, engravings, appeared in books or were issued in single sheets for sale to pilgrims as souvenirs of visits to religious shrines, much as postcards are sold today. Few people knew how to read, and these didactic prints played a large part in the spiritual life of the people, who easily recognized the symbols, often decorated with colored stencils. These prints had only broad and simple outlines, but by the end of the century a system of shading with parallel or cross-hatched (densely criss-crossed) lines was developed, blending shadows towards the white of the paper in order to indicate various tones and textures; it was so well done that color was not longer considered necessary. Particularly in the small compass of most prints, color was too insistent and distracting; black and white had its own dramatic effectiveness.

It is generally believed that the earliest woodcuts came from the workshops of carpenters or manuscript illuminators in Germany. The artist either made his design on paper, which was then pasted on the surface of a plank, or drew it directly on the wood. Yet woodcuts generally do not look much like drawings. Their lines do not have the same free sweep, nor can their tonal gradations be as smoothly shaded. Their aesthetic charm lies in their bold and striking appearance, and their usefulness in an almost unlimited reproductive capacity. They were often cut by specialists who painstakingly used knives and gouges to remove everything but the lines that were to be printed, thus preserving the artist's original image. These raised designs impressed their marks on paper, very

8

much like an ordinary rubber stamp. Woodcuts were reinked and reprinted until the wood wore down. Some eighteenth-century blocks are known to have produced almost a million impressions.

Soon after the introduction of woodcuts, line engraving, which produced more tightly controlled images, was developed in south Germany by metalsmiths whose skills were very highly advanced. Engraving required great physical strength and a steady hand to push the sharply pointed tool, or burin, into and across the slippery metal (usually copper), incising V-shaped furrows below the surface of the plates. After a thin strip of metal, or burr, is gouged out, the rough edges (burr) are smoothed down. To create a print, ink must be rubbed into the grooves, the plate then wiped clean and rolled through a press along with dampened paper. The enormous crush of the rollers extracts the ink from the recesses, producing lines with a knife-edged ridge that print with great clarity and distinctness, as in an engraved business card. The metal plate is reinked for each subsequent impression. Early examples, of course, are the freshest; with continual use the metal begins to show wear and the recessed lines become shallower and less capable of holding ink. At that point, all the original sparkle and brilliance of the engraving are gone.

I. Germany

Only a few woodcuts from the period shortly after 1400 have survived, since they were mostly cheap throw-away items that were discarded when they got torn or dirty; most of those that remain had been tucked away in old books or pasted in boxes. The earliest dated print is of *St. Christopher*, 1423, or possibly the *Madonna with Four Saints*, 1418, although there are questions as to the authenticity of these dates.

With the advent of movable type at mid-century, literacy increased, and after about 1460 printed books with woodcuts appeared on the market and soon became cherished possessions. The pictures were often awkwardly drawn and provincial in appearance, lacking Italianate spatial qualities, but the books were generally affordable and frequently quite handsome. Their illustrations were visually well adapted to the accompanying texts, and because woodcuts are a relief process, their type-high blocks could be rolled through the presses simultaneously with the type for the written material. However, wealthier buyers still preferred elegant handwritten and hand-illustrated manuscripts, which continued to be produced in the monastic institutions where most artists received their training.

By 1475, woodcutting techniques had advanced sufficiently so that the forceful likeness of the Turkish art patron and conqueror of Constantinople Mohammed II, although flat and bordering on caricature, was relatively successful. (Fig. 8) Since portraiture was forbidden in the Moslem religion, Mohammed risked the displeasure of his people by sitting for artists whom he imported for just that purpose. Another very early

portrait woodcut was that of Bishop Friedrich von Hohenzollern, 1487, particularly interesting since it was printed (not painted by hand) in several colors, separate blocks of wood being required for each hue.

Because of the greater fineness of their lines, engravings had a greater appeal and were considered a step above the more primitive-looking woodcuts. Although there certainly were prior examples, the first dated engraving is from the *Passion of Christ* series, 1446, by an anonymous artist known as the Master of 1446. At least as popular as these holy figures were playing cards, both as woodcuts and as engravings. Considerable effort was devoted to an engraved set dating from 1461, using different suits from those with which we are familiar; according to tradition, Charles VII of France was the model for the King of Shields.

Unlike woodcuts, engravings are not compatible with letter-press because their lines lie below the surface of the plate. When they were included in books, a different press than that for typesetting was required, and they had to be bound in on separate sheets of paper.

In about 1480, an artist known as the Master of the Amsterdam Cabinet engraved a group of heads with individualized features, but the first true portrait engraver in Germany, known only as W♯B completed four plates between 1480 and 1485 which are almost certainly modeled after real people. The elaborate cutting of the dress and headpiece in one of these prints, *Head of a Young Woman*, quite obviously reveals its goldsmith origins. (Fig. 9) In relation to the size of the plate the head is rather too large, the eyes bulge unnaturally, and the shading is awkward. It is interesting to compare this plate with the earliest engraved self-portrait, that of Israhel van Meckenem and his wife, of about 1490. (Fig. 10) Again the heads are moved forward to the front plane and placed before the border. Like the W♯B print they are out of proportion to the narrow shoulders; in these Gothic holdovers there was not yet sufficient skill in drawing the body. But Meckenem, who left almost six hundred prints, was a cleverer technician than W♯B, and his heads are more finely engraved. The expression on his own face suggests self-absorption as well as the cunning required by a business man accustomed to living by his wits. The few years that separate these two prints show the rapid improvements that were being made in printmaking. While very few artists drew themselves before the second half of the sixteenth century, this plate enabled Meckenem to advertise himself as a qualified portraitist to an eager public. Self-portraiture was a relatively new artistic expression in which every effort was directed to the artist's knowledge of his own inner being. If the date of 1490 is correct, it precedes by three years what was probably the first painted self-portrait in Europe, in which Albrecht Dürer presented himself with both the natural uncertainty of a twenty-two year old and the novel Renaissance concept of the artist as a man of stature.

Opposite, left: Fig. 8. Anonymous. *Sultan Mohammed II*. Courtesy Staatliche Museum, Munich. *Right*: Fig. 9. Master W♯B. *Head of a Young Woman*. Courtesy Royal Print Room, Berlin.

Fig. 10. Israhel van Meckenem. *Portrait of the Artist and His Wife, Ida.* Courtesy National Gallery of Art, Washington, D.C., Rosenwald Collection.

The greatest engraver of the fifteenth century, about whom we fortunately have considerable information, was Martin Schongauer, a painter and printmaker who was strongly influenced by Netherlandish artists. (Dürer was familiar with his work and made a special trip to see him, only to arrive shortly after he died.) The elimination of excessive detail in Schongauer's later prints, as well as his sparkling clarity and ability to model forms, placed him well ahead of contemporary Gothic provincialism and identified him with the transition to the Renaissance. He had an extraordinarily delicate control over the burin and was gifted with originality and wit. From one of the parable stories in the Gospels he engraved a set of virgins, wise or foolish according to whether they remembered to carry enough oil for their lamps. The seductive half-figure of *A Foolish Virgin,* c. 1475–91, with its obvious sensuality and bold confrontation, hardly suggests sexual innocence, but it is almost certainly a portrait and was possibly influenced by Italian compositions. (Fig. 11)

By now we can already trace those qualities which were indigenous to German artists. A trend towards facial expressiveness, which developed out of the anxiety and agitation of medieval life, has persisted from the fifteenth century to the twentieth. German artists never tried to flatter their sitters. This alone divided their work stylistically from masters elsewhere. Although most early printmakers were clearly minor artists, technically

Fig. 11. Martin Schongauer. *A Foolish Virgin*. Courtesy National Gallery of Art, Washington, D.C., Rosenwald Collection 1958.

they were quite capable and their plates were crisp and well printed. Their systems of laying lines became the conventions which were accepted and further refined by Dürer and his followers. They laid the foundations for the more distinguished engravers of the next generation and conditioned the public to expect highly detailed and carefully shaded features that formed specific and often penetrating likenesses.

II. Italy

The cultural and intellectual capital of the western world was Italy. In spite of the wars and rivalries between the heads of the many political entities, it had a societal unity and cohesiveness unknown in Germany. Its dukes and doges sponsored the greatest development of art since the glory days of Greece. Although early Italian printmaking had its derivation in Germany, it assumed a classical rather than a religious orientation. Whereas the Bible was the first book to be printed in Germany, in Italy a less doctrinal influence was already felt in the first book we know of there,

Left: Fig. 12. Anonymous. *Paolo Attavanti. Right*: Fig. 13. Anonymous. *Bernardo Bellinzone.* Both figures courtesy Dover Publications, Inc.

a fourth century philosophical treatise by Lactantius Firmianus, a heathen convert to Christianity who was not very well informed about the Scriptures.

Possibly the first Italian portrait print was that of the author Paolo Attavanti, 1479, from a volume produced in Milan, a city particularly famous for books illustrated with woodcut portraits. (Fig. 12) The artist attempted to convey three-dimensional space, but he was not very successful in spite of the fact that the science of perspective was well advanced in Italian painting. Another Milanese example, dating from 1493, is more schematic than true portraiture. It depicts the writer Bernardo Bellinzone at his desk, and is interesting because its everyday setting and relaxed pose indicate the new secular approach to life. (Fig. 13) Leonardo da Vinci has been suggested as the artist, but as far as is known, he never attempted printmaking, experimental though he was.

In 1497 Boccaccio's popular *De Claris Mulieribus (Of Famous Women)* was issued in the large publishing center of Ferrara. Some of the clearly drawn woodcuts were taken from mythological sources or the Bible, but several were contemporary portraits that suggest specific personalities. According to William Ivins, Jr., a former curator of the Metropolitan Museum of Art, "its illustrations may be said to be the first collection of woodcut portraits of human beings as distinct from those of cigar-store Indians." In an earlier German edition of the book, one print, of a more intimate nature than portraiture, may have guaranteed its large sales. We learn from it that couples engaged in amorous activities wore no clothes, although the current fashion evidently required turbans or hats.

In Italy, where the Greek tradition was still very much alive, engravers were more concerned with idealized than with realistic portraiture. They recorded features without seeking intrinsic character. While this simplified style made for grandeur, their images seem impersonal, and while well-modeled, they suggest a quality of isolation in their calm and static appearance. This classicism was perpetuated largely through familiarity with the ongoing excavations of ancient Roman ruins. Florence was still the center of archeological interest as well as the home of the goldsmith craft, and the earliest prints there, dating from about 1461, naturally reflect antique grace and refinement, order, and unity. At first, contours were almost entirely drawn with a continuous line, but as greater printmaking skills developed, there was a noticeable increase in delicacy and spontaneity through the use of freer, broken outlines. However, although Italy produced supreme masterpieces in painting and sculpture, her best artists never specialized in printmaking as did Germany's, possibly because Italian taste ran more to monumental figures and large and colorful decorations needed to beautify her churches. Nor were Italians as successful as their northern colleagues in producing firm, vigorous prints. The tones of their impressions tend to be gray in contrast to the strong black and white of the Germans.

The engraving *Profile Bust of a Young Woman* has been attributed by some experts to Leonardo because of its sensitive "painterly" and rhythmic draftsmanship. (Fig. 14) (The artist's tool appears to have slipped and made an unintentional cut above the forehead, suggesting a hand unfamiliar with the burin.) However, the calligraphy is more typical of someone trained as an engraver, perhaps Zoan Andrea or Antonio Pollaiuolo. Some Florentine painters, such as Sandro Botticelli, seem to have had close working arrangements with printmakers who absorbed their highly polished styles. The anonymous Florentine engraving *Portrait of a Lady*, 1460–1465, with its incisive contour, lack of interior shading, and cool unapproachable appearance is a characteristic specimen. (Fig. 15) The elaborate headdress is indicative of its goldsmith origins, while the delicate mouth and chin suggest a particular individual. Like most Italian examples, these heads correspond well to the size of the plate and have a harmonious balance that even such a northern master as Schongauer was unable to match.

Classic design is also apparent in the *Man in a Fantastic Helmet*, from about 1470 to 1480. (Fig. 16) The anonymous Florentine engraver used close parallel lines to achieve his shading in low relief, whereas in the north, shadows indicated by cross-hatching produced a more sculpturesque effect. While the print's complex details were obviously derived from the goldsmith's highly convoluted flourishes, the clarity of the profile was borrowed from the painting styles of Andrea del Verrocchio and Pollaiuolo. Such headpieces, incidentally, were frequently designed by Leonardo, among others, to be worn in pageants that were popular diversions at that time.

Printmakers have always taken some of their compositions and stylistic techniques from contemporary painters; two early examples will suffice here. Jan van Eyck's *Man in a Red Turban*, 1433, possibly a self-portrait and surely an unforgettable Flemish masterpiece, was perhaps the

Top: Fig. 17. Jan van Eyck. *Man in a Red Turban*. Courtesy National Gallery, London. *Bottom*: Fig. 18. Pierro della Francesca. *Federigo da Montefeltro*. Courtesy Uffllizzi Museum, Florence.

Opposite left: Fig. 14. Anonymous. *Profile Bust of a Young Woman*. Courtesy British Museum. *Center*: Fig. 15. Anonymous. *Portrait of a Lady*. Courtesy British Museum. *Right*: Fig. 16. Anonymous. *Man in a Fantastic Helmet*. Courtesy National Gallery of Art, Washington, D.C., Rosenwald Collection 1943.

first painted portrait since ancient Egyptian times to show a sitter openly and naturally contemplating the viewer. (Fig. 17; see also Fig. 4) The newly developed oil paint technique and the three-quarter view contribute to its very realistic presence. This type of pose, painted at close range and combining the accuracy of likeness that is possible in the full face with the precision of the profile view, has remained a staple portrait design. Van Eyck's delicate contouring and careful handling of features, the natural use of highlights and shadows to accent details, and the spaciousness around the head to make the picture appear uncramped, all had a great influence in northern Europe and soon took root in Dürer's paintings and prints.

Piero della Francesca, one of the few Italian painters who didn't recoil from the imperfect and inelegant, also had a seminal role in portrait engraving. After about 1470, when the knowledge of oil painting moved south, he caught a wonderful likeness in the profile portrait *Federigo da Montefeltro*, in which the duke's moles and broken nose were prominently displayed. (Fig. 18) It is one of the earliest in a long line of great Italian portraits, and is typical in showing only the head and shoulders. Federigo exists not only as a symbol of authority and political power but as a living being, with his large head dwarfing the Urbino landscape over which he ruled. The painting's clear lines and general simplicity appeared fifty years later in the engravings of Marcantonio Raimondi.

Much of what passed for artistic style, particularly in Italy, emanated from the theories of Leon Battista Alberti, which influenced painters and printmakers in the second half of the fifteenth century and later. Alberti was a remarkable example of the Renaissance man, successfully active as a writer, papal secretary, sociologist, educator, architect, politician, religionist, animal behaviorist, inventor, and city planner. He believed in the classical ideal of selecting only the most beautiful in nature. Since most people, such as the Duke of Urbino, were not as beautiful as Alberti might have wished, Italian portraiture was somewhat handicapped by his rather narrow strictures. He also insisted on the merits of high relief to the derogation of other styles. "I shall praise those faces," he wrote, "which seem to project out of the picture as though they were sculptured, and I shall censure those faces in which I see no art but that of outline."

But some artists were unwilling to subject their works so completely to a single theoretical system, and prominent painters such as della Francesca developed their ideas independently or in defiance of the classical ideals of facial perfection. They turned to the study of anatomy in order to achieve valid likenesses and a surer indication of personality. Possibly some of them already knew the importance of suggesting the many muscles around the eyes, mouth, and forehead that control facial expression and psychological immediacy. It was their experimental work which prepared the way for the realistic portraiture developed to a high level of excellence by sixteenth century Italian printmakers.

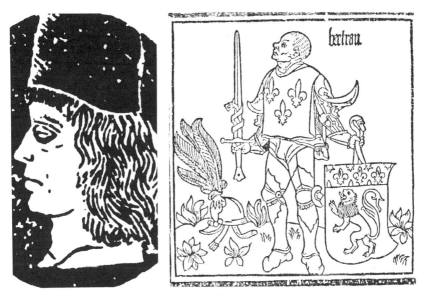

Left: Fig. 19. Anonymous. *John of Westphalia*. *Right*: Fig. 20. Anonymous. *Bertrand du Guesclin*. Both figures courtesy Dover Publications, Inc.

III. The Netherlands

The Netherlands was an important book publishing center, but did not yet have the caliber of printmakers in Germany or Italy. Printers there occasionally used their own likenesses as printer's marks in books issued between 1475 and 1484. The small cameo-like woodcut profile of John of Westphalia (Fig. 19), and a similar one of his brother Conrad, though not typical of such devices, are possibly the first portraits of known, ordinary people, and reveal the Renaissance notion of self-worth, regardless of political or social status.

IV. France

France, too, has a long tradition of printed books, but not of fine prints. Once in a while an illustrated portrait of an author was used as a frontispiece, showing him writing a manuscript or offering it in homage to royalty. Occasionally a portrait seems to have been made for no other reason than to honor a hero: the woodcut based on a lifetime portrait of a fourteenth century warrior Bertrand du Guesclin appeared in Abbeville in the book *Le Triomphe des Neuf Preux* (*The Triumph of Gallant Knights*), 1487, and showed him wearing his armor and a rather truculent expression. (Fig. 20)

These were difficult times in Europe, seething with violence, corruption, and economic ferment. Yet the fifteenth century artist carried on his work despite the stresses and turbulence around him. Knowledge increased vastly and information was widely disseminated, propelled by the invention of movable type and the ability to print what William Ivins has called "exactly repeatable pictorial statements." Substantial numbers of the expanding middle class were thereby able to educate themselves and participate in the Renaissance. They developed global commercial enterprises and bankrolled the fleets that hauled cargoes of salt, wines, furs, grains, precious metals, and above all, wool from one busy port to the next. Europe began to change from an agricultural civilization to one based on trade and industrialization. Civil authority and the control of wealth gradually passed from the Church to secular aristocratic families. While these advances helped to modernize society, they also caused radical disruptions in daily life, resulting in polarization and unease in the religious world as well as political and social upheavals among the general public.

In 1492 Europe began its overseas acquisitions while centralizing and strengthening its monarchies. By 1500 the horrors of the plague had subsided, the Hundred Years' War between England and France had ended, and Joan of Arc had burned. The Church, whose grim hold on men's imaginations was almost absolute at the beginning of the century, was being resisted at its end; it could no longer maintain religious unity, nor could it choke off vexing questions regarding its temporal or nonspiritual role. The final rupture was partly attributable to the books and printed pictures that spread information of its improprieties. Although attempts at reform had been made periodically, the scandals were too deeply imbedded and too widely known to be surmounted. The stage was set for the Reformation as Europe turned the corner into the next century.

Yet in spite of confusion and agitation, a climate of optimism defied the times and created a surge of art in Italy that has persuaded posterity that man had indeed experienced and explored his own rebirth. The Renaissance soon moved north, spearheaded in part by woodcuts and engravings. Northern printmakers adapted them to their own taste and went on to invent the great technical advances that dominated the art for the next hundred years.

Chapter 3

The Sixteenth Century

Life for most people in the sixteenth century was vexatious and grim. War, pestilence, and religious convulsions absorbed their strength and ravaged their land. However, growing communities were slowly turning away from an agricultural base, and with the spread of commerce resulting from the explorations and colonizations of the New World, the old local feudal system broke down. As central authority increased, nationalism and expansionism emerged in many parts of Europe. Northern Italy, which had been under French domination, was invaded by the Spanish, who substituted one style of tyranny for another. In Rome a great plague flared up and overwhelmed the population. Before the city could recover, it was sacked in 1527 by Charles V leading Spanish and Protestant German armies. (See Fig. 34) The disaster caused a terrible loss of lives and an incredible destruction of books and works of art. Although Charles was a staunch Catholic, in his efforts to overcome what he considered the immorality of the clergy, his troops, in eight brutal days, killed scores of priests and nuns, lodged their horses in St. Peter's Cathedral, and used the Vatican as their military headquarters. In his drive for control of Europe, he obstructed the consolidation of Germany and contributed to the fragmentation of Italy. As a result, both countries lagged behind in the development of nationhood until almost the twentieth century.

The Spanish grip extended to the Low Countries under the rule of Charles' son, Philip II, who was more repressive than his father, particularly in the imposition of taxes and the persecution of heretics. The Protestant north (Holland) and the Catholic south (Belgium) responded in 1567 with an uprising that lasted over forty years, although north and south soon were fighting against each other (the south recognized Philip, but insisted on important areas of autonomy). After Philip's initial victories, he lost his armada in 1588 to stormy weather and the superior maneuverability of the English fleet, and with that, his hopes for a Spanish conquest and Catholic domination of Europe.

When Francis I came to the French throne in 1515 he was every inch a splendid fellow—tall, charming, athletic, twenty years old. Unfortunately, he involved his country in a series of mostly profitless wars against his archrival, Charles V, and arranged for a system of loans that undermined the French economy for generations. To his credit, however, he provided patronage to humanists and artists and honored Leonardo da Vinci in his last years. According to the not always reliable Giorgio Vasari, who wrote a book on the lives of Italian painters, Francis held the old man in his arms when he died; for this, much may be forgiven.

As the century progressed in France, so did Protestantism, gaining strength in spite of frequent repression until 1562, when mutual hatred led to a series of religious wars which were to last forty years. Under the leadership of Admiral Gaspard de Coligny the Protestants won occasional reprieves, but they were thwarted by his murder at the massacre of St. Bartholomew in 1572. (See Fig. 39) The bloodletting was instigated by the ruthless queen mother Catherine de Medici, who feared losing political control of her weak son, Charles IX, to Coligny. For twenty-five more years the image of France was muddied by the slaughter of thousands of Huguenots. Eventually, the Protestant Henry IV, a capable politician and systematic administrator, brought the religious dilemma to an end by converting to Catholicism and granting what turned out to be an often perfunctory tolerance to the Protestant population. (See Figs. 46, 55) His efforts resulted in prosperity and peace for France and his own assassination.

England was Catholic until Henry VIII was excommunicated for marrying Anne Boleyn in defiance of the pope's refusal to grant him a divorce; under the reign of their daughter, the Protestant Elizabeth, England experienced its greatest cultural development. (See Figs. 52, 53) The religious status quo was carefully balanced, marred by occasional revolts in the northern and western parts of the country, and by a more serious Catholic rebellion in Ireland. As queen, Elizabeth, in spite of her desire to provide an heir to the throne, rebuffed a dozen of Europe's royal bachelors eager for a political alliance, if not a romantic union. After the rout of the Spanish Armada, the country expanded its commercial trade, but stepped up the persecution of its schismatic Puritans, who then emigrated to Holland and America. Towards the end of her life Elizabeth wistfully looked back: "To be a king and wear a crown," she said, "is a thing more glorious to them that see it than it is pleasant to them that bear it."

The troubles in Germany were largely philosophical and theological. Erasmus encouraged humanism in the belief that through changes within the Church the Protestant split might be prevented. (See Figs. 27, 28) Luther rebutted the argument that the Church was capable of moral, economic, or political self-reform. (See Figs. 31, 32) A collision resulted between those who wished to maintain unity and those who demanded the creation of a new denomination. Luther and other Protestants such as Calvin led the Reformation away from Catholicism; Erasmus and his followers remained loyal to it. By mid-century the conflict had hobbled German vitality and helped shift concerns such as art and humanism to countries which, in the next generations, were to prove more hospitable.

This receptive atmosphere was partially brought about by the Catholic Counter-Reformation as expressed in the Baroque movement, in which artists responded to Church pleas for greater discipline in art through a renewed sense of communication, naturalism, and passion in their works.

But the sixteenth century should be remembered for the glory of its culture as well as the burdens of its political and religious history. The Renaissance art of Leonardo, Michaelangelo, Raphael, Dürer, and a thousand brilliant painters, sculptors, architects, and craftsmen dominated not only its own time, but the art of the next three hundred years. Music was a great solace to the people; kings as well as merchants composed and sang as though armies were not dying in the field. Organ and lute soloists were sure of a welcome wherever they traveled, and were often accompanied by singers and dancers to the delight of both the royal courts and the humbler commoners.

It was a century of unsurpassed storytellers — Shakespeare in England, Rabelais in France, and Ariosto in Italy — among a plenitude of poets and dramatists all over the continent. (See Fig. 89) Great chateaux and palaces were built in the Loire Valley, at Fontainebleau and at Hampton Court, that desperate and futile last-gasp gift to Henry VIII from Cardinal Wolsey.

It was a period like many others history has witnessed, of splendor and prosperity coexisting with inglorious war and degrading squalor. Classical scholarship and theological dogma struggled for man's intellect and soul. The temporal claims of the Church, no match for Europe's rising chauvinism, clashed with the religious faith of sincere priests and pious laymen.

It was a frightening and wondrous age.

I. Germany

By the beginning of the sixteenth century it was clear that an intellectual class was emerging in Germany and the Netherlands under the influence of humanists such as Erasmus of Rotterdam, and eroding or contesting the powers of religious authorities. In 1517, when the monk Martin Luther broke with Catholicism, he decried the cult of the Madonna and the role of the saints as intercessors between man and God. For Protestants this meant, among other things, the abrupt end of the most popular subjects in art — the lives of the saints and the Virgin. People looked closely at the paintings around them and equated them with the luxury of the papacy they abhorred. Calvinists in particular questioned whether there should be any role at all for art, whether the simplicity they demanded of their church was not fundamentally in conflict with the gorgeous colors and opulence of Renaissance painting. In parts of northern Europe even some Biblical themes no longer were acceptable, and artists had to explore other topics if they were to continue their work. The prosperous lay community replaced the Church as patron of the arts and commissioned nonreligious works suitable for private homes, such as prints, easel paintings, and illustrated books. So we find, after about 1520, intellectuals, Protestants, and those with secular interests looking with fresh eyes at nondevotional art: landscape, genre, and the portrait.

Portraiture thus became an important element in European art because of Protestant prohibitions and the rise of an influential bourgeoisie that had the necessary means and leisure to aggrandize themselves. An interest in art also spread among the many legal, financial, and diplomatic advisors who were necessary for the expanding business of the community. For this growing middle class the Church no longer was the principal avenue for upward mobility, nor was it perceived as the sole arbiter of philosophic or artistic matters. People began to trust their own judgment as to what constituted proper subject material and felt free to choose mundane works for their homes. They dared to adopt the dress and deportment of the aristocracy, and, as self-confident sitters, sought out artists who previously had limited their talents to the high-born and royal. Portraiture, which had been of relatively minor interest, was suddenly in vogue among the socially prominent and the socially hopeful.

It was from Germany—that most Gothic and intensely emotional milieu—that one of the greatest painters and printmakers in the world emerged. Albrecht Dürer—that most Gothic and intensely emotional artist—was to revolutionize the graphic arts and elevate printmaking from negligible to major artistic significance. He not only invented subtle new engraving techniques that rendered textures realistically and produced a luminous or silvery quality, but also introduced creative ideas and innovative compositions. He brought about an exchange of northern and Italian styles as a result of his travels from Nuremberg to Venice and the Low Countries. These visits were of monumental importance in the history of art, since he took with him the flagging clichés of the Middle Ages and returned with the knowledge and attitudes with which to launch the Renaissance in Germany.

From the Italians he acquired a somewhat freer and less linear approach, a greater sense of space, proportion, and simplicity, and a feeling for gradations of light in his shadows, though he never learned how to indicate distances well. He helped to reestablish the notion that the function of art was not necessarily to depict man as the personification of some ideal, nor simply to record his obvious physical appearance, but rather to examine him with understanding and to set down the truth. Although his heads conformed to a system of classical proportions, he taught his own generation how to endow a fixed and unmoving image with the appearance of mental capacity, animation, and the illusion of an actual presence. His success may be measured against the countless numbers of dull, static portraits that fail in these basic requirements. Not until Rembrandt's day was the ability to enter into the emotions of another personality so fully revived again.

Dürer was trained as a goldsmith by his father and learned print-making as an apprentice in the workshop of Michael Wolgemut. He painted his first self-portrait in 1493 with tentative self-satisfaction and again five years later as master of his world. One might think that the chief interest of the young dandy in the latter painting was his silk and tassels and golden curls. But Dürer was not simply recording a fashion plate. The face is calm and intelligent; the eyes are already knowing and wary, ingeniously highlighted with reflected light to give the portrait its expressive reality. The half-figure occupies most of the canvas and is brought very far forward as though to help the viewer take in every splendid detail.

Towards the end of his career Dürer took up the study of portraits on wood and copper. He was one of the first artists to devote himself to the human model, having all his life drawn and painted many of the people he knew, from the most casual of acquaintances to the emperor himself. He printed eight portraits, six on copper, two on wood. None were of himself, although the man dressed in an oriental costume in his landscape etching *The Cannon*, 1518, has been identified by some scholars as the artist. His first engraved portrait, in 1519, was of Cardinal and Imperial Chancellor Albrecht of Brandenberg, a widely read humanist who encouraged intellectuals, such as Dürer, to travel to Italy. (Fig. 21) He played an unsuspecting role in Christian history when he appointed a Dominican friar named Johann Tetzel as his agent to solicit contributions from the townspeople in exchange for indulgences or pardons offered by Pope Leo X. The money was allegedly intended for the completion of St. Peter's Basilica in Rome, but actually it went into the chancellor's pockets to finance the purchase of a higher office for himself. When Martin Luther was asked to corroborate the claims made for the indulgences, he not only refused, but wrote out a list of ninety-five theses objecting to many existing Church practices, and on October 31, 1517, tacked them to the door of the Castle Church in Wittenberg. At that moment the Protestant Reformation began, although no one, including Luther himself, could have guessed the significance and consequences of that protest. With a reckless audacity Luther sent a copy of the theses to Albrecht, who was an archbishop at the time.

When a cardinalship became his, Albrecht, aged twenty-nine, decided to have his portrait engraved and distributed throughout his jurisdiction as a symbol of his political and spiritual power. It was delicately modeled, though unmercifully drawn with drooping flesh and arrogant eye. Dürer sent him two hundred impressions and received in return two hundred gold guilders and twenty arm's-lengths of damask. Whatever its success as propaganda, it is perhaps Dürer's finest and most effective portrait engraving, although the coat of arms and list of titles add nothing to its artistic value. The excessive detail typical of the north has been avoided and the tones kept within a narrow range so that all the emphasis remains on the strong face.

In 1523 Dürer sent Albrecht five hundred copies of a second engraving, *The Large Cardinal*, as a bookplate for his collection. (Fig. 22) Here

ALBERTVS·MI·DI·SA·SANC
ROMANAE·ECCLAE·TI·SAN·
CHRYSOGONI·PBR·CARDINA·
MAGVN·AC·MAGDE·ARCHI·
EPS·ELECTOR·IMPE·PRIMAS·
ADMINI·HALBER·MAR·CHI·
BRANDENBVRGENSIS

M·D·X·X·IIII
SIC·OCVLOS·SIC·ILLE·GENAS·SIC·ORA·FEREBAT·
ANNO·ETATIS·SVE·XXXIIII

ALBERTVS·MI·DI·SA·SANC·ROMANAE·ECCLAE·TI·SAN·
CHRYSOGONI·PBR·CARDINA·MAGVN·AC·MAGDE·
ARCHIEPS·ELECTOR·IMPE·PRIMAS·ADMINI·
HALBER·MARCHI·BRANDENBVRGENSIS·

Top: Fig. 21. Albrecht Dürer. *Albrecht of Brandenberg*. Private Collection.
Bottom: Fig. 22. Albrecht Dürer. *The Large Cardinal*. National Gallery of Art,
Washington, D.C., Rosenwald Collection.

· CHRISTO · SACRVM ·
· ILLe ·Dei· VERBO· MAGNA· PIETATE· FAVEBAT ·
· PERPETVA · DIGNVS· POSTERITATE·COLI ·

· D· FRIDR· DVCI· SAXON· S· R· IMP·
· ARCHIM· ELECTORI ·
· ALBERTVS· DVRER· NVR· FACIEBAT ·
· B· M· F· V· V ·
· M · D · XXIIII ·

BILIBALDI· PIRKEYMHERI· EFFIGIES ·
· AETATIS· SVAE· ANNO· L· III ·
VIVITVR· INGENIO· CAETERA·MORTIS·
· ERVNT·
· M· D· XX · IV ·

Top: Fig. 23. Albrecht Dürer. *Frederick the Wise, Elector of Saxony.* Courtesy Staatliche Museum, Berlin. *Bottom:* Fig. 24. Albrecht Dürer. *Wilibald Pirkheimer.* Courtesy Staatliche Museum, Berlin.

Dürer portrayed him in sculpturesque relief as though on an ancient medallion. Because it is in profile, some of the personality of the sitter is lost, although it, too, is a forceful image. (A group of eleven etched profile portraits, including those of Luther and Erasmus made earlier in the century in Augsberg, Germany, by Daniel Hopfer and his son, Jerome, may have suggested the pose.)

Another of Dürer's patrons was one of the leading humanist supporters of the Reformation, Frederick the Wise, Elector of Saxony. (Fig. 23) After Archbishop Albrecht instructed Tetzel to turn the papal indulgences into cash, Frederick forbade their further sale in the territories over which he ruled. When those orders were flouted, Luther took up his pen and brought on the Reformation. Dürer admired Frederick, who protected Luther from the fury of the pope, and engraved his portrait in 1524, representing him as a hard and imperious man. The hat, the beard, the fur collar, all wonderfully engraved, compete for attention, but the piercing eyes and fat, homely face of the elector dominate the picture.

Wilibald Pirkheimer was Dürer's closest friend, a well-known business man, art lover, and philosopher, whom Erasmus called the "chief glory of Germany." (Fig. 24) In 1524, as a gift bookplate for his large library, Dürer engraved his portrait at the age of fifty-three, concentrating on the character of the fleshy, jowly countenance and bulging eyes. The head almost fills the sheet, each stroke describing the fullness of the face and the modeling of its features. There isn't a line that could be removed without destroying the vitality of the whole, a criterion which, according to Alberti, was the quintessential test of beauty. However, since Dürer never completely lost his Gothic stiffness, his work tended to be compressed and cramped; Alberti would have insisted on greater classical ease than Dürer's often awkward lines. But awkward or not, Dürer developed and extended the standards which influenced the next generation of artists — finer gradation of tones that yield softer and more painterly treatments, discrimination between different textures and color values, and greater variety in the cross-hatched and parallel lines.

Although Dürer never met Luther, in 1526 he made a brilliant portrait of an important member of his circle, Philip Melanchthon, a professor of Greek characterized by Luther as a man who "walks softly and silently, tills and plants, sows and waters with pleasure, since God has gifted him richly." (Fig. 25) Elsewhere, however, in a less kind moment, Luther described him as a "scrawny shrimp." Melanchthon won fame with his succinct analysis of the new Protestant religion, coming down very hard on those who deviated from what he believed was God's word. The inscription below the portrait reads, "Dürer could depict the features of the living Philip, but the skilled hand could not depict his mind." In another portrait of Philip, 1530, by a contemporary engraver, Master I.B., the great reformer is presented in a more conventional, straightforward manner. (Fig. 26) Dürer caught the soul of the fanatic; Master I.B. missed it completely.

In 1526 Dürer also engraved the portrait of Erasmus of Rotterdam, which he based on his own charcoal life drawing sketched in Flanders in 1520-21, and on works by Quentin Massys which Erasmus sent him to refresh his memory. (Fig. 27) Erasmus was a scholar and philosopher, a critic of the Church who nevertheless remained a sincere Catholic. He had hoped to reconcile the warring parties by persuading Rome to reform, but events had gone too far to avoid the final break. Dürer's design indicates nobility and strength, but not the spiritual resources of the sitter. The print has not been thought to be a good likeness. In fact, Erasmus hardly recognized himself and tactfully suggested that he must have aged since the two had met. However, it does resemble a portrait painting of Erasmus by Hans Holbein the Younger made about the same time as Dürer's preliminary sketch. Holbein also made a woodcut of Erasmus in about 1535, likewise expressing dignity and the spirit of humanism, but with a line quality far less complicated than Dürer's. (Fig. 28) Erasmus, more a "presence" than a "portrait," stands under an elaborate arch with his hand resting on the head of Terminus, the allegorical figure representing the vanity and termination of mortal life. Art critic H. Knackfuss has described the print as "decorative and rich, yet pure and distinguished in its forms, perhaps the most beautiful thing produced in that period in book design."

Dürer's portrait has been criticized for being too much of a still-life crowded with details and accessories, but perhaps this was his way of distracting attention from the face he may not have remembered too well. It is, however, expertly engraved in a wide tonal range and all parts are carefully studied. It is the only portrait in which Dürer refrained from his virtuoso quirk of showing a reflection of a window within the pupils, the eyes, of course, symbolizing the mirror of the soul.

Although Dürer was aware of what the Italians had accomplished in modeling with their long sweeping strokes, he nevertheless seemed to prefer the decorative possibilities of intricately winding lines. His portraits show a stronger bone structure, greater angularity, and more delineation of facial muscles than the smooth, rounded Italian ideal; his approach was more investigative or scientific in the study of proportion and anatomy, and he is among the few eminent portraitists who successfully intertwined psychological awareness with technical resourcefulness.

Dürer's woodcuts, of course, differed considerably in appearance from his engravings — bolder and even more direct, far fewer lines, but equally convincing. Shadows in woodcuts are usually indicated by parallel lines which remain as distinct or separate elements rather than blending gradually into the white of the paper. Cross-hatching, which melts shadows more evenly, is seldom attempted on wood because of the great difficulty in cutting between its tightly meshed lines. However, since Dürer, like most artists, designed but did not cut his own blocks, he must have tried the patience of the "formschneider" who laboriously hollowed out the thousands of tiny squares on the hat in the portrait *Ulrich Varnbüler*, 1522. Varnbüler was a chancellor of the Supreme Court of the Holy

Top: Fig. 25. Albrecht Dürer. *Philip Melanchthon*. Courtesy Brooklyn Museum.
Bottom: Fig. 26. Master I. B. *Philip Melanchthon*. Courtesy Staatliche Museum,
Berlin.

Fig. 27. Albrecht Dürer. *Erasmus of Rotterdam*. Courtesy National Gallery of Art, Washington, D.C., Rosenwald Collection.

Roman Empire and Dürer's "friend unequaled." (Fig. 29) In his portrait, the large hat overshoots the upper border as though Varnbüler's presence could barely be contained within the prescribed space. When the wood developed cracks about a hundred years later, another block was introduced to camouflage the damage and, incidentally, add a color tone. Chiaroscuro, as this technique is called, typically used several blocks to represent various tones of light and shade, and was probably invented in Germany by Lucas Cranach the Elder in 1508 to imitate wash drawings.

Dürer's other woodcut portrait, that of Emperor Maximilian, 1518, was made from his life drawing several months before the emperor died,

ER·ROT

TERMINVS

Corporis effigiem si quis non uidit Erasmi,
Hanc scitè ad uiuum picta tabella dabit.

the strong relief and the proud set of the head attesting to the essence of majesty. (Fig. 30) Around the broad shoulders he placed the Order of the Golden Fleece, a mythological emblem symbolizing the sovereign's relationship with his knights; perhaps as an egalitarian gesture he omitted any royal insignia. The pomegranate design on the coat may have represented Maximilian's personal qualities — "rough on the outside, an overabundance of sweet seeds underneath." An athlete and scholar who was knowledgeable in music, art, and eight languages, Maximilian had an important role in sixteenth century graphic art because he commissioned many prints to record his life and enhance his reputation. He distributed his portraits as political gifts, which then as now were presented at foreign courts as marks of courtesy. Although he was unsuccessful in war, his reign achieved improvements in commerce, education, and government. His financial resources, however, were limited, and he had to scrimp in order to give his administration some measure of regal tone. Unlike Henry VIII of England, who sent Hans Holbein to half the capitals of Europe to dispense paintings of his portly self as well as to portray various wifely candidates, Maximilian had to satisfy himself with the many impressions of which a single block or plate was capable.

Though Dürer was his country's best-known artist, he never lost interest in the intellectual passions of the day; all his life he studied geometry, architecture, music, science, writing and philosophy. He became caught up in the Reformation, the single greatest struggle of the sixteenth century, and sympathized with many of its goals. Following a spiritual crisis, he converted to Lutheranism.

A flourishing school of portraiture developed during and after his life, imitating or reflecting his style in Germany, Italy, and the Netherlands. But his was not the only influence affecting engravers. Classic designs from the south stimulated the work of a group of German printmakers known as the Little Masters; the small size of their prints was intended to induce more concentrated observation. These artists combined the detailed intricate patterns of Dürer with the broader, more harmonious compositions of Italy, and pioneered an eclectic mini-style of their own.

Of the Little Masters working during Dürer's lifetime and for a generation after his death, Albrecht Altdorfer was the senior artist, interested primarily in picturesque landscape. The lines of his woodcuts tend to twist and turn in a manner incompatible with that medium, but in 1521, before he gave up printmaking for more prosaic duties, he did an excellent little woodcut portrait of Luther after one of Cranach's engravings. (Fig. 31) Cranach was primarily a painter, although he took time off to engrave eight plates, seven of which were portraits, two of them of his good friend Luther as an Augustinian friar, made in 1520 and 1521. A woodcut of 1522 shows the pious scholar as a handsome thirty-nine-year-

Opposite: Fig. 28. Hans Holbein the Younger. *Erasmus of Rotterdam.* Courtesy Cleveland Museum of Art, gift of the Print Club of Cleveland.

Top: Fig. 29. Albrecht Dürer. *Ulrich Varnbüler.* Courtesy Philadelphia Museum of Art, given by Mrs. Horace C. Jones. *Bottom:* Fig. 30. Albrecht Dürer. *Maximilian I.* Courtesy National Gallery of Art, Washington, D.C., Rosenwald Collection.

IMAGO MARTINI LVTHERI EO HABITV EX
PRESSA, QVO REVERSVS EST EX PATHMO
WITENBERGAM. ANNO DOMINI 1522.

Top: Fig. 31. Albrecht Altdorfer. *Martin Luther. Bottom:* Fig. 32. Lucas Cranach
the Elder. *Luther as an Augustinian Friar.* Both figures courtesy National Gallery
of Art, Washington, D.C., Rosenwald Collection.

Top: Fig. 33. Barthel Beham. *Emperor Ferdinand I. Bottom:* Fig. 34. Barthel Beham. *Charles V.* Both figures courtesy National Gallery of Art, Washington, D.C., Rosenwald Collection.

old with carefully curled hair and beard. (Fig. 32) Cranach's devotion to Luther is apparent in these descriptive portraits, which reflect idealism and determination. However, they do not show the hard side of his character, which demanded the death of thousands of peasants rebelling against serfdom, nor the anti–Jewish bigotry which Germany accepted and which, in part, it used to rationalize genocide in the twentieth century. In 1509 Cranach engraved three portraits of Frederick the Wise, who appointed him court painter, and also copied Dürer's *Albrecht of Brandenberg* in 1520. None of these portraits has the power or sensitivity of those he did of Luther. His son, Lucas Cranach the Younger, was not one of the Little Masters, but he also designed woodcut portraits, one of which was a full-length study of Emperor Ferdinand I dated 1548. It is mainly of costume interest, with a beautifully cut brocade coat and heavy gold neck chain.

The emperors Ferdinand I and Charles V were grandsons of Maximilian. Charles was the most powerful man of his time, but was not as well liked as his brother. In 1531, at ages twenty-nine and thirty-one, they sat for two of the choicest portraits of the century. (Figs. 33, 34) These were engraved by Barthel Beham, who, with his brother Hans Sebald and their friend, Georg Pencz, may have been Dürer's pupils. Although they were the finest of the Little Master artists, all three were exiled from Nuremberg for taking up the cause of the Peasants' Revolt in 1525. Barthel, who is generally credited as the most innovative of the group, probably studied in Bologna and Rome, where he modeled his work on the Marcantonio school as well as on Dürer. The vivacity of the drawing of Ferdinand is compelling. The open-mouthed figure, about to move and speak, is a masterpiece of lifelike representation. The portrait of Charles, from whom Ferdinand inherited his throne, is almost as successful. He thought his jutting jaw and narrow face made him look ugly, but he had a lively expression about the eyes which Beham captured. Engravings of Charles' portraits were mostly copies of popular paintings by Titian, who lent his patron a majesty he may not have actually possessed — which could have been the reason Charles preferred him to any other artist.

Georg Pencz engraved only one portrait, that of John Frederick the Magnanimous, Duke of Saxony, in 1543. (Fig. 35) The duke was a devoted Lutheran who spent five years as a religious and political prisoner of Charles V, earning his cognomen because of his fortitude under those trying experiences. His favorite sports were hunting and drinking, but he spent time and money to encourage learning, founding and supporting two universities. Pencz's delicate dotting to create uniform tonalities was borrowed from Italian sources, but the overwhelming detail in costume and border is still in the German style.

Another of the Little Masters, Heinrich Aldegraver, is best known for the inventiveness of his ornament designs, but one of his most interesting prints is his graceful Italianate *Self-Portrait* at the age of twenty-eight. (Fig. 36) There is a sensual quality in this fashionable likeness of 1530 with its broad hat and handsome collar. The outturned eye, too obviously

peering in a mirror, creates an awkward and jarring note in the otherwise well composed work. Perhaps he had heard that, in a three-quarter pose, when the eyes look back, an alert expression may be achieved.

The decline of the German school of engravers is represented by Jacob Binck, also an ornamentalist, who engraved the portrait of the ill-fated brother-in-law of Charles V, Christian II of Denmark and Norway. (Fig. 37) Christian conquered Sweden, but was so repressive that he was overthrown and condemned to prison, where he died in 1559. Binck's design, 1529, engraved with such softness that it has been mistaken for an etching, was probably made after a drawing by Jan Gossaert (Mabuse), a Flemish painter and engraver who never left a restful, undecorated spot in his work if he could help it; the engraving likewise leaves no parts unlabored, although the face is powerfully drawn. Hans Brossamer, of lesser importance, who made a few engraved and woodcut portraits of Luther and some German counts, died about 1560, and with him the fineness and quality of the school ended.

The etching technique was derived from armorers' workshops, where it had been used since the mid fifteenth century for embellishing metal, but not for printing on paper. Etchings are made by covering a plate with an impervious varnish or wax ground through which the artist is able to draw freely with a sharp instrument, removing the ground as he goes along, leaving the design visible on the bared metal. The plate is then exposed to acid, which eats into the unprotected lines, eroding them to whatever depth the etcher chooses. The grooves become microscopically corroded, resulting in a slightly ragged appearance; the less time the plate remains in the acid bath, the thinner and shallower are the incised U-shaped furrows. When the plate is sufficiently bitten, the protective coating is washed off, and the etching can then be inked and printed exactly as an engraving. The etched line can be differentiated from engraving because its ends are blunt rather than pointed. The objective was a quick imitation of the engraved line's disciplined and formal style; neither etching's warmth or range of tone nor its intrinsic sketchy and spontaneous properties were fully exploited until Rembrandt made use of its unrealized and undeveloped potential. In the nineteenth century Seymour Haden contrasted it with engraving as "the pen to the plough."

The first etchings originated in the early years of the sixteenth century with the Hopfer family of armorers in Augsburg, Germany. Daniel Hopfer already had some understanding that freer lines were possible in etching and that he could indicate texture and tone by varying lighter and heavier strokes. One of his etchings was a portrait of Maximilian, which no doubt also made the rounds among European princes. His best-known

Opposite, left: Fig. 35. Georg Pencz. *John Frederick the Magnanimous*. Courtesy Staatliche Museum, Berlin. *Center*: Fig. 36. Heinrich Aldegraver. *Self-Portrait*. Courtesy Philadelphia Museum of Art, Charles M. Lea Collection. *Right*: Fig. 37. Jacob Binck. *Christian II of Denmark and Norway*. Courtesy Staatliche Museum, Berlin.

work, from about 1500, is *Kunz von der Rosen*, Maximilian's court jester, thought to be copied from an earlier drawing by an unknown artist, since, with the exception of this portrait, Hopfer specialized in profiles. (Fig. 38) The exact date of the print is unknown, but it is very possible that it is the first extant etching, anticipating by perhaps ten years one by the Swiss engraver Urs Graf, dated 1513. There were a number of German etchers other than the Hopfer family, but their portraits do not compare in quality to this lusty and rugged example.

Jost Amman's work should be mentioned as an exception, however, because of some innovative touches in his fifteen etched portraits. He created an unusual print in his *Gaspard de Coligny*, 1573, where the background serves the extraordinary purpose of illustrating the death of the French admiral and Protestant leader in the St. Bartholomew massacre. (Fig. 39) The violent action is depicted below the portrait, etched a year after Coligny was stabbed, thrown out of his window still breathing, decapitated, and dragged through the crowd. So much for human pity. The psychological and narrative elements which Amman introduced were dramatic extensions of the scope of portraiture. A looser technique was shown in his portrait of Thessalonus II, Prince of Bavaria. (Fig. 40) The elaborate costume has its own interest, while the full-length composition suggests greater importance than the typical head and bust. The aesthetic appeal of the graceful man dominating the receding vista anticipates Jacques Callot in the next century. (See Fig. 56) Amman's portrait of the shoemaker poet *Hans Sachs*, 1576, shows the overstated emotionalism that would cling to German art through the twentieth century.

Little more need be said of the remainder of portrait printmakers in Germany. Hans Sebald Lautensack, like Altdorfer, is best known for his attractive landscapes, one of which is visible through the window in his etched portrait of Dr. Georg Roggenbach, 1554. (Fig. 41) His ability to indicate textures was inadequate, and the figure has a flat quality; it makes an anemic comparison with the powerful, almost mirror-image of von der Rosen. (See Fig. 38) Matthias Zündt etched a few portraits, as did Augustin Hirschvogel and Hans Burgkmair the Younger, the latter very largely influenced by the Italian school. Hans Baldung (Grien), Dürer's best pupil and one of the better German printmakers, designed an occasional portrait; his woodcut of the botanist Otto Brunfels is full of personality. Finally we mention Hans Burgkmair the Elder for a woodcut equestrian design of *Maximilian* of 1508, the first dated chiaroscuro and another of the prints commissioned by the emperor in his pursuit of immortality. (Fig. 42) However, since the eye, nose and mouth are only partly visible within the full armor, the portrait serves to illustrate not the man, but the splendor of his person. Jost de Negker of Antwerp cut the design on two blocks and printed them in black and gold on vellum, and in black and white on colored papers—elegant statements indeed. It was one of a projected two hundred and eighteen woodcuts based on Maximilian's life; one hundred and thirty-five were completed.

Fig. 38. Daniel Hopfer. *Kunz von der Rosen*. Courtesy British Museum.

By the middle of the sixteenth century most of these artists were dead, and with them German graphic art died, too. Throughout much of the century Germany experienced such severe political and social instability that the equilibrium it had enjoyed at the beginning of the 1500s disappeared. The country suffered through religious upheavals, peasant uprisings, and loss of its overland commercial traffic because of Portuguese discoveries of alternate trade routes by sea. The cumulative effect of this turmoil was financial disaster and the decline of the central government after the death of Charles V. Germany crumbled into a conglomeration of principalities continually warring among themselves. There no longer was an atmosphere that might warrant another Maximilian to patronize the arts or encourage artists to immortalize the great figures of their day.

Fig. 39. Jost Amman. *Gaspard de Coligny*. Courtesy Metropolitan Museum of Art, Harris Brisbane Dick Fund, 1943 [43.4]

II. The Netherlands

While a great deal is known about the life of Dürer, much of Lucas van Leyden's is lost to us. If 1494 is accepted as the year of his birth, he was an artistic prodigy, having produced excellent work by the age of fourteen. He exchanged prints with Dürer and probably had seen engravings by other German artists, but he developed his own technique and evolved a personal style in his very early years. Most of his themes were derived from religious or Biblical sources, but he also had a Flemish interest in animal, genre, and landscape

Fig. 40. Jost Amman. *Thessalonus II*. Private collection.

subjects, and in these he even surpassed Dürer in the suggestion of atmosphere and deep perspective. By keeping his background lines shallow so that they would print faintly in the distances, and using a heavier needle for the foreground, he was able to achieve a delicate variety and gradation of tones. Unfortunately, his plates suffered early deterioration since the fine lines wore down quickly under the weight of the printing press, making good impressions of his plates much rarer than Dürer's. Later Dutch printmakers followed his system, and unlike the Germans, purposely kept their plates in his lighter tones. Rembrandt admired Lucas' work and owned a group of his engravings.

Lucas engraved an elaborately costumed *Portrait of a Young Man with a Skull*, about 1519, which may be a self-portrait, since it corresponds with a later written description of him. One of his finest prints is the portrait of *Maximilian*, 1520. (Fig. 43) It was probably based on Dürer's woodcut (See Fig. 30) rather than on a life drawing, Maximilian having died in 1519. Lucas had made a portrait of the emperor during an earlier royal visit to Leyden, but whether or not that was a source for the print is unknown. Lucas added an architectural background to Dürer's design and, to help locate the figure in real space, a parapet in front where Maximilian rests his hand. The portrait is of additional interest because it is the first time that engraving (on the head) and etching (on the background) were combined in a single plate; both media are used on the costume. This innovation of mixing techniques subsequently was widely adopted for the sake of speed, with etching used as a shortcut to lay in the basic design in the earliest versions of the plate, and the burin to reinforce and complete the details. Etchings made before this time had been on very hard iron; this is the first on copper. The softer metal doesn't rust, and it produces a more fluent and delicate line quality than the coarser results on iron.

Fig. 41. Hans Sebald Lautensack. *Dr. Georg Roggenbach.* Courtesy Philadelphia Museum of Art, the John S. Phillips Collection, acquired with the Edgar V. Seeler fund (by exchange) and with funds contributed by Muriel and Phillip Berman.

During much of the sixteenth century many thousands of prints of all descriptions were turned out in the Netherlands, where printsellers commissioned and published them to fill the demand for book illustrations and inexpensive art. The Mannerist style in which many of these prints were designed developed in part as a reaction against the clarity and symmetry of the High Renaissance. Beginning with the period following Raphael's death in 1520, and for almost a hundred years after, artificiality outweighed natural representation. It was a rather narrow style, more concerned with aesthetic expression than with spatial or internal logic, gaining recognition in the north beginning about 1550 through the dissemination of complex and unnatural looking prints. Harmonious compositions and classical arrangements of space gave way to excessively refined details, unbalanced overwrought designs, and intricate surface decoration. Paintings were reproduced with extraordinarily subtle gradations of tone, marvelous imitations of luxurious fabrics, and white highlights to create brilliant sculptural effects. The Mannerists reacted to the religious and political anxieties of the times very much as many twentieth century artists did, by breaking away from traditional forms and dramatizing their apprehensions in irregular and ungainly distortions of the human figure.

In portraits, profuse or exaggerated detail was often introduced, with sitters appearing in self-conscious, affected poses, concealing their

Fig. 42. Hans Burgkmair the Elder. *Maximilian*. Courtesy Staatliche Museum, Berlin.

emotions behind mask-like faces. Such anti-classical Mannerist show-pieces, or rather show-off pieces, while becoming models for the Rubens school of reproductive printmaking in the seventeenth century, were repudiated by the Nanteuil school of French portrait engravers as more suitable to painting than printmaking. (However, brilliantly executed elaboration proved almost irresistible, and the flamboyant Drevet school brought it back again in a modified way in the eighteenth century in France.)

The first and greatest engraving virtuoso of the Mannerist school was Hendrik Goltzius of Haarlem, who worked in the latter part of the six-teenth century and the early years of the seventeenth. Not only was he a great success at home, but when he traveled to Italy he had the pleasure of hearing his work praised as he stood by unknown to his admirers. His hand had been crippled by a childhood burn, forcing him to use his shoulder and arm to control and direct his engraving tool. This method worked to his benefit, resulting in long, sweeping lines that were thicker in the middle and tapered at either end, allowing endless variations of sur-face textures, color relationships, and shading. The lavishly detailed ac-cessories in his *Self-Portrait* — moiré patterned background, curled beard, ruffled neckpiece, and fur collar — display great technical skill, but have in them more of strained craftsmanship than artistry. (Fig. 44) Because the print is not signed, some scholars attribute it to Goltzius' pupil and stepson Jacob Matham, who may have engraved the plate after the master's unfinished self-portrait drawing.

Goltzius' posthumous portrait of his teacher, *Dirck Coornhert*, the humanist poet, engraver, and activist in the Dutch revolt against Spain, was engraved from a life sketch when the sitter was sixty-eight years old. It dates from about 1590 and is an intense character study with its very large head permitting a great amount of detail and a sparkling and strongly lit finish. While the lack of tonal gradations, particularly in the forehead, creates a rather lumpy effect, such knotted surfaces of the body, as well as compressed space, are characteristic of Goltzius' Mannerist style.

A more unusual engraving, dating from 1597, is a portrait of his apprentice, Frederick de Vries, the son of a painter with whom Goltzius was friendly. (Fig. 45) The purpose of the Latin inscription was to inform the father that his son was well and cheerful. Portraits of children were still quite rare at this time, possibly because only adults were considered important family members. Domenico Ghirlandaio and Dürer were the first major artists, in the latter fifteenth century, to give serious consideration to very young sitters, Dürer fancying himself of sufficient consequence to draw his self-portrait when he was only thirteen. The de Vries engraving is the earliest printed portrait of a child, which may account for the inelegant and mature demeanor of Frederick; the Mannerist tendencies towards unnatural posture and movement could be responsible for the pose, although the infant Jesus was often represented by northern artists with an adult face and awkward appearance. Portraiture was a serious business in Protestant countries, and until the seventeenth century even children had to conform to a sober and solemn demeanor. Goltzius incorporated various allegorical or contrived elements, the dog perhaps representing fidelity and the bird, innocence. The inconsistency of the shadow on the left of the boy's jacket and the squeezing of the figure into a shallow space between the dog and the tree are typically Mannerist, although there are fewer such devices in Goltzius' portraits than in his other prints.

Goltzius also engraved a number of very small portraits on silver and gold which, because of their size, are less exaggerated than his usual work. Although they were not meant for printing, since their inscriptions were engraved in the normal reading direction, bright clear-cut impressions have been taken from them.

He chose to depict few of the nobility or churchmen, but left a gallery of the Flemish middle class — physician, merchant, mathematician, and fellow engraver. Sitting for their portraits gave these dignified burghers an illusion of social equality with the aristocracy; later artists such as Van Dyck and Rembrandt catered to the same aspirations. However, in his *Henry IV*, King of France, about 1600, Goltzius created an image that is unquestionably regal and executed it with rare insight and sympathy. (Fig.

Fig. 43. Lucas van Leyden. *Maximilian*. Courtesy National Gallery of Art, Washington, D.C., Rosenwald Collection.

46) It is the best of the many engraved portraits of Henry, the leader of the Huguenot party, who managed to save himself from the massacre of St. Bartholomew only to be killed in 1610. He was a very popular ruler, though unfortunately not to his assassin, François Ravaillac, who had a vision that God wanted to save France from Henry's Protestantism. God evidently did not communicate that message widely, for Henry was mourned by Catholic and Protestant alike.

Religious disturbances in the Netherlands affected not only daily life, but a great deal of Christian art too: stained-glass windows, paintings, and statues were destroyed by Calvinist zealots; there is very little left of pre-seventeenth century work in Holland today. Prints, however, were often exempted, and artists such as the Wierix brothers of Amsterdam continued to produce thousands of detailed and delicate impressions of well-known people, more in the style of Lucas van Leyden than of Goltzius. Jan Wierix's portrait of Marie de Medici, 1600, the wife of Henry IV, is attractive, but lacks the intuitive qualities and energy that Goltzius gave her husband. Marie and Henry were the grandparents of Louis XIV, through whose personal interest and support portrait engraving achieved its greatest advances in the next century.

III. Italy

Fig. 44. Hendrik Goltzius. *Self-Portrait*. Courtesy Rijksmuseum, Amsterdam.

Great art in great abundance was produced in Italy in the sixteenth century. Much of it was pagan or secular in character, mythological figures and nude studies rivaling religious subjects. For the uneducated masses who could not understand the classical references in High Renaissance art, and religious people who would not admit profane works in their homes, portraits, which needed neither scholarly interpretation nor dispensation from the priest, became a major source of pictorial information.

While northern portrait artists emphasized craftsmanship, detail, and meticulous drawing, the Italian school stressed ideals of facial beauty, academic refinement, and breadth of design. Raphael, for instance, harking back to Aristotle, said that he preferred to portray his sitters not as they were, but as they ought to be. The Renaissance concept that "man is the measure of all things" not only helped generate the philosophy of humanism, but increased the sensitivity of artists to all the possibilities inherent in portraiture.

The full face, for example, offered the best opportunities for character analysis and solid modeling of features; it was therefore used more often than the profile by the great masters. Leonardo's *Mona Lisa* of about 1504 was one of the earliest portraits in Europe to take advantage of this approach, transcending mere factual reporting in its inscrutable and mysterious otherworldliness. The contours of her face blend imperceptibly into the background, while the sensitive focus on the corners of her eyes and mouth gives the painting its emotional expressiveness. This softer, shadowy type of facial representation, known as sfumato, began to replace the more linear, clear-cut style, or what Vasari called the "dry and hard manner," of many fifteenth century works. It influenced the techniques of printmakers, who followed Leonardo's lead and imitated painterly effects through the placement of dots and flicks that also blurred features and outlines.

Although many artists traveled back and forth between northern and southern centers and clearly influenced each other, Italian printmakers never developed the wide-ranging skills of their northern colleagues; the greatest Italian artists, Raphael, Leonardo, Michaelangelo, Titian, chose paint and canvas or chisel and stone over the printmaker's tools. Nevertheless, they had a weighty impact on engravers working in the Netherlands. The costume details and extravagant compositional devices of the anti-classical Italian Mannerists also found their way into many northern prints.

Italy did produce one engraver who, while not an innovative genius like Dürer, nor a dazzling technician like Goltzius, established a reproductive school that influenced more practitioners than anyone before or since his time. Marcantonio Raimondi was born in Bologna and lived about the same time as Dürer, occasionally copying his work in order to learn his techniques. In spite of a lawsuit, the plagiarism continued, although he was no longer permitted to use Dürer's monogram; ironically, some people preferred his imitations to Dürer's authentic prints.

Marcantonio was associated with Raphael for about ten years, translating and elaborating many of his drawings into engravings for sale to tourists, thus helping to spread the High Renaissance vocabulary throughout Europe. His most important contribution to printmaking, aside from the introduction of reproductive rather than original engraving, was the development of a standardized procedure of cutting lines, which he derived from a union of northern and southern ingredients. Italian painters had always incorporated a strong feeling for volume, which printmakers learned to represent with sweeping sinuous outlines. Dürer and his followers, on the other hand, emphasized surface pattern — fur, textiles, wood, flesh — using dots, cross-hatching, and closely laid lines that followed curves and boundaries in order to indicate gradations of tone and shading in depth.

Marcantonio was able to combine the three-dimensional Italian manner of indicating volume and roundness with Dürer's method of shading to describe surface contours and textures. He classified all kinds of lines, including those used by German woodcutters, into a clear system that could be taught almost by rote. This meant that a skilled craftsman could learn to reproduce the work of great artists in the print medium by schematically representing dimension, shading, and tonal values according to a prescribed technique. More and more engravers now began to copy existing works rather than inventing their own compositions. Unfortunately, this opened the flood gates to uncounted numbers of mindless reproductive prints, including portraits, most of which may be overlooked in the interests of charity. The practice contributed to the deterioration of creative printmaking, and had an enormous effect on portrait painting too, since many canvases were produced primarily to be translated into saleable prints. The onus of commercialism and the widespread use of reproductive printmaking resulted in a negative view of re-creative art.

Marcantonio, who had everything but originality in design, was the inventor and leader of this reproductive school and turned out hundreds of plates, a few of which were portraits. An early work was a likeness of the author and musician Philotheo Achillini (*The Guitar Player*), in which

he helped himself to a number of Dürer's ideas—the background landscape, for example, and the device of hanging his name from a tree branch. Towards the end of his career he engraved a stately portrait, *Pietro Aretino* with a richer range of color than usual. (Fig. 47) The style here is fuller than some of his other work, the hat and costume finely detailed, and the expression of the face vivacious. Marcantonio had learned to indicate consistent lighting from a single source, thereby adding verisimilitude to his work. Giorgio Vasari thought this engraving was the "most beautiful of all that were executed by Marcantonio." The portrait may have been based on an anonymous, probably Florentine, engraving of about 1523, after a painting by Titian of 1510. Marcantonio's version of about 1527 is slightly different, lacking the border design, and showing Aretino older-looking and with a larger beard. Aretino was, among his many other accomplishments, the writer of some notorious verses which were illustrated by Marcantonio's equally scandalous engravings. The result, according to one story, was temporary banishment for the artist and a narrow escape to Venice for the poet. But Catholic Italy wasn't the only place nervous about obscenity; England, afraid of an onslaught of vulgarity, also invoked strict censorship, leading Shakespeare to fume about "art made tongue-tied by authority."

Marcantonio had a number of followers, like himself mostly reproductive engravers, but without his extraordinary gifts. Agostino de Musi (Veneziano) engraved some original designs, among them the 1535 portrait of the Moslem admiral and ally of Francis I, Khar-Ed-Din-Barbarossa, whose defeat by Charles V secured the release of thousands of Christian slaves. (Fig. 49) The artist paid attention to the penetrating eyes and fine mouth of the old warrior, using tiny dots in the flesh to suggest softness, but overall, the tonal gradations are poor, the lines meager, and the body narrow and flat. Another Venetian, Agostino Carracci, who with his brother and cousin enjoyed great popularity all over Italy, dominated artistic activities in Bologna's cultural and financial centers. He copied Titian's painted self-portrait in 1586 in a proto–Baroque style ten years after the master's death. The engraving expresses Venetian interest in rich color and texture with wonderful incisiveness, and clearly differentiates fur from fabric from hair. Nicolas Beatrizet, Enea Vico, Martino Rota, and Niccolò della Casa all were portrait engravers, some of them unusually descriptive, but too profuse in their details. An early Venetian etched portrait, whose lines are more widely spaced than most of the engravings of the period, is *Doge Pasquale Cicogna*; this portrait was successful in capturing dignity and mental concentration. (Fig. 50) Although it is signed "Tintoretto" in the plate, it is regarded as anonymous.

Woodcut-illustrated books continued to be popular with collectors, and publishers had no trouble selling them to an increasingly literate and

Opposite, left: Fig. 45. Hendrik Goltzius. *Frederick de Vries*. Courtesy Rijksmuseum, Amsterdam. *Right*: Fig. 46. Hendrik Goltzius. *Henry IV*. Courtesy Grunwald Center for the Graphic Arts, UCLA.

Fig. 47. Marcantonio Raimondi. *Philotheo Achillini* (*The Guitar Player*). Courtesy Albertina Museum, Vienna.

affluent public. In 1507 a Milanese work by J. L. Vivaldus, *Opus Regale* (*Royal Book*), was published with a profile portrait, *Marquis of Saluzzo*. (Fig. 51) With very few interior lines the artist was able to suggest the aging face with its sagging throat and tired eyes. *Orlando Furioso*, the greatest love poem of the Renaissance, was issued in 1532 with a woodcut portrait of its author, *Ariosto*, designed by Titian, and cut by Francesco Marolini. This is Titian's only documented book illustration. A chiaroscuro likeness of Charles V, possibly by Guiseppe Nicole (Vicentino), was one of the earliest Italian examples of this technique, although it also appeared as a conventional black and white print. Chiaroscuro cutting had been introduced into Italy by Ugo da Carpi in about 1518, ten years after its probable invention in Germany.

By the mid-sixteenth century woodcuts were slowly being superseded by metalcuts, which were capable of much finer detail. Where wood was still in use, primarily for book illustration, it was not generally for its aesthetic merits, but because it was cheaper than engraving. Once publishing establishments recognized the potential for wide sales of reproductive images after famous artists both in books and as single sheets, commercial printmaking began its great expansion. In 1572 a print publisher in Rome issued one of the earliest known catalogues. Helped by such advertising, prints became very widely circulated. They were important because they educated Europe in connoisseurship, providing the best information about great original works until the invention of the camera.

The Sack of Rome in 1527 disrupted every aspect of life. Marcantonio supposedly fled the city and was forced to remain in exile along with many of his colleagues. No more of his history is known, and without his leadership, Italian engraving declined in quality and soon petered out. He had furthered the creation of a vast, appreciative audience for prints, among whom was Robert Browning. In his poem *A Likeness*, 1864, Browning describes how his print collection contributed to evenings of convivial pleasure:

All that I own is a print,
An etching, a mezzotint; . . .
When somebody tries my claret,

Top left: Fig. 48. Marcantonio Raimondi, *Pietro Aretino*. Courtesy Metropolitan Museum of Art, Joseph Pulitzer Bequest, 1917 [17.50.40]. *Top Right*: Fig. 49. Agostino de Musi (Veneziano). *Khar-Ed-Din-Barbarossa*. Courtesy British Museum. *Bottom left*: Fig. 50. Anonymous. *Doge Pasquale Cicogna*. Courtesy Dover Publications, Inc. *Bottom Right*: Fig. 51. Anonymous. *The Marquis of Saluzzo*. Courtesy Dover Publications, Inc.

We turn round chairs to the fire,
Chirp over days in a garret,
Chuckle o'er increase of salary,
Taste the good fruits of our leisure,
Talk about pencil and lyre,
And the National Portrait Gallery:
Then I exhibit my treasure.
After we've turned over twenty,
And the debt of wonder my crony owes
Is paid to my Marc Antonios, . . .

IV. England

Elizabeth came to the English throne in 1558 and set about restoring strength and confidence after the short, divisive reign of Bloody Mary. She understood the value and uses of propaganda and therefore encouraged artists in England to preserve her appearance for her subjects and ultimately for posterity. However, her vanity soon overcame her desire to proliferate her image, for in 1563 she issued a warning that only approved paintings of herself would be permitted. "Hitherto," she proclaimed, "none hath sufficiently expressed the natural representation of her Majesty's person, favor, or grace, but most have also erred therein." She appointed an artist to paint an acceptable portrait of herself from which copies could be made because she "perceiveth that a great number of loving subjects are much grieved and take great offence with the errors and deformities already committed by sundry persons in this behalf." She then ordered her ministers to "reform the errors already committed."

Because of these restrictions, portraits of her became more and more vague or diagrammatic, with most of the interest centered on her costumes and regality rather than on her face. All her portraits are frontal and symmetrical, conveying a sense of majesty and power, and represent her almost as a religious icon; they record posture, pose, dress, and background rather than likeness. Artistically, they were several steps backwards from the realistic portraits painted by Holbein for her father.

There are two engravings of her by Thomas Geminus, a Flemish surgeon who was the first known printmaker to work in England. One, the first engraving ever made there, and almost as early a portrait of her as exists, appeared on the title page of a translation of Vesalius' *Anatomy* in the edition of 1559. (Fig. 52) A similar one dates from a few years later. Other Flemings working in England in the 1560s to the 1580s were the brothers Franciscus and Remigius Hogenberg, minor engravers who turned out Biblical illustrations, architectural views, maps, and portraits of the queen.

Crispin van de Passe the Elder, following the style of the Wierixes in their very close hatching, made an engraving of Elizabeth after a copy of a drawing from about 1595 by the miniature painter Isaac Oliver. (Fig. 53)

Left: Fig. 52. Thomas Geminus. *Queen Elizabeth*. Courtesy British Library. *Right*: Fig. 53. Crispin van de Passe the Elder. *Queen Elizabeth*. Courtesy National Gallery of Art, Washington, D.C., Rosenwald Collection.

Elizabeth was about sixty-two when she posed for him, but the print was not issued until after her death in 1603. She is shown in the elaborate dress (she had about three thousand) which she first wore in 1588 at the great celebration of victory over the Spanish Armada. It is said that her gowns, extravagantly covered with precious jewels, were so heavy that wooden supports were required to keep her upright, since it was impossible to stand unassisted in such edifices.

Most of the artists worked in the Holbein tradition. As there was very little patronage available for native craftsmen, most of the artists were foreign, with the exception of court portraitists and mapmakers. The first English-born engraver of any note, William Rogers, made three decorative, though very flat and stiff, portraits of the queen. One of them, *Eliza Triumphans*, 1589, is a crudely drawn, full-length depiction in which she is flanked by Victory, Plenty, and other allegorical figures. Rogers, about whom nothing is known except that he probably began his career as a goldsmith, also engraved eight portraits in 1602 of eminent court personalities, including a rigid but nonetheless charming figure of Elizabeth's favorite, the *Earl of Essex*. Although these prints appear rather forced and excessively ornate, and clearly reflect the immature state of the printmakers' art in England, they created a demand for portraits that was soon filled by engravers and the printsellers who marketed them in great quantities. By the end of the sixteenth century, innumerable engraved portraits had been churned out, often crowded with symbolic allusions, most of them of no interest except to their sitters. But they were ultimately successful because they created an appetite for portraiture that was met by the beautiful mezzotints that appeared a hundred years later.

Left: Fig. 54. Leonard Gaultier. *Jeanne d' Albret*. Private Collection. *Right*: Fig. 55. Thomas de Leu. *Henri IV*. Courtesy Musée Louvre, Rothschild Collection.

V. France

France, like England, lacked an early tradition of fine engraving; neither the court nor the upper classes encouraged it. Although Francis I delighted in Mannerist prints illustrating the decorations of his Fontainebleau Castle and brought Leonardo and the *Mona Lisa* to France, engraving did not play much of a role in his patronage. Most of the paintings and ornaments he commissioned are now gone and the only information about the lost originals is provided by the drawings and reproductive prints that remain. At the time, there were a small number of Italian and Flemish engravers working in France along with a few native etchers who had learned their trade in Italy. Other than the Fontainebleau artists, most of the printmakers in France were illustrators of books, and most of the few illustrations were portraits, either of the author, the hero, or the person to whom the book was dedicated. Paris and Lyons were the chief publishing centers, but their productions did not equal the standards reached in Italy. Most of them date from mid-century and were series of famous men or kings of France, but since the artists worked from rather poor models of dead people, by and large the prints were not of much artistic significance. Not even the marvelous portrait drawings and paintings by the Clouet family were sufficient inspiration to raise the level of engraved work in France.

The situation was not, however, entirely bleak. Leonard Gaultier, originally from Germany, engraved a number of meticulous portraits such as that of Jeanne d' Albret, 1596, Queen of Navarre and mother of Henry III. (Fig. 54) Thomas de Leu, who was probably Flemish, and appears to have learned his profession in the Wierix school, worked in France and engraved several plates with great delicacy, particularly *Henry IV*, 1599, although that portrait suffers greatly by comparison with Goltzius' version. (Fig. 55; see also Fig. 46) Jean Duvet engraved an Italianate portrait, *Pope Adrian VI*, that is fine; René Boyvin also produced some creditable work. Their portraits represented both the close of a stylistic period and the points of departure for the distinguished French engraving school of the seventeenth century.

Chapter 4

The Seventeenth Century

European history in the seventeenth century can readily be split down
the middle — before and after 1650. The first half of the century witnessed
the Thirty Years' War begun in 1618, the culmination of the religious
dissension that had originated a hundred years earlier with the Reformation. Its destructive power was unprecedented, yet when it was over almost
nothing had changed. The continent was still divided, Protestant against
Catholic, with both sides hell-bent to rid the world of popery or heresy.
At the same time, Charles V was trying unsuccessfully to bring three
hundred rival princes of the Lutheran German-speaking states into a
strong centralized monarchy. France, Spain, England, and the
Netherlands all had their own religious, legislative, and military priorities.
The rich continued to live in splendor between worrisome periods of
peasant uprisings, and the poor in desperate poverty, with occasional
opportunities for revenge.

After 1650 Europe finally accepted the fact that religious pluralism
was entrenched and would not go away, that people could not be united
under a single denomination or dogma. The new direction that Europe
took after the Thirty Years' War was symbolized by the terms of the treaty
that ended it. For the first time in history, an assembly that was almost
completely secular gathered in 1648 to arrange the peace negotiations. It
attempted to bring the nations together in a spirit of cooperation and
interdependence — not through church leadership, but through international law. No longer would Europe be perceived as a monolithic unity;
the Holy Roman Empire was weakened, the pope was no longer censor of
Europe's conscience, individual sovereign states were recognized, each
with its own unique and independent goals. By 1650 modern Europe had
been born.

The French survived the war best of all. As early as 1624, they were
well on their way to establishing a strong central government. Cardinal
Richelieu, the powerful minister of Louis XIII, had gathered up the loose
ends of the realm and imposed royal dominance over the nobility, the
Church, and the army. He died before the war was over, and was succeeded

by Cardinal Mazarin, who strengthened his policies. At Mazarin's death, the teen-aged Louis XIV took the reins of government into his own hands and ruled like a king, but in his pursuit of glory he confused the glitter of his court with the radiance of the planets; he became *le Roi Soleil*, the Sun King, and left his stamp for better or worse on all of Europe. He was lucky in his counselors. First with Mazarin and then with his financial and cultural advisor, Jean Baptiste Colbert, Louis united the country and humbled most of Europe.

The wars in the second half of the century, mostly stirred up by France, were fought for military conquest and commercial considerations and were not basically religious in origin. The key principle of diplomacy was now balance of power, meaning Europe, especially Holland, versus France. The Dutch had prospered from their overseas colonies and had built enormous trading organizations such as the Dutch East India Company, which threatened Louis' expansionist dreams and England's shipping interests.

French Protestants, English royalists, and Spanish and Portuguese Jews offered their brains and financial resources to make Holland the leading commercial and banking nation in the world. Its colonial outposts extended from the New World to Asia. When its trade began to interfere with England's lifeline—its sea power—the two countries began a twelve-year, mostly inconclusive war. France, taking advantage of Holland's preoccupation with England, and hoping to extend its own boundaries, attacked the Spanish Netherlands (present-day Belgium). England and Holland then effected a dramatic reconciliation and united with Sweden to stop the French, although that alliance had only a temporary restraining influence. In 1672 Louis, angry at the Dutch for preventing his advances into Spanish Netherlands, invaded Holland, and with England's help, won victory after victory. The Dutch, in desperation, bravely took the only action left to them: they opened the dikes and flooded the land. It took another set of alliances to force a French retreat, effectively deadlocking France and bringing her ascendancy in Europe to an end. The balance of power remained intact.

Nevertheless, Louis raised France to a power and glory unknown in modern history and governed it with a prodigal civilizing genius. Later, his shortcomings threw his most worthwhile accomplishments into the shade. He reinstated an inquisition against Protestant Huguenots. In perversity or folly, he drove thousands of his most prosperous and hardworking subjects to tolerant Holland. He led wars of aggression which broke his fortunes and turned Europe against him. His profligacy exhausted the national treasury. The people suffered greatly from unemployment and hunger, while ruinous taxes wrenched from farmers, laborers, and merchants brought on local uprisings. When he finally realized that his wars were destroying France, he became resigned to peace and in 1697 concluded a humiliating treaty with Holland, Spain and England. He lived on until 1715, securing the throne of Spain for his grandson, but sacrificing a million lives along the way and losing control of the seas. The Sun King had set.

While the continent was wrestling with the problems of unification, military adventurism, and absolute monarchy, England was developing a parliamentary system of government. Queen Elizabeth I had died in 1603 after a reign that gave England the age of Shakespeare, commercial expansion, and naval superiority. She had ruled with a headstrong power that postponed civil war for a time, but ultimately it could not be avoided. Her Stuart successors were no match for her. During the first half of the century the intelligent but ineffectual James I and the foolish and ineffectual Charles I unraveled many of her achievements. By mid-century civil war erupted between the Calvinists (in England called Puritans) and the Church of England (known to lean towards Catholicism). It was fought partly over religious issues and partly over control of Church wealth, with the Catholics supporting the king and the Puritans supporting the constitutional Parliament which Charles had arbitrarily bypassed. Parliament rebelled. Charles insisted on his divine rights. In 1649 he paid with his head for his recalcitrance.

After his death, the Puritans achieved supremacy for eleven years under the Commonwealth and Protectorate of Oliver Cromwell, but the resulting overdose of asceticism helped bring about the restoration of the monarchy under Charles II. With the return of the royal court in 1660, the pent-up spirits of the populace exploded in intellectual vitality and wicked morals. But not for long. Tiring of the licentious excesses and the Catholicism of Charles' successor, James II, the citizens again demanded sober Protestantism and the protection of their rights under the law. Parliament deposed James and invited the Dutch William and Mary (she was James' daughter) to share the throne. After their coronation in 1689, they united the recent enemies, England and Holland, against France, and assured a Protestant dynasty to England.

From the 1630s on, the New World became the haven of some twenty thousand Puritans. They left England, abandoning their homes and every familiar attachment for a no-man's-land where, known as the Pilgrims, they founded a society in which they could choose their own God and elect their own leaders. However, their extreme fanaticism, combined with local hysteria, brought on the Salem witch trials in 1692 in which twenty people were put to death and hundreds more imprisoned.

Beginning in 1690, and continuing for seventy years, efforts to control the fur trade led to wars between the French, English, and Indians. The outcome was the end of major French influence in the Western Hemisphere and the beginning of English as America's mother tongue. As the incipient communities developed into permanent settlements, they were beset by religious and civil struggles. Yet out of the problems and troubles of the young colonies came the birth of a new political entity: the democratic representative government of the United States.

I. France

In 1545, when Charles V and Pope Paul III convened a council in the Italian city of Trent, they resolved to deal once and for all with the growing expansion of Protestantism. From these sessions, ending in 1563, came the Counter-Reformation, which coped with heresy by reinvigorating and renewing the religious fervor of Catholics. For a time stricter morality prevailed in literature and art—possibly even in life. Artists, particularly in Italy, covered up some of the more blatant nudes; even Michaelangelo's *Last Judgment* did not escape the addition of loincloths on its naked sinners.

Art was now intended to inspire devotion and piety and to reject the grimmer aspects of Protestantism through a greater appeal to the senses. The result was the somewhat theatrical style known as Baroque, originally a Portuguese word meaning a rough or imperfect pearl. As a reaction to the classicism of the Renaissance and the excesses of Mannerism, it encouraged religious works, often melodramatic in nature, which revealed different national characteristics as the style moved from country to country. It responded to a variety of local needs and expectations, serving to enhance aristocratic aspirations in England and Catholic Flanders, to accomodate the spiritual intensity of the bourgeois Protestant Dutch, and to promote the political regime in France. Printmakers did not try to seize the imagination by depicting their sitters gazing heavenward in reverent poses, but rather kept portraiture as a descriptive art designed to produce satisfying likenesses. They used the Baroque vocabulary of vivid gestures, dignity of form, and dramatic lighting to interpret mood and personality and to yield a sense of the accidental in their postures and facial expressions.

Influenced by the painter Nicolas Poussin and furthered by Charles Lebrun, the artistic dictator under Louis XIV, a rational classical impulse developed in France, directing all the arts towards national priorities. French engraving had earlier been under foreign influences, which emphasized a miniaturist approach and provided thorough craftsmanship, but not an overall harmony. Broader design principles were introduced with the inception of a true native school of French printmaking begun by a non–Frenchman, Jacques Callot. He was born in 1592 in Nancy, part of the Duchy of Lorraine. Although that area was officially independent of France until 1766, it was considered French, having from time to time been overrun by French armies.

In his forty-three years Callot produced almost fifteen hundred prints, a few of which were portraits. Unlike most graphic artists who were also painters, he restricted his talents to printmaking alone. His work served as a bridge from the sixteenth century Mannerism of the Low Countries to a distinctly French Baroque style in the seventeenth. In a relatively short lifetime he developed a number of techniques that profoundly affected the history of etching. One of these discoveries was a hard varnish, borrowed from the lute makers, which made it possible to produce cleaner-cut lines than the softer wax grounds had permitted. He generously shared this invention with Anthony Van Dyck, who used it for his own portrait anthology, *The Iconography*. Callot also designed the échoppe, a special implement which permitted his lines to taper and swell in imitation of engraving. (The etched line typically is even throughout its length.) He introduced the process of "stopping out." This technique involved repeated immersions of the plate, or multiple bitings, with the lighter marks successively covered by additional ground to protect them from further erosion, permitting continued etching of the exposed lines. The furrows therefore vary in depth and consequently in the amount of ink they can hold. Etchers in this way are able to control the shadings of their designs from faint to very deep blacks.

Callot's ingenuity made technical advances possible; his artistic skills established new criteria for excellence. When he was appointed court engraver in 1623, he etched a portrait of the illegitimate prince and commander-in-chief of the armies Louis de Lorraine, who had hoped to gain the throne in spite of the impropriety of his birth. He had Callot represent him as a monumental figure on a rearing horse, dominating a battle scene in the distance; unfortunately, he was killed in the Thirty Years' War. This unusual print helped to initiate a number of related equestrian compositions, such as *Louis XIII* (of France), 1630, by Michel Lasne, an engraver who had studied with de Leu and Gaultier. Callot collaborated with Lasne on this large print, which commemorated Louis' expulsion of the Spanish armies from Italy, contributing the landscape and military exercises depicted in the background.

In 1627 Callot visited the great print market in Antwerp, where Van Dyck painted his portrait. That picture, now lost, was subsequently engraved by Lucas Vorsterman, a member, like Van Dyck himself, of Rubens' workshop. After returning to Nancy, Callot etched a full-length portrait of an old friend and professional rival, the elegant *Claude Deruet with His Son*, 1632. (Fig. 56) Children were included more often now in art works, pointing up their growing significance in middle class society. As in the portraits of aristocratic families, the youngster's ornate costume enhanced the father's prestige. The two dandified figures are presented in a theatrical setting complete with a curtain, a platform suggesting a stage, and an impressive backdrop represented by the white paper. The slightly ironic, self-indulgent facial expressions of the pair are Callot's own invention, and reappear periodically in French portraiture.

Callot was a transitional figure, standing somewhat apart from the classical principles that the French school soon adopted. His etched lines remained as tight as an engraver's at a time when Rembrandt's and Van Dyck's work was far more spontaneous. He clung to his stylized, elongated Mannerist figures with their small heads and dainty extremities, while simultaneously developing the formal line and order of French Baroque art.

In spite of many lucrative commissions, his life in Nancy became

Fig. 56. Jacques Callot. *Claude Deruet with His Son*. Courtesy St. Louis Art Museum, gift of Henry V. Putzel.

increasingly unhappy. The Thirty Years' War was raging in Europe. The duel between the Holy Roman Empire of the German Hapsburgs and Louis XIII of France resulted in foreign invasions of Lorraine, and his beloved city of Nancy was afflicted with plague and famine, plunder and rape. He died of ulcers in 1635, quite possibly brought on by the wretched horrors around him, which he depicted in the first great pictorial outcries against human depravity, *Miseries of War*. These two series stripped battle of romanticism and pageantry and presaged by almost two hundred years the even greater *Disasters of War* by Goya.

With the death of Callot the story of French art moves to Paris, which soon became the cultural center of the world, unchallenged until the middle of the twentieth century. Serious interest in the arts had been initiated by Cardinal Richelieu, whose love of beauty rivaled his love of political intrigue. He recognized the need for a strong central government that could unify the individual fiefdoms controlled by the Church and the nobility. Because he saw an important role for art in strengthening the country's stature and consolidating its territory, he decided to encourage a native school of painting. He arranged for a number of artists from the Low Countries to come to Paris, among them Peter Paul Rubens and Philippe de Champaigne, much as the Medici family had provided patronage for artists in Florence more than a hundred years earlier.

Rubens soon returned home, but Champaigne, aged nineteen, stayed to become the first great portrait painter in France. He quickly dropped his early grandiose tendencies absorbed from exposure to Rubens and Van Dyck and developed an unidealized (though still aristocratic) style, expressed with dignity, stability, and simple naturalism, that became the basis for French portraiture; only its lack of warmth prevents a greater appeal. His paintings, and those of his colleagues who followed him, lent themselves well to translation into engravings. They were straightforward and consistent and conceived in linear terms, which made them compatible with printmakers' lines. (In *linear* art, such as the paintings of Botticelli or Raphael, the main focus is on the clear outlines of the work; in *painterly* art, the edges or contours are blurred and lose themselves in undefined or indistinct forms. Linearity in painting is therefore technically compatible with the line quality of engraving. On the other hand, paintings such as Frans Hals' or Rembrandt's are conceived in terms of shadows and tones, and are much more difficult to render into prints.)

A group of French engravers, stimulated by the Netherlandish printmakers working in France, soon formed around Champaigne and other portrait painters, translating their works, and creating a school of engraving that included both reproductive and original artists, a school that has never been equaled. Once these printmakers understood and assimilated the current rational and sober style, they transmitted it relatively unchanged from master to master until the end of the eighteenth century, when the needs and the nature of portraiture were redefined after the French Revolution.

The first of the great portrait engravers was Claude Mellan, who learned his technique in Rome but produced his most important work in Paris. His method was original and never attracted many followers, but it marked the beginning of the simplicity and objectivity that characterized engraving until the end of the Louis XIV period. His procedure consisted of engraving long parallel strokes and eliminating almost all cross-hatching and contour lines. Instead, he shaded his designs either by thickening his lines or by placing them closer together. Without cross-hatching it is difficult to indicate textures and color-values smoothly. He often produced restless and exaggerated patterns, but his work, though too mechanical, fortunately was balanced by his unusually fine draftsmanship, clarity, and sense of individuality.

Left: Fig. 57. Claude Mellan. *Fabri de Peyresc*. *Right*: Fig. 58. Claude Mellan. *Henricus Ludovicus Habert de Montmar*. Both figures courtesy Musée Louvre, Rothschild Collection.

His masterpiece, the portrait *Fabri de Peyresc* of 1637, was done from life, every line suggesting directness and sincerity. (Fig. 57) It avoids his usual unevenness through well-defined strokes and color-values. Peyresc was an intimate friend of Rubens and a lover of artistic bric-a-brac. "No ship entered a port in France," wrote an acquaintance, "without bringing for his collections some rare example of the fauna and flora of a distant country, some antique marble, a Coptic, Arab, Chinese, Greek, or Hebrew manuscript, or some fragment excavated from Asia or Greece." He was not unique. Collecting reached manic proportions in the seventeenth century. Jean de la Bruyère, a French author, poked a little fun at the frenzy that apparently drove a number of addicts into a passion, often unrequited:

> "You wish to see my prints," says Democenes, and he forthwith brings them out and sets them before you. You see one which is neither dark nor clear nor completely drawn, and better fit for holiday decorations on the walls of the Petit Pont or the Rue Neuve than to be treasured in a famous collection. He admits that it is engraved badly and drawn worse, but

hastens to inform you that it is the work of an Italian artist who produced very little, and that the plate had hardly any printing; that, moreover, it is the only one of its kind in France; that he paid much for it, and would not exchange it for something far better. "I am," he adds, "in such a serious trouble that it will prevent any further collecting. I have all of Callot but one print, which is not one of his best plates, but actually one of his worst; nevertheless, it would complete my Callot. I have been looking for it for twenty years, and, despairing of success, I find life very hard, indeed."

This charming paragraph illustrates the support given to the print market by well-to-do patrons such as Henricus Ludovicus Habert de Montmar, a court secretary in charge of government petitions. (Fig. 58) Mellan's lively and animated engraving of him in 1638 has more richness of tone and suggestion of color than is typical of his work. Most of his other plates do not exhibit as much descriptive detail and are usually faulted for the excessive use of unbroken, almost nonstop, lines. Yet Mellan was an effective and inventive artist, setting the pattern for the French school with his series of dignified personality studies. The fine preparatory sketches for many of his prints still exist and demonstrate that his grasp of character was even better expressed in drawing than in engraving.

His contemporary, Jean Morin, likewise an important printmaker with a unique style, did not attract any real following either. While he and Mellan essentially had a monopoly on portrait commissions in the first half of the century, they had no effect at all upon each other. Morin was always a reproductive artist, working after the paintings of Champaigne and Van Dyck in his best prints.

He was chiefly concerned with the expression and character of the face; his backgrounds and accessories were secondary and not engraved with his usual careful finish. He used a combination of engraving and etching on the costumes and frames, while etching the faces with minute dots and lines in order to reproduce the nuances of skin color; indeed, his rendering of flesh was extremely skillful and unobtrusive. Occasionally his tones are jarring and do not blend well, depriving his prints of a seamless quality. He avoided a precise regularity in his strokes, which gives his work individuality, a distinction that too few later artists of the French school could boast of.

For the first time in portrait printmaking, Morin was able to produce almost all the modeling and variety of lights and shadows that could be achieved with a few brush strokes on canvas, though with far greater effort. However, his stipple-like etching technique is so difficult to do well that only he and Van Dyck were successful in attempting it. (A little-known, though sensitive, Italian portrait engraver, Ottavio Leoni, used a similar method in his faces, but there is no evidence that either Morin or Van Dyck knew his work.)

The 1623 portrait of Cardinal Bentivoglio, papal representative to the court of Louis XIII, is an outstanding example of subtle modeling and richness of tones. (Fig. 59) The sober plate is after a painting by Van Dyck, although it suggests neither Van Dyck's freedom nor his bravura. Bentivoglio was one of the judges who returned a guilty verdict against Galileo in the Inquisition for insisting that the earth revolves around the sun. It is said that the cardinal might have been elected pope, but he died during the voting procedure after suffering through eleven sleepless nights because of a fellow prelate's snoring in the next cell.

Morin was as unconventional in his way as was Mellan, often forfeiting an unstrained quality in his work by paying too much attention to little details. But he had a fuller range to his tones, was richer in his contrasts and highlights, and had a softness made possible by the etching technique. He portrayed the court of Louis XIII with an unpretentiousness learned from Champaigne, and a methodology adapted from Flemish printmakers. His fifty solemn and distinguished portraits, most of them set into octagonal frames, were, with Mellan's, the inspirations from which Robert Nanteuil derived his even more remarkable prints.

Nanteuil was the greatest portrait engraver of all time, although he lacked the emotional charge of contemporary etchers in the Low Countries. Born in or about 1623, he appropriated some of the innovations of his predecessors and distilled them into a style that was preeminent in his own day, and, of its kind, has never been surpassed. His portraits, rendered in a clear and full light, show supreme self-confidence, absolute control over his burin, and the reserve and self-control that disdain affectation of pose or dazzling technique. He concentrated his powers on depicting his sitters with moderation and nobility, which is exactly the way they wished to be remembered. His original portraits were commissioned by noblemen, high churchmen of France, friends in the legal, medical and writing professions, and the royal family—a breed of men (he chose very few women) who have reached posterity as masters of their time. He portrayed Louis XIV eleven times, from ages twenty-six to thirty-eight, in such fine likenesses that the queen-mother, taken with a preparatory pastel drawing, reportedly said to her daughter-in-law, "Come and look at your husband, Madam, he seems about to speak."

He was fortunate in having Louis, the world's most generous benefactor of the arts (as long as the works were classical in style) as his supporter. In 1660 the king issued a proclamation in Nanteuil's honor establishing engraving as a liberal, rather than a mechanical, art. This meant that engravers would no longer be considered as craftsmen, but rather as creative artists equal in rank with painters and sculptors. He approved the formation of an engraving school in 1667, housed in the Louvre under the direction of Colbert, his most powerful advisor and the actual leader of much of the government. Like Richelieu before him, Colbert was anxious to increase and tighten control in a period of rising nationalism and a new merchant class. He thoroughly understood how to use the arts to serve French needs.

Nanteuil was only one of many to invoke the printmaker's skills. Even

Fig. 59. Jean Morin. *Cardinal Bentivoglio*. Courtesy Musée Louvre, Rothschild Collection.

in artistically backward Russia, the printed portrait was to play a consequential political role. The princess Sophia, hoping for equal status with her brothers, the Tsars Ivan and Peter, had a portrait of herself engraved in which she was depicted with the crown, scepter, and orb, royal objects she had no business wearing. The print, distributed not only in Moscow but also in the great capitals of Europe in 1687, was considered a daring and ominous challenge to the throne, a possible threat to depose the lawful government. An accompanying poem brazenly accorded her a place in the company of the Empress of Byzantium and Queen Elizabeth, a dangerous idea, dangerously expressed in the powerful medium of the print. Her scheme, however, proved unsuccessful, for Peter confined her to a convent from which she was no longer able to meddle in imperial affairs.

Propagandic engraved portraits of the mighty were distributed much as campaign posters are today. (Peter was familiar enough with them to wonder whether the splendid French images he saw were not all of kings!) Particularly in France they were major public relations tools meant to influence or intimidate vast numbers of Catholic peasants as well as the still-persecuted Protestants. Ambitious students also used them as frontispieces for their academic theses with the hope of receiving favors from the great personages to whom they were dedicated. Thus, the heroic and noble style of portraiture was at least partly imposed on artists, and if they hoped to prosper, they turned out designs meant to glorify the Glorious, and to reassure or distract the populace concerned over the extravagances of court life or the vast expenditures on projects such as Versailles.

Versailles was the largest palace in the world, built under the king's direct supervision, and became the nerve center of cultured Europe, a paradigm of etiquette, style, and beauty. The leaders of the aristocracy made merry in an atmosphere of exquisite and dissolute intrigue, and quite forgot that it was their duty to make Louis accountable to France. When the king declared that he was accountable only to God, they smiled and went on dancing, whiling away the time that might otherwise have been spent on conscientious government. Yet in spite of the fact that people rebelled at various times because of high tariffs, burdensome red tape, and military and economic blunders, homage to the king almost replaced worship of the saints. In manners, life, and the arts, Louis encouraged and provided for the elegance, flair, and grace that were such stuff as dreams are made on.

He particularly enjoyed engravings, and as collectors began to amass them in large numbers he offered to buy and bring them together, forming the basis for the holdings now in the Bibliothèque Nationale. During the seventeenth century alone, perhaps half a million etchings and engravings, many of which were portraits, were assembled there. The buying and selling of prints became a popular commercial business. The English artist and critic John Evelyn advised Samuel Pepys to collect portrait engravings, particularly those of Nanteuil. "Some are so well done to the life," he wrote, "that they may stand in competition with the best paintings. This were a cheaper and so much a more useful curiosity as they seldom are without the names, ages and eulogies of the persons whose portrait they represent. I say you will be exceedingly pleased to contemplate the effigies of those who have made such a noise and bustle in the world, either by their madness and folly, or a more conspicuous figure by their wit and learning."

There is an anecdote to the effect that Nanteuil began his profession by sketching the picture of a young man and showing it to a group of Parisian college students, pretending to enlist their help in locating an old friend. Some of the students admired his skill, commissioned portraits of themselves, and recommended him to their acquaintances; he was an instant success.

Early in his career Nanteuil imitated Mellan, and in his plates of the early 1650s he often used the same kind of parallel lines to define his modeling. Other portraits clearly show Morin's influence in the dotting on the faces. But although he reflected their manner, his work was derived from his own lively imagination. He was probably familiar with Dutch portrait engravers such as W. J. Delff and Jonas Suyderhoef, but their prints, although in some respects technically similar, come nowhere near his excellence. Not only are his portraits farther advanced in color-values and variations of texture in the hair, skin, armor, and fabrics, but each face is touched with greater temperament and spirit. His technique broke with the more "artistic," or art-conscious, style that was basically linear, and substituted a more readily learnable cross-hatching method that could better imitate the tonal qualities of paintings. This skill was later misused by engravers who appropriated his systematized network of lines without his moderation and good taste or his understanding of every line's potential. The result was that engraving lost much of its function as original art and became instead a reproductive tool used almost exclusively to replicate paintings. Nanteuil, however, was a creative master; his style, polished with the help of Champaigne, developed rapidly and by 1657 reached its maturity. During the next five or six years he engraved a dozen or so plates that are unrivalled in the history of portrait engraving.

His beautiful design of the first president of Parliament, Pompone de

Bellièvre, 1657, is a tour de force that has been called the greatest master-piece of French engraving. (Fig. 60) Actually, it is deficient in his usual vigor, having been reproduced from a painting by Charles Lebrun; it lacks the unique grasp of character and personality that informs much of his original work, although he was careful not to let the accessories overwhelm the face. But it is certainly meticulous, with a finespun softness in the skin and fur, and unmatched in its rendering of texture. Most of his prints were entirely his own, however, and it is by these that he must be judged. Only thirty-eight of his plates out of a total of two hundred and sixteen were reproductive.

Prime examples of his work include the superb psychological studies of the brothers Basile and Nicolas Fouquet, 1657 and 1661. (Figs. 61, 62) Nicolas, having raised himself by intrigue and fraud to the high govern-mental post of finance minister, amassed the largest personal fortune in France and surrounded himself in a magnificent palace with art objects, feminine and otherwise, of such splendor that Louis himself was jealous. He eventually undid himself by inviting the king to a party of an opulence and profusion that royalty itself could not afford. Among the six thousand celebrants was Molière, whose comedy Les Fâcheux was written for the oc-casion and performed outdoors on a stage set up in front of a huge man-made waterfall. It took the king just nineteen days to figure out the enor-mous extent of the embezzlements; Fouquet was arrested by one of Dumas' musketeers and spent the rest of his life in prison. Louis requi-sitioned his architect, gardener, and decorator, and began Versailles.

Nanteuil engraved Nicholas' portrait shortly before the great ban-quet; for subtlety and ability to capture the man behind the self-satisfied smirk, this is an extraordinary document. During the legal proceedings Basile, a handsome fellow not unaware of his impact on women, at-tempted to pick up bits of court gossip that might be helpful to his brother. Nanteuil's descriptive portrait of him captured the vanity of the man who flirted tirelessly with all the ladies, hoping they might disclose some useful information. Unfortunately for Nicholas, they did not.

Nanteuil had discovered a successful formula—once mastered, he hardly experimented with it. Almost always he used a bust design; almost always a three-quarter view. In his rather blunt depiction of his good friend, the poet and satiric writer Jean Loret, 1658, he added a personal touch not always found in his more formal studies of high-ranking officials. (Fig. 63) He concentrated on the vitality of the face, modeling his tones gradually and delicately, in order to give the print a harmonious quality; its proportions are perfectly adapted to the frame.

He summed up the distinctly French portrait art of the Louis XIV period; in this lie his strengths as well as his weaknesses. Other printmakers expressed color with better fidelity and clarity. Rembrandt imbued his sitters with a deeper and more moving insight. Van Dyck suggested greater elegance along with spontaneity and livelier animation. Because Nanteuil rarely portrayed anything but the head and shoulders, he sacrificed the

Top left: Fig. 60. Robert Nanteuil. *Pompone de Bellièvre.* Courtesy Musée Louvre, Rothschild Collection. *Top right:* Fig. 61. Robert Nanteuil. *Basile Fouquet.* Private Collection. *Bottom left:* Fig. 62. Robert Nanteuil. *Nicolas Fouquet.* Courtesy Musée Louvre, Rothschild Collection. *Bottom right:* Fig. 63. Robert Nanteuil. *Jean Loret.* Courtesy Grunwald Center for the Graphic Arts, UCLA.

descriptive possibilities inherent in the rest of the body, as well as a sense of movement and an existence in space which is denied to bust portraits. But one of Nanteuil's contributions, like Marcantonio Raimondi's, was the development of a logical technique that could be transmitted from master to pupil. He perfected a carefully balanced system that avoided extremes, a calm, intellectual discernment of character, and an unerring grasp of the sitter's identity. It is true that there is an element of sameness to his plates, particularly after 1660, but his alert, sometimes satirical expressions, natural lifelike faces, and superb draftsmanship have always been greatly admired. He had the combined gifts of originality and unusually refined taste; each of his portraits was a separate study of human nature, and it is that which constitutes the best in art. He died a relatively young man in 1678, highly regarded by the king, never lacking for patrons, and always handsomely rewarded for his work. He was the finest biographer of the French court.

Other engravers, encouraged by his success, advanced his technique still further. Some of his immediate followers — Jean Lenfant, Peter van Schuppen, and François de Poilly — often produced very attractive portraits, but too often technical virtuosity was their first priority. Nanteuil's heads are always far more interesting. The work of Antoine Masson, however, has a particular importance because he, like Nanteuil, often worked from his own designs. His original prints, on that account, show individuality and a search for the uniqueness of his clients, although his impeccable craftsmanship can also be appreciated in his reproductive plates. In the engraving *Pierre Dupuis*, 1663, after Nicolas Mignard, Dupuis' fur hat, the glitter of his chain, his intelligent face, all have a very direct appeal; Masson has hardly a rival for the power and brilliance of his plates. (Fig. 64) His most famous print, that of Queen Maria Theresa's secretary, *Guillaume de Brisacier*, 1664, also after Nicolas Mignard, is known as the Grey-haired Man. (Fig. 65) Brisacier has come down to history as a fraud and imposter. He falsely claimed to be the illegitimate son of John III Sobieski, the King of Poland, and Maria Theresa, the first queen of Louis XIV, and was able to trick her into signing a bogus confession admitting their liaison. That letter, together with a generous bribe, persuaded Sobieski that he might have been guilty of a forgotten indiscretion and that he should acknowledge his "natural son" to Louis. Brisacier coveted a French dukedom and hoped that this revelation would qualify him for a noble rank. Instead, he spent a short time in jail for larceny before returning to Poland, again managing to swindle the king, this time out of enough money to get himself to Russia, where he died before he had a chance to plan any further mischief.

Like many of Masson's works, the print has been criticized for its excessive attention-getting devices, although given the rascally subject, Masson may have thought he was reasonably entitled to include some extra embellishments. Unfortunately, his preoccupation with minutiae detracts from the unity of the design. The exaggerated contrast between the dark background and Brisacier's white hairs was produced by laborious scoring, but the technique is more appropriate to woodcutting and generally outside the natural limitations of the burin. Masson's prints were admittedly sparkling, but he didn't always know when to stop. Compared with Nanteuil, his tones and lighting were abrupt and harsh and he lacked the greater master's solidity and restraint.

Gérard Edelinck, who was Nanteuil's nephew-in-law and closest to his abilities, did some particularly effective work in the last quarter of the century. He had originally come from Antwerp, perhaps invited by Colbert, and promptly adopted Nanteuil's methods and Champaigne's style. Although he was not as gifted a draftsman as Nanteuil, and did not create his own original compositions, his large engraving after Champaigne's *Self-Portrait* of 1676 is one of the most expressive works of the period. (Fig. 66) It was his own favorite and is considered his masterpiece, beautifully arranged, modest in treatment, and with most of the best qualities of the French school. It is particularly noteworthy in that it introduced something radically new to the classical engraved portrait — an increasingly complex design with more of the body than just the head and shoulders, and with the figure placed before a landscape instead of the ubiquitous cross-hatched background. His style evolved from the solemnity of Champaigne to the grandiloquence of Hyacinthe Rigaud.

In his portrait of the genealogist to the royal family, *Charles d'Hosier*, 1691, after Rigaud, Edelinck stretched his technique to accommodate the abundant details of the painting, including the royal family tree, and effectively reproduced every nuance of its color and intricate decoration. (Fig. 67) But it might have been wiser for him to choose a better exemplar than the archetypical Baroque artist Rigaud, who, although the most popular portraitist in France, was often pompous and repetitive; the graceful half-closed hand with pointing index finger, for example, found its way into too many of his paintings. Since Rigaud charged extra for coming up with innovative poses, Edelinck had to use all his ingenuity to make the familiar stereotypes look less cut and dried.

Rigaud overemphasized the accoutrements of his sitters' professions or places in society, forcing the trappings of wealth and rank to explain or characterize the individual. The convincing depiction of mental activity, which is the most difficult challenge to the portrait artist, was usually beyond his reach, but his style, which lasted until the French Revolution, introduced an elegance and ornamentation that was much admired by the Louis XV court.

In some ways Edelinck improved on Rigaud's originals, supplying a dash and energy that were often lacking; mountainous drapery effects, for instance, were less aberrant and more skillfully executed in the engraved renditions. When he felt it was appropriate he eliminated whole sections of the paintings, changed backgrounds, and accentuated the frames, creating intelligent translations rather than obedient reproductions. His two hundred or so portraits disseminated the images of the greatest figures

of the day — Colbert, Lebrun, the poet John Dryden, René Descartes, the greatest philosopher and metaphysician that France has produced, and the architect Jules Mansard, of whom Louis said: "I can make twenty dukes or peers in a quarter of an hour, but it takes centuries to make a Mansard."

Portrait designs began to loosen and change by 1690 after the deaths of Champaigne and Lebrun. During their lifetimes the Academy attempted to raise the professional reputations of its members and to serve as a teaching center. But, by maintaining rigid classical standards which reinforced the fantasy of France's artistic descent from a once-mighty empire, it stifled deviation from what it decreed as acceptable, and insisted on specific rules and formulas which it alone defined. In the two hundred years during which the Academy dominated the art world, it became a dead weight to creative and experimental artists until it was virtually ignored by the end of the nineteenth century.

Yet in spite of its heavy hand, the seventeenth century artists were fortunate to have lived under a ruler who supported a great in-gathering of talent with an unprecedented profusion of money and encouragement. They responded by dedicating their skills to the glory of France and the honor of the king.

II. Spanish Netherlands (Belgium)

The Baroque style found a welcome home during the Counter–Reformation in Catholic Spanish Netherlands. Its greatest exponent, Peter Paul Rubens, embraced its self-confident exuberance and incorporated its vitality and expansive movements into his paintings. He spent most of his creative life in Antwerp, where as a young man he became familiar with the enigmatic sixteenth century Mannerist style; later he went to Italy and absorbed the energetic designs of the High Renaissance masters. He then traveled to other major European centers, leaving behind hundreds of brilliant paintings, many of them portraits. Although today he is thought of primarily as an artist, in his own time he was at least as well known as an ambassador to foreign courts, a diplomat who spoke six languages and was entrusted with many of his country's most delicate missions. When Charles I of England knighted him, it was not for his paintings but for his skill in promoting a peace treaty between their countries. However, diplomacy did not suit him as well as art, and when he returned to Antwerp he was grateful to be relieved of further government service. He spent his remaining years painting.

Although his works consistently won the highest praises, he was somewhat dissatisfied because their impact was necessarily limited to a

Opposite, left: Fig. 64. Antoine Masson. *Pierre Dupuis.* Private Collection. *Right:* Fig. 65. Antoine Masson. *Guillaume de Brisacier.* Courtesy Musée Louvre, Rothschild Collection.

Fig. 66. Gérard Edelinck. *Philippe de Champaigne.* Courtesy St. Louis Art Museum.

relatively small audience. He decided to popularize them through engraved reproductions, and encouraged a number of printmakers, some of whom he or his pupils trained, to interpret his pictures. While he himself probably was not an engraver, he guided those who were, and they learned to do exceptionally graceful, varied, and lively prints which found their way all over Europe.

Among his engravers were Goltzius' pupils or colleagues Jan Muller, Jacob Matham, and the Bolswert brothers, their methods well suited to Rubens' sketchy brush strokes. Muller's elaborate prints of 1615, after Rubens, of the Archduke Albert and his wife Isabella, rulers of the Netherlands, show Muller's talent in suggesting color, rendering costumes and lace, and conveying the dignity of their highnesses. (Fig. 68)

The country had reached its artistic culmination during the years of Albert and Isabella's joint reign, when both Rubens and Van Dyck were producing some of their most dramatic and virile compositions. Isabella

Fig. 67. Gérard Edelinck. *Charles d' Hosier*. Private Collection.

was the daughter of Philip II of Spain and the granddaughter of Charles V. When Charles retired to a monastery, he turned over to Philip his Spanish territories, which included the Low Countries; nations made attractive gift items for royalty. But the Belgians were very unhappy with Philip, who kept them in the shadow of his Spanish troops, imposed ruinous taxes without their consent and persecuted not only the local Calvinists, but also the nobility, who had been reasonably tolerant of the heretics. In hopes of placating the people who wanted their own sovereigns, Philip arranged for the marriage of Isabella to Albert of Austria and proclaimed them regents of the country. When the couple died childless, Belgium reverted to Spain, to continue a pawn in the wars of Europe.

This was the political background in which Rubens moved. But when he was fully able to devote himself to his artistic life, he assembled a group of pupils and organized a printmaking workshop under his own dictatorial supervision. His best students were Paul Pontius and the two Lucas Vorstermans, father and son. The pupils interpreted his paintings with a

Top: Fig. 68. Jan Muller. *Archduke Albert of Austria*. Courtesy National Gallery of Art, Washington, D.C., Rosenwald Collection. *Bottom*: Fig. 69. Paul Pontius. *Peter Paul Rubens*. Courtesy Teylers Museum, Haarlem.

refreshing freedom, eliminating some of the typical minutiae in favor of broader masses. Their dramatic darks and lights produced sparkling plates, but neither their color-values nor the clarity of their printing was quite up to the French standard.

Pontius' rare and beautiful engraving after Rubens' painted *Self-Portrait*, 1607, is particularly fine in the depiction of surface qualities and gradations of tones. (Fig. 69) The original was painted when Rubens was thirty and already an aristocrat. The roughness or carelessness seen in some of his paintings is absent from this finely composed portrait. Pontius succeeded in indicating the warm skin textures for which Rubens was famous.

Another Rubens follower, Christoffel Jegher, was a woodcutter. His three-tone chiaroscuro block *Doge Giovanni Cornaro*, after a Rubens drawing, is composed with painterly values. He was able to approximate the color balance as well as the vitality of the original sketches because Rubens provided precise and finished drawings for his associates. But although there were some skillful practitioners who did pleasing work, woodcutting did not become popular again until the late nineteenth and early twentieth centuries. At that time, Expressionism demanded the emotional symbolism characterized by the strong and dramatic outlines of woodcutting.

Most of the printmakers who worked after Rubens reproduced the paintings of Anthony Van Dyck as well, turning out vast numbers of prints after both artists. As a young man of nineteeen, Van Dyck joined the Rubens workshop, where his job was to draw black and white copies of the master's paintings to be used as engravers' models. When he grew tired of that, he went to Italy for six years and learned to paint with southern fluency. On his return to Antwerp in 1626 he experimented with engraving and etching although at first without much success. He was, of course, familiar with the highly finished reproductive engravings after Rubens' virile compositions, but he preferred etching as a freely drawn suggestive art, concentrating on a less forceful, more dignified style. The latitude and flexibility of his needle was very unlike the formal engravings that had wide public acceptance.

During the next six years he etched eighteen likenesses of his fellow artists, intimate friends, and himself as the celebrities they were. With the exception of *Phillipe Baron Le Roy*, all were included in a collection of portraiture called the *Iconography*. They were made with as few lines as possible in a loose and open manner, using stipple and a little cross-hatching for shading. His combinations of dark tonalities and sinewy lines animate his surfaces and accent his forms. He varied the thickness of his needles in order to give the prints an added verve. As he left them, the etchings have the quality of original drawings. Their ability to imply the whole figure eliminates the need for more explicit description. The heads are well defined, some of the costumes and backgrounds minimally indicated, others carried more or less to completion. They bear only the

Top: Fig. 70. Anthony Van Dyck. *Self-Portrait.* Courtesy National Gallery of Art, Washington, D.C., Rosenwald Collection. *Bottom:* Fig. 71. Anthony Van Dyck. *Self-Portrait.* Private collection.

Top: Fig. 72. Anthony Van Dyck. *Frans Snyders.* Courtesy National Gallery of Art, Washington, D.C., Rosenwald Collection. *Bottom:* Fig. 73. Anthony Van Dyck. *Frans Snyders.* Private collection.

most essential notations and were done with rapid, dashing strokes, flowing with energy and grace. But since only fully developed designs covering the plate from top to bottom were highly valued at the time, all but five of them were later augmented with engraving by other artists to include more of the costumes and settings.

Whether or not Van Dyck was aware that the etchings would be greatly valued is a permanent riddle. That he printed only a few impressions would imply that he either found no market for them or did not consider them important or complete. Because of his inclination to please his public, we can only wonder whether, in order to make them more saleable, he approved of the additional work. Perhaps he thought of the etchings, in their first sketchy states, as preparatory or experimental. He had only hinted at their completion, allowing the viewer's imagination to fill out the details; his engravers "finished" them in more ways than one.

Each change made in a plate, such as the addition or subtraction of a line, constitutes a new variant or "state." The final state is the artist's last word unless, as in the case of Van Dyck, others have had access to the plate. These considerations, while generally not of great moment to the casual print collector (though of prime importance to the specialist), are vital to the understanding of Van Dyck's prints. Five of his eighteen etchings were left in their first states; six had engraved backgrounds added, probably after Van Dyck's death; seven more were heavily engraved throughout, possibly under his own supervision. Fortunately, examples of the scarce first states still exist.

The best way to appreciate his prints is to compare the clear draftsmanship of the early etched states with those that had engraved additions. His own *Self-Portrait*, so beautifully placed on the sheet, so direct and insistent in its glance, was probably intended an an introduction to the *Iconography*. (Fig. 70) Perhaps Van Dyck planned to develop the plate further himself; if so, it is a pity that he didn't get around to it, because it loses almost all its appeal in Jacob Neeffs' awkward bust atop the world's homeliest pedestal. (Fig. 71) The portrait of the still-life painter and Rubens' chief assistant, *Frans Snyders*, did not suffer quite as bad a fate, but even here the engraving of the costume, which Neeffs added after Van Dyck's death, weakens the interest of the face. (Figs. 72, 73) The head is now out of proportion to the body, and the introduction of the square pillar draws attention from the features. Van Dyck's own images were charged with intensity, but the supplementary work by various printmakers tended to destroy much of their effectiveness by the complexity and profusion of their lines. In their original "unfinished" states, the etchings are very rare and are among the grandest treasures of art; superb and convincing, they stand alone. They had some influence in France in the eighteenth century, but no real following until the nineteenth, when etchers in England and America looked back and revived their deceptively simple and easy style.

From about 1627 to 1632 Van Dyck drew or painted eighty portraits of his patrons and associates. These were subsequently engraved by others and published in the *Iconography* in 1645 along with the seventeen etchings; the Neeffs version of his self-portrait served as the frontispiece. It is not known whether Van Dyck had planned to include the etchings, since the book was not published until four years after his death. The collection was eventually expanded from the original eighty to one hundred and ninety. Most of these portraits were wish-fulfilling likenesses, meant to please the sitters and charm their friends, and no doubt they were a sensation. Pontius, Vorsterman and Peter de Jode the Younger were the main engravers of the project, and they were joined by other skilled craftsmen of the Rubens workshop. One of the reproductive portraits from this set is that of the Flemish painter and architect Deodat Delmont, engraved by

Fig. 74. Lucas Vorsterman. *Deodat Delmont.* Courtesy Grunwald Center for the Graphic Arts, UCLA, gift of Mr. Joel Hirsch.

Vorsterman in 1626–1627. (Fig. 74) Delmont was one of many prominent persons who flocked to Van Dyck in Antwerp and later in London, where Van Dyck became court painter to Charles I.

Van Dyck's international reputation for portraiture is due in great part to the wide circulation of the *Iconography* in edition after edition until 1851, when the plates were finally sold to the Louvre and electroplated so that the copper would be permanently protected from further wear. These nineteenth century impressions were catalysts for the etching revival beginning in the 1860s.

Van Dyck enjoyed mixing with an intelligent aristocratic crowd that had become increasingly curious about the art world and eager to include artists in its circle. Critics have charged that because of his aspiring social ambitions, he flattered his sitters and represented them all as elegant, well-bred courtiers (this is often more valid in his paintings than in his prints). It is probably true, as Samuel Butler once pointed out, that a great portrait is as much a likeness of the painter as the painted. This may be particularly so in the case of the elegant, well-bred Van Dyck, but there is no denying the irresistible force of his works.

He died when he was only forty-two, in spite of the large reward the king offered to any doctor who could save his life. He bequeathed his grand-manner painting style to the next generation of artists working in England, Peter Lely and Godfrey Kneller, and following them, Reynolds,

Gainsborough and other nineteenth century fashionable portraitists. They adopted his graceful poses and, like him, set their figures in pleasant, artificial indoor or outdoor surroundings. He was unusually responsive to his patrons, possibly because many of them were his friends. His prints were not as vigorous as those after Rubens, nor as intimate as Rembrandt's, but it is only fair to remember that at forty-two, Rembrandt had not yet produced his most penetrating and emotional portraits. Compared with the work of his French contemporaries, his designs were more dramatic and dynamic. His contribution to the extraordinarily high level of seventeenth century portrait printmaking was enormous in an extraordinary artistic period — in France, in Belgium, but perhaps above all in Holland.

III. Holland

It is not known whether Van Dyck and Rembrandt van Rijn were familiar with each other's work, but if they were, they remained mutually uninfluenced. They could hardly have been more different in their mature styles, one patrician and sophisticated, the other plebeian and intense — although in his younger days, Rembrandt certainly painted handsome pictures of his handsome countrymen. He was born in 1606 in Protestant Leyden, the son of a thriving miller, and was already a successful portrait painter at twenty, the same year that Peter Minuit was buying real estate on Manhattan Island. In 1632 he made a permanent move to Amsterdam, married two years later, and was content to remain in Dutch surroundings the rest of his life. Amsterdam was the brightest star in Holland. Its cleanliness, the charm of its canals and windmills, and the friendliness of its burghers made it a mecca for jaded travelers. Everything was available there. It had the most famous red-light district in Europe and the greatest number of book publishers. Both had a loyal following.

The Dutch used their money freely to invest in the art market, a boon for the painters, who were kept busy by well-heeled middle-class patrons convinced that posterity would want to know what they looked like. Although Rembrandt had many commissions for fashionable portraits, he also painted and etched everything he saw — beggars, rustic landscapes, his neighbors and family, and whatever religious imagery touched his soul. His etched self-portraits are among the most interesting of his works, because in them can be traced not only his professional development, but the story of his life.

Like Van Dyck, Rembrandt invented a portrait model as a young man. There doesn't seem to be a source from which he drew his ideas, although he collected prints and benefited from studying Callot's drawings and etchings. Every likeness, including his own, became a separate study into the mind and spirit of his sitters. He examined each face for what it could tell him and recorded its pain and drama. The inexplicable effect of his work on those who have been touched by his human sympathy goes far beyond mere skillful technique. Robert Browning might just as well have had Rembrandt in mind in his poem about another artist, *Fra Lippo Lippi:*

> Your business is not to catch men with show,
> With homage to the perishable clay,
> But lift them over it, ignore it all,
> Make them forget there's such a thing as flesh.
> Your business is to paint the souls of men — ...
> Give us no more of body than shows soul!

Rembrandt did just that. His first dated print, a small introspective etching, *The Artist's Mother,* 1628, was a splendid beginning because it already indicated his understanding of the medium and his ability to make emotion visible. Three years later he etched another portrait of her, compassionate, yet uncompromising in its realism. (Fig. 75) He conveyed old age not only through the wrinkled skin, sagging facial contours, and worn hands, but in her whole posture.

In his early works he often avoided outlines, used close hatching, squiggles that turn and twist, and glittering dots that melt into velvety darkness. The treatment of light, shadow, and atmosphere were the magical elements of Dutch art, preoccupying Jan Vermeer and others as well as Rembrandt. It is no coincidence that the study of light waves, the microscope, and the telescope all had their inception in light-conscious Holland.

His technical repertoire was expanding all the time. Where he wanted richer tones he added drypoint — lines scratched into the plate with a pointed tool to raise a metal ridge or burr on either side of the furrow. Unlike engraving, the burr remains, holding the ink and printing with a soft, furry texture. Unfortunately, because it wears down quickly under printing pressure, the number of good impressions of which drypoint is capable is very limited. He experimented with acids and different types of inks and papers to achieve painterly effects that ranged from delicately spare to heavily shadowed. Within these unforced lines and suggestive tones lies the emotional impact of his portraits.

The 1630s were the most fruitful of his professional life; his *Self-Portrait in a Velvet Cap with Plume*, 1638, shows him affluent and self-satisfied. (Fig. 76) He posed for himself in a variety of exotic costumes, colorful fabrics, swords, furs, foppish hats. He grimaced and scowled, examined himself with pride and curiosity, in brooding and serene moods. He etched himself thirty-seven times, more than 10 percent of his entire print output. If ever an artist searched for his own nature as it changed over the years, Rembrandt was that man. No one else ever etched his own portrait with such continuous familiarity and honesty.

In 1639, when he was thirty-three and still popular and optimistic, he portrayed himself in *Self-Portrait Leaning on a Stone Sill*, after attending an Amsterdam auction where he studied some sixteenth century Italian portraits. (Fig. 77) He took the suggestion for the stylish pose from Titian's

Fig. 75. Rembrandt van Rijn. *The Artist's Mother*. Courtesy Teylers Museum, Haarlem.

painting *Portrait of a Man*. From Raphael he appropriated some of the design elements of a portrait of the courtier and author Baldassare Castiglione, particularly in the coat, the sharply tilted hat, and the placement of the arm, although the etching, as might be expected, is more intimate.

In the next decade personal problems began to pile up. His mother, his wife Saskia, and three of their children all had died by 1642. He became more reclusive and less interested in self-portraiture. Fashionable externals meant less to him, character and spirituality more. He now began to exploit such Baroque elements as asymmetry, to describe volume through dense and arbitrary cross-hatching, and to achieve even greater dramatic intensity through stronger contrasts and hidden light sources.

His tender description of Saskia's guardian, the Mennonite preacher Jan Cornelis Sylvius, was made in 1646, with the Baroque device of an open hand extending beyond the oval frame to reach out to the spectator. (Fig. 78) Although the print is composed of etching, drypoint, and engraving, it doesn't have an unnecessary stroke; even the beard is rendered with relatively few lines. He shaded the face and hand to simulate the wash of drawings, possibly pitting the plate with minute amounts of powdered sulphur to produce a faint tint. Such chiaroscuro effects, which he used more and more in his later period, were much admired by those who preferred his more finished "printed paintings" to his sketchier style.

Another of his richly toned prints is the portrait of a Jewish doctor and scholar, *Ephraim Bonus*, 1647. The subject seems anxious about the patient he has just seen, or perhaps he is dwelling on the sufferings of his people for whom Rembrandt had such great sympathy. (Fig. 79) The deep facial shadows impart spiritual depth and dissolve form, while the contrasting white collar and cuffs supply strong highlights. The dark background pushes the figure forward and invites close rapport.

In 1648 he used himself as a model for the last time in etching. *Self-Portrait Drawing at a Window* reveals the accumulated sorrows and disappointments of his middle years. (Fig. 80) Gone are the illusions he may have assumed as a young man. There are darker shadows, fewer details, and more concise lines, but the eyes remain as alert and penetrating as ever.

Left: Fig. 76. Rembrandt van Rijn. *Self-Portrait in a Velvet Cap with Plume.*
Right: Fig. 77. Rembrandt van Rijn. *Self-Portrait Leaning on a Stone Sill.* Both
figures courtesy Teylers Museum, Holland.

It was hardly surprising that he lost most of his well-to-do patrons, and
with them, his fortune and art collection. He refused to flatter his sitters,
and they balked at his blunt truthfulness. His critics harped on his
preference for the expressive over the beautiful, but they evidently could not
see that every one of his portraits had a soul inside its face.

By 1661 his eyesight was beginning to fail and he had to give up etching.
He died eight years later, out of fashion, having explored the human state
from youthful exuberance to the final limits of old age. He influenced only
a few etchers in his own lifetime because his unsystematic method was so
personal and difficult to follow that few artists pursued his lead. Not until
the nineteenth century was his intuitive work fully appreciated.

However, he did have some students and disciples who were unusually
gifted and who retained a sense of his spiritual depth. One of his assistants,
Ferdinand Bol, made a few etchings that are reminiscent of the master's. Jan
Lievens, whose own fine work was sometimes attributed to Rembrandt by
cataloguers, shared a studio with him for a time. Though his lines are
somewhat too compact and the hand badly drawn, Lievens' portrait of
Ephraim Bonus is also a worthy rendition; in his version Bonus' self-
confident bearing is derived more from Van Dyck than from Rembrandt.

Fig. 78. Rembrandt van Rijn. *Jan Cornelis Sylvius*. Private collection.

(Fig. 81; see Fig. 79) Lievens also made some excellent woodcut portraits, but the immediacy of etching was much preferred at that period, and wood-cutting languished.

So did engraving. Nevertheless, book publishers continued to feed a demand for engraved portraits whose tonal variations, completer designs, and dimensional values still attracted customers all over Europe. A few portrait engravers carried on distinguished work. Cornelis Visscher, who died young, was the equal of the members of Rubens' workshop, differing in his added use of etching for warmth of tone. His portrait *Gellius de Bouma*, 1656, of a seventy-seven year old preacher sitting among his books, has very effective dark and bright accents. (Fig. 82) Gossips reported that Bouma had more than a passing interest in the bottle; if that is true, it could account for the flushed skin and heavily lidded eyes.

Visscher skillfully indicated textures and surface qualities, setting off the softness of the beard against the stiffness of the ruff. His Dutch realism is evident in the drawing of the thick and powerful hands; note the difference of national styles in Edelinck's graceful fingers. (See Fig. 66)

Cornelius van Dalen the Younger was a pupil of Visscher and, like his teacher, an excellent craftsman. His *Charles II of England*, after Peter Nason, is a forceful study. Jonas Suyderhoef engraved some fine portraits after Frans Hals, Rubens, and Van Dyck, imitating Hals' strong brush strokes in a bold style. His rendering of the hand and face of the philosopher and mathematician *René Descartes*, after a painting by Hals, was meticulous.

Until this time printmaking had been essentially an art of descriptive line work. As a graphic convention this was universally accepted, although, of course, there are no lines in nature; what we see are shapes or masses which painters are able to indicate by brush strokes. Attempts to transfer tonal qualities into the print medium had been made from time to time in a variety of techniques — chiaroscuro woodcuts, minute dotting, dense cross-hatching, and even Rembrandt's trick of leaving some ink on the plate itself; none of these alternatives adequately depicted the uninterrupted transition from lighter to darker shadings.

Therefore, when Ludwig von Siegen, an amateur portrait painter who was living in Amsterdam, invented an engraving process that could produce continuous tones, a new printmaking method became available. Gradual coloration from the palest suggestion of grey to the richest blacks was now possible in a system of halftones — mezzotint — that was able to convey a more realistic impression of paintings than had yet been possible. The need to draw with lines was eliminated, although mezzotint printmakers often added etched or engraved strokes to underscore and strengthen their plates, particularly around the eyes, nose, and mouth. In Von Siegen's procedure the copper was pricked with a serrated or spiked wheel which was rolled over those areas where shadows or darker values were wanted. This raised a burr which held ink and printed darker or lighter, depending on the depth and closeness of the prick marks; the image took shape as the burr was scraped or filed down in accordance with the emerging design, finally yielding the desired form and intensity of tone. Where blank or white areas were desired, the plate was left untouched.

Von Siegen's first dated mezzotint, 1643, was a portrait of the widow regent of Hesse-Cassel, Germany, *Amelia Elizabeth*, after his own drawing. (Fig. 83) It is a bit coarse in its gradations, but considering its earliness, it is remarkable for its fine modeling and the transparency of the starched collar. Von Siegen originally tried to keep his invention to himself, but in 1654 he went to Brussels and shared the secret with Prince Rupert of Bohemia, grandson of James I of England. The prince, an amateur artist himself, made a few mezzotints in the 1650s, including a fine *Self-Portrait* with even deeper tones than von Siegen's; the velvety blacks were particularly admired. (Fig. 84)

By the last quarter of the century the technique was already widely known. Among its most prominent practitioners were Wallerant Vaillant, Abraham Blooteling and Gérard Valck, all of whom worked in Amsterdam. But by this time the great printmaking schools of the Low Countries had had their day. Glorious works of portraiture, perhaps the finest that have ever been etched, appeared suddenly in the second quarter of the century; fifty years later the momentum of the Golden Age was over.

IV. England

While Catholic and Protestant leaders were taking turns running the country, Catholic and Protestant citizens were taking turns desecrating each other's churches. Tolerance made tentative, but mostly unsuccessful, progress, although Parliament initiated some modest reforms in 1683. It took many generations before the government finally came to the startling conclusion that, regardless of restrictive state policies, people insist on the right to choose their own style of denominational worship. Nations are fascinated by this lesson; they rediscover and relearn it over and over.

Five years after the return of the monarchy in 1660, London suffered through a plague in which some seventy thousand people died. In 1666 a great fire destroyed two-thirds of the city north of the Thames River. Charles II offered a young scientist the opportunity to become an architect: Christopher Wren rebuilt the churches and public buildings over a fifty-year period, giving London much of the appearance it has today. In the etchings of Wenzel Hollar, which are our main source of information about the city in the seventeenth century, we can still see what it looked like, both before and after the fire.

Where was art during these dreadful years in England? It was becoming an important institution, particularly after the establishment of the Ashmolean Gallery in 1683, one of the first genuine museums in the world. In painting, the fashion was above all for portraiture. Neither war nor pestilence nor persecution curbed the desire of the aristocracy to sit for the foreign artists working in England—Sir Anthony Van Dyck and Sir Peter Lely from the Low Countries and Sir Godfrey Kneller from Germany. England, having almost no native artists of any stature, gratefully knighted those who came from abroad. These European masters provided most of the original paintings from which vast numbers of engravings were reproduced during the seventeenth and eighteenth centuries. The sheer volume of printed material created a shortage of rags, from which paper was made. Laws were passed in England and elsewhere prohibiting their wasteful disposal. Parliament banned graveclothes because the fabric

Opposite, left: Fig. 79. Rembrandt van Rijn. *Ephraim Bonus. Right*: Fig. 80. Rembrandt van Rijn. *Self-Portrait Drawing at a Window*. Both figures courtesy Teylers Museum, Haarlem.

Fig. 81. Jan Lievens. *Ephraim Bonus.*
Courtesy Teylers Museum, Haarlem.

could be used for paper production; not until the end of the eighteenth century was wood pulp substituted for rags in paper manufacture, which unfortunately resulted in a brittle, rapidly perishable product.

As an example of the extent of the craze for portrait prints, William Willshire in his *Introduction to Ancient Prints* refers to the contents of a single collection for which he gives these statistics: one hundred eighty-four portraits of James I, of which one hundred thirty-five are from different plates; seven hundred forty-three of Charles II, of which five hundred seventy-three are from different plates; three hundred seventy-three of Cromwell from two hundred fifty-three plates; two hundred seventy-six of James II; one hundred seventy-five of Mary II from one hundred forty-eight plates; and four hundred thirty-one of William III, of which three hundred sixty-three are from separate plates. Willshire continues, "We have known the passion for collecting portraits so strong as to lead an amateur to relinquish every other branch for its prosecution, to amass heaps of all kinds and descriptions of likenesses, and apparently to think and dream of nothing else but portraits."

Although Elizabeth's interest in printmaking was only moderate, her successor, James I, showed considerable enthusiasm for scholarship and the arts, commissioning the poetic King James version of the Bible; to judge by some of his behavior, however, it is doubtful that he ever read it. It was during his reign, which covered the first quarter of the century, that a demand first developed for the stiff and awkward images that served as frontispieces for books or were sold singly. The Earl of Gloucester in Shakespeare's *King Lear*, written in 1607, also may have found a practical use for printed portraits. When he was afraid that his son, who he believed was guilty of conspiracy, would attempt to flee the country, he ordered the seaports watched; "his picture I will send far and near, that all the kingdom may have due note of him...." Perhaps that was the first "Wanted" poster.

The publishing business grew rapidly as interest in illustrated books developed. Renold Elstrack, a Fleming, who may have been a pupil of William Rogers, was a prolific engraver who contributed most of the

Fig. 82. Cornelis Visscher. *Gellius de Bouma*. Courtesy Teylers Museum, Haarlem.

highly detailed portraits for a 1618 edition of *Baziliologia, The True and Lively Effigies of All Our English Kings*. His engraving from that series of the mother of James I, *Mary, Queen of Scots*, is more ornamental than realistic, but it underscores the qualities of royalty. (Fig. 85) Mary had hoped for the English crown, but she plotted too eagerly to depose Elizabeth, and was beheaded for conspiracy. The engraving was made a generation after her death, presumably based on a miniature by Nicholas Hilliard, the first good native-born painter to specialize in portraiture.

AMELIA ELISABETHA,D.G.HASSIÆ LANDGRAVIA &c.
COMITISSA HANOVIÆ MVNTZENÆ:

Fig. 83. Ludwig von Siegen. *Amelia Elizabeth*. Courtesy British Museum.

Francis Delaram, imported from Flanders, engraved the portraits of many outstanding personalities of the day, mostly from life. Willem and Simon van de Passe of Utrecht, sons of Crispin, were among the busiest printmakers working in England. They turned out portraits of the nobility containing a great deal of information relating to contemporary costume design; occasionally a less than wooden facial expression emerges from these decorative prints. When the Indian princess Pocahontas visited England, everyone was curious to see what an American "savage" looked like. Simon van de Passe engraved her likeness after an anonymous painting, 1616, the year before she died. (Fig. 86) She was dressed in the latest English fashion, with gratuitous feathers in her hat and hand.

Simon's pupil John Payne should be mentioned chiefly as the link between two prominent engravers whom he trained. George Glover was an artist of unusual originality and the first native-born engraver of consequence; William Faithorne was the best engraver of the period. Unfortunately, Payne preferred merry company to teaching and printmaking, and soon drank himself to death. During the Civil War, Faithorne, along with the etcher Wenzel Hollar and the poet Richard Lovelace, was arrested for Royalist sympathies. During that internment Lovelace wrote his famous lines:

Stone walls do not a prison make,
Nor iron bars a cage

and

I could not love thee, dear, so much,
Loved I not honor more.

The latter verse appeared in Lovelace's book *Lucasta*, for which Faithorne had the honor of providing an engraved title-page. While in custody, he also engraved a refined and sensitive portrait of Sir Thomas Fairfax, c. 1644, after a painting by Robert Walker. (Fig. 87) Fairfax was the general of all the English forces until Cromwell usurped his job. His face was already well known through an anonymous woodcut that had

Fig. 84. Prince Rupert. *Self-Portrait*. Courtesy British Museum.

appeared in 1643 in England's first illustrated newspaper. Faithorne's early engraving was modeled after Claude Mellan's long parallel lines and distinctive manner of characterization. After he was sentenced to exile in France, he exchanged Mellan's system for the cross-hatched tonal effects of Nanteuil, with whom he has been favorably compared. He returned to England with the Restoration and continued a distinguished career, engraving dozens of precise, high-quality portraits of the best people, including King Charles' mistress, Lady Barbara Castlemaine, 1666, after Lely. (Fig. 88) Samuel Pepys said that Faithorne's preliminary drawing was the "finest thing I ever saw in my life, I think." He hung it in his home

MATOAKA ALS REBECCA FILIA POTENTISS: PRINC: POWHATANI IMP: VIRGINIA

Ætatis suæ 21. A.
1616

SERENISSIMA MARIA REGINA
IACOB: MAG: BRIT: REG: MATER

Left: Fig. 87. William Faithorne. *Sir Thomas Fairfax*. Courtesy British Museum.
Right: Fig. 88. William Faithorne. *Lady Barbara Castlemaine*. Private collection.

in addition to buying three impressions of the print. She looks pensive as she leans her head on her hand, her wavy hair falling over one shoulder, her bosom generously exposed. Pictures of the royal playmates were very popular and each new favorite occasioned the production of dozens of engravings. They were the cover girls of their day.

Pierre Lombart, a Dutch contemporary of Faithorne, also worked in the French style in England, where he engraved, after Van Dyck, a series of countesses from the court of Charles — a fascinating gallery of the ladies behind the men behind the king. In one of his most notable plates, based on a composition after the style of Van Dyck, Lombard burnished out and replaced the head as different rulers came to power. The equestrian figure bore in turn the heads of Louis XIV, Cromwell, Charles I, and Cromwell again as an older man. Such substitutions were by no means unique; in print publishing, as in any other business, time saved was money earned. Buyers simply bought the version that was consistent with their partisan views.

Not only heads of state, but important scientists, artists, writers, and nobility had their likenesses taken by printmakers. Simon van de Passe

Opposite, left: Fig. 85. Renold Elstrack. *Mary, Queen of Scots. Right*: Fig. 86. Simon van de Passe. *Pocahontas*. Both figures courtesy British Museum.

gave us portraits of Sir Francis Bacon and Sir Walter Raleigh, among many others. Faithorne engraved a moving *John Milton* with blinded eyes. *William Shakespeare*, 1623, engraved by the Dutch Martin Droeshout as the frontispiece for the first four folio editions, would be of even more interest were it not for the unfortunate ineptitude of the artist. (Fig. 89) The head appears to have been cut out and pasted onto the collar. Shakespeare died in 1616, but it is possible that in 1609 a member of Droeshout's family had made a painting on which the print is based.

The portrait, which some scholars are reluctant to associate with the great poet, has been called the "blank face of a country oaf" and a "pudding-faced effigy." The eyes are on different levels, the hair is longer on the right side than on the left, the body is out of proportion to the head, and the inconsistent lighting creates unnatural shadows on the face. In the eighteenth century, the painter Thomas Gainsborough was commissioned to ennoble the bard's features in an idealized image, but he evidently gave up when he saw the engraving, saying, "I never saw a stupider face. It is impossible that such a mind and such a rare talent should shine with such a face and such a pair of eyes."

David Loggan, originally from Danzig, engraved portraits as well as topical views. His pupil, Robert White, also produced some good portraits, but their work was of uneven quality. With White, English engraving had come about as far as it was to go until the next century, when William Hogarth took up the burin.

Very few etchers were doing portraits of any value with the conspicuous exception of Wenzel Hollar, who brought continental criteria to English printmaking. He was born in Prague, although most of his work was done in England, where he was sponsored by the great patron and connoisseur of art, the Earl of Arundel. Hollar was enormously prolific, specializing in minutely detailed architectural landscapes; like Callot, he was one of the first artists to use the magnifying glass. He depicted fur, silk, lace and feathers with scrupulous care, even though only one of his eyes was functional. He produced many costume prints as well as portraits of famous people both of his own design and after other masters. His life spanned the reigns of Charles I and II and James II, all of whom he etched in a delicate and elegant, though tight, engraving style.

One of his loveliest portraits is the *Lady Seen from the Front*, 1645, presumably his wife, Mistress Tracy, a lady-in-waiting to the Countess Arundel. (Fig. 90) It has all the familiarity and spontaneous grace of domestic intimacy, its sensitive treatment testifying to genuine affection. After the earl escaped to Europe in the disruptions of the Civil War, Hollar was barely able to earn a living, although he produced almost three thousand plates in his lifetime. The king tried to help him after seeing his print *The Coronation of Charles II in Westminster Abbey*, but not enough patronage came his way, and he died penniless. The best of his few followers was Francis Place, whose portraits were etched with light dotting and little strokes, giving his plates a pleasant airy appearance.

Fig. 89. Martin Droeshout. *William Shakespeare*. Courtesy British Museum.

While most English printmakers imitated the European style, none of them had the power or intensity of either Van Dyck or Rembrandt, or the intellect and brilliance of Nanteuil. English collectors, including Samuel Pepys and John Evelyn, patronized continental artists, although Pepys also had many of Faithorne's works in his collection of about three thousand portrait prints. Pepys organized these engravings in albums according to the rank or prestige of the sitters: "royal family; sovereign princes foreign; noblemen, great ministers; ambassadors; gentlemen, virtuosi, men of letters, merchants; ladys & virtuosae; seamen; soldiers, churchmen; lawyers; physicians, chirurgeons (surgeons), chymists; poets, comedians, musicians; paynters, gravers, statuarys, architects; trades art's mechanics,

Fig. 90. Wenzel Hollar. *Lady Seen From the Front.* Private collection.

exempts as not comprehended in any of the praeceding classes." It is a revealing analysis of the stratification of seventeenth-century English society.

When the soft tonal process of mezzotint engraving was introduced, England finally discovered a preferred style and some home-grown talent, and adopted the method as its own. During its heyday it was almost exclusively an English specialty and was known in Europe as *la manière anglaise.* Invented by von Siegen and improved by Prince Rupert, mezzotint was brought to England with the Restoration. Rupert showed the technique to John Evelyn, himself an etcher, author, and incidentally, an early environmentalist through whose suggestion hundreds of trees, which still provide welcome greenery in London, were planted. Evelyn wrote the first book about mezzotint, the *Sculptura* in 1662, but he did not include the secret of how it was done. "I did not think it necessary, that an Art so curious and, as yet, so little vulgar," he noted, "was to be prostituted at so cheap a rate, as the more naked describing of it here would too soon have exposed it to." However, he offered to teach it to anyone who asked. It didn't remain a mystery for very long, but soon became the most popular type of portrait engraving; the rage lasted until the end of the eighteenth century and then was over almost as quickly as it had begun.

It was mostly a reproductive medium, wonderfully equipped to translate the massed shadows, unbroken flows of darks and lights, and softer outlines of the seventeenth and eighteenth century paintings it interpreted. English paintings were well suited for the purpose because their color-values were expressed in cool, toned-down shades and atmospheric effects that lent themselves to mezzotint engraving. Mezzotint, which could not show the details that were possible with engraved lines, was meant to be seen from a little distance rather than closely scrutinized. Because it could suggest painting, it was ideally fitted for the reproduction of beautifully costumed figures, whereas line engravings, more limited in their tonal resources, functioned better in the traditional head and shoulders format. When French engravers attempted full-length transcriptions rather than bust designs, they often became entangled in webs of minutiae. French paintings were generally more linear and higher keyed in their coloring, especially in the eighteenth century, and therefore could not be as successfully rendered in mezzotint. Actually, the French seemed to prefer the greater expressiveness as well as the precision of the incised line, and although there were a few practitioners, mezzotint never caught on in France or anywhere else on the continent. Only J. M. W. Turner, in the nineteenth century, used it successfully as an original medium. In the late 1970s, mezzotints as well as other "handmade" techniques made something of a comeback among artists who reappraised the "mechanistic" serigraphic work of the 1960s and wished to return to a more personal style.

The first dated mezzotint print in England was published in 1669 with a dedication to Prince Rupert. It was a rather coarsely scraped portrait of Rupert's cousin, the merry monarch Charles II, engraved by William Sherwin, Rupert's pupil. (Fig. 91) Sherwin was one of a group of mezzotinters that included Evelyn, Gérard Valck, and Francis Place who did good quality work in spite of the difficulty of producing very fine gradations of shadow. Fortunately, that problem was mostly cleared up when the Dutch Abraham Blooteling came to England about 1672. He based his work on Rupert's improvements of von Siegen's methods. Instead of selective pricking, he roughened the surface of the entire plate. (The print would appear as a solid black at this point.) For this technique, a curved tool with spiked edges was

Top: Fig. 91. William Sherwin. *Charles II. Bottom*: Fig. 92. Abraham Blooteling. *James, Duke of Monmouth.* Both figures courtesy British Museum.

invented, capable of being rocked back and forth over the copper in dozens of directions to produce the innumerable little tooth-points or burr that give the characteristic velvety blacks to the plates when they are inked and printed. This procedure, usually carried out by trained assistants, also provided a closer grain which allowed greater detail and subtlety than was previously possible. As the rough surfaces were scraped down, they held ever less amounts of ink, thus reducing the blacks tone by tone until lighter shades were achieved and the image appeared. Where whites were needed, the burr was entirely smoothed away. Blooteling's method is *subtractive* since it went from darks to lights. Von Siegen's roulette, rendered more or less obsolete, was *additive* in that it created tones or patches progressively only in the places where they were wanted. Mezzotints, like drypoints, must be seen in early impressions before the burr wears down, since the delicate gradations, particularly in the darker parts, generally disappear after only a few dozen impressions are taken. Plates can be reworked, but their fragile tonal balance cannot be restored; much of their aesthetic and commercial value would be lost.

Blooteling's splendid portrait of the bastard son of Charles II, *James, Duke of Monmouth*, 1675, after Sir Peter Lely's painting, is a good example of his work, and pleased Lely too. (Fig. 92) The duke attempted to usurp the throne in 1685, but was captured and executed for treason. Blooteling also left us a portrait of Rupert, as did the prince himself. (See Fig. 84) Fortunately for mezzotint enthusiasts, Rupert made a few engravings before he fell in love with a young actress; after he lost his heart to her, he lost interest in printmaking. The lady was Margaret Hughes, probably the first woman to appear as an actress in the English theatre. She played Desdemona in a 1660 version of Shakespeare's *Othello*, an indication of the greater permissiveness of the Restoration period, when boys were no longer required for female roles.

To John Smith goes the distinction of creating the best seventeenth and early eighteenth century examples of mezzotint portraits. While his work is uneven, the lights are often sparkling and the tones well organized and carefully graduated. His very fine draftsmanship raised the level of mezzotint to first-rate competence. Smith was a pupil of Isaac Beckett, also an able and very popular mezzotinter. They both worked after Kneller's many portraits of poets, philosophers, artists, musicians, and actors. Smith engraved after his teacher as well as after Kneller, from whose paintings his best prints were made. He portrayed everyone — kings, queens, and every duke and duchess who longed to be noticed. Kneller invited him to live and work in his house and chose him to reproduce one hundred thirty-eight of his paintings. Smith's mezzotint of Kneller's *Countess of Ranelagh* is as luminous as any from this period. (Fig. 93; see also Fig. 111) His faces are a little more than just pretty and his ability in drawing hands was especially noted. This was no mean accomplishment, since one way the aristocracy prided themselves was through the delicacy of their fingers, which distinguished them from the less fortunate.

Fig. 93. John Smith. *Countess of Ranelagh*. Courtesy British Museum.

After the Restoration everyone in London was eager to spruce up and shine again. The demand for fashionable portraits was so great that only a small number could be real personality studies. Too many were turned out mechanically by artists who were more interested in merchandising than in excellence. Even the best painters, Lely, Kneller, and Van Dyck, were not able to give individual attention to every gentleman and lady. Expert technicians did most of the costumes, backgrounds, and even some of the faces, but in their finest work, both the painters and the engravers often showed a true feeling for character delineation. In the eighteenth century the superiority of paintings by Sir Joshua Reynolds and Thomas Gainsborough permitted even higher quality mezzotints.

But the immediate business of English portrait artists was not to define the inner man, his thoughts, or the expressive aspects of his face.

Fig. 94. John Foster. *Mr. Richard Mather.* Courtesy American Antiquarian Society, Worcester, Mass.

The English patron wanted an elegant image, cultured and aristocratic in appearance, and that is what he got in fully modeled and gracefully posed pictures. They were meant to be beautiful and decorative, and they were.

V. America

After years of struggling to free itself from Spanish rule, Holland signed a truce with Philip III in 1609 which granted greater religious toleration. The armistice attracted groups of English Protestants, who emigrated to Holland hoping to share in these wider freedoms. However, the cease-fire was only in effect for twelve years, and in 1620, when it became apparent that hostilities and persecution would be resumed, a handful of refugees, determined to find a place where they could live in safety, boarded the *Speedwell* in Rotterdam and headed for the wide ocean. When the ship became unseaworthy, they turned back, transferred to the *Mayflower*, and sailed for the New World.

Eighteen years later the first printing press in America was already in operation in Cambridge. By 1686 Boston had eight bookshops. In 1690 the first American paper mill was founded in Pennsylvania. An experiment in newspaper publication was attempted in that same year in Massachusetts, but it was suppressed after the first issue because of the fear that printing would lead to "disobedience and heresy."

Amateur artists arrived from time to time from the Old Country, and although their skills were limited, they provided a bit of civility for the settlers. Aside from some announcements and other ephemera, they produced two main categories of prints — maps, which were necessary, and portraits, which were not. The latter could hardly be ignored, however, where the social hierarchy was still fluid and a reputation of consequence might be made. For the modest and frugal Puritans, printed portraits had a distinct advantage over large colorful paintings — they were less pretentious and they were cheaper.

The earliest surviving American print is a woodcut portrait that served as a frontispiece for the biography of *Richard Mather*, Boston's first preacher. (Fig. 94) For unknown reasons the woodblock was cut in two; the halves in the three extant impressions do not meet in correct register, but that evidently did not bother anyone since its purpose was more documentary than artistic. Despite the crude workmanship, self-possession and fortitude are vividly conveyed; the simple black and white shapes make a bold and attractive design. The proportions are faulty — the pince-nez is more fit for a doll than a man, and the thumb bears no resemblance to any digit in existence — but they hardly detract from the lively presence of the New England clergyman. He was the grandfather of Cotton Mather, the Puritan scholar who has been blamed, to some extent unjustly, for exacerbating the witchcraft frenzy in Salem.

The print was cut in 1670 by John Foster, a Native American school teacher who may also have been the engraver of an ABC primer for Indian students. As an amateur he was probably more acceptable than a European-trained printmaker to the straitlaced Pilgrims for whom art was suspect at best, and sinful at worst. As it was, perhaps a few eyebrows were raised at the portrait, made in obvious disregard of the Second Commandment, which forbade graven images.

Throughout the seventeenth century, settlements grew, rapidly along the seaboard, more slowly towards the west. Incoming colonists arrived steadily, bringing with them paintings and prints which local artists borrowed. Poses, costumes, and even furnishings and backgrounds were copied and recopied until skills improved sufficiently for an indigenous style to develop. But printmaking as a fine art in America still had a long way to go.

Chapter 5

The Eighteenth Century

The Age of Enlightenment opened on the continent with battles royal. Occasional treaties of peace interrupted the hostilities until intrigue or opportunism renewed the tugs of war. In 1715 Louis XV, aged five, came to the French throne; when he grew up he was hampered by a weak intellect, meddling mistresses, humiliating political blunders, and military defeats in which France lost most of her colonies in North America and India. To his successor he handed down a country fairly well on its way to ruin. The reign of his grandson Louis XVI had some important positive elements, but its life-style was so extravagant and corrupt, and the costs of aiding the American independence movement so heavy, that the economy broke down. The government finally succumbed to the Revolution in 1789 partly because of riots by the over-taxed and monstrously burdened peasantry and partly because the land-owning upper classes resisted impoverishment as the country's wealth shifted to the bourgeoisie.

The Age of Enlightenment also generated a passion for learning and a conviction that reason and experience would promote happiness. The intellectual atmosphere, kindled by Rationalist philosophers such as Montesquieu, Rousseau, and Voltaire, and stimulated by the successful American Revolution, had aroused popular sentiment around the ideals of the rights of man. The best minds of both the middle and upper classes contributed to the expansion of commercial enterprises as well as the arts and sciences. All of cultured Europe spoke French. Parisian elegance was *de rigeur*. French art pervaded all aspects of refined taste.

But by the century's end everything came unstuck. Mobs, hungry for bread, and thwarted by their failure to bring about liberty, equality, and fraternity, went mad in a Reign of Terror and guillotined thousands of their countrymen, including the king and his unpopular queen, Marie Antoinette. Unemployment, food shortages, and political uprisings were universal. The prestige and authority of French leadership collapsed, the worn-out classical spirit faltered, imagination weakened. When it seemed as if nothing could moderate the alienation and disillusion, a young Corsican general pulled together the demoralized country, suppressed

106

further violence, averted a civil war, and established himself, for good and evil, as dictator of France.

Meanwhile, England, despite recurrent war and troubles with the American colonies, enjoyed enough peace to permit great strides in commerce and industry, anticipating the achievements of the Industrial Revolution. Seaport towns grew prosperous through trade with colonial outposts. Improved health care and the control of some devastating diseases raised the birth rate and lowered the death rate so that by the end of the century the population had about doubled. Unfortunately, the country couldn't absorb the numbers of workers entering the marketplace, resulting in the malnutrition and squalid housing that Dickens would later describe.

The leadership of Europe that France had sought through military campaigns, England was able to secure by avoiding war on its own soil, by wresting control of the seas from the Dutch, and by its monopoly of the pernicious African slave trade, the profits from which built much of its large naval fleet. Not until 1833 were slavery and the slave trade abolished throughout the British Empire.

A new spirit of religious toleration infused the country with vitality and hope. Catholics found welcome gestures of conciliation, and Jews, after almost four hundred years of exclusion, were returning in considerable numbers. These recently approved Englishmen, together with Protestants who had come as refugees from Louis XIV's persecutions, now helped England to outstrip the continent in financial and industrial undertakings. But the gulf between the classes grew wider than ever. Although the poor had very little to show for their grinding drudgery, the moneyed people had the leisure and security to become patrons of art and scholarship. English superseded Latin in learned works, literacy was extended, and reading became a popular pastime; the first circulating public library was founded in 1740. By means of a gradual progression, the country moved on a high road from oligarchic government to the beginnings of modern constitutional rule. Napoleon alone was still a menace.

Spain, which had hardly acknowledged either the Renaissance or the Reformation, lay at the crossroads of Italian, Moslem and northern European civilizations. Her early heritage included splendid Moorish buildings, beautifully illuminated manuscripts, religious erudition, and a deep spiritual commitment by her people; the great explorations of Columbus, Cortes, and Balboa to distant and unheard-of places were Spanish in origin. But the later events of her history reflect a stunted political and philosophical development, an irremediably corrupt government and repressive Church, an entrenched illiteracy of the peasantry, and the fanaticism of the Inquisition against her Jewish and Moslem populations who refused conversion to Catholicism. This doctrinaire shortsightedness emptied the country of a large number of its most valued artists, merchants, and scholars.

France decided in 1702 that Spain was an easy target and would make an excellent appendage; much of Europe thought otherwise and began a war that lasted eleven years. When it was over, France's attempts to dominate Europe and to destroy the balance of power finally failed. For a short period of time, during which Spain was under the reign of Louis XIV's son and grandsons, its intellectual and aesthetic level was raised by the influx of enlightened Frenchmen. The harshness of the Inquisition, which had in the previous fifty years alone burned almost eight hundred victims at the stake, was modified. Under French rule Spain achieved relative prosperity, but by 1788 the empty-headed Charles IV and his disreputable queen Maria Luisa Teresa, both of whom Goya painted with searing contempt, assumed power, and along with her lover, the wily Manuel de Godoy, delivered Spain into Napoleon's empire. However, Godoy is remembered gratefully by engravers, if by no one else, because he was agreeable to their inclusion in the Spanish Royal Academy at a time when printmakers had not yet attained similar privileges in England.

Europe's major economic connection with America was through the tobacco, flour, and cotton trades. The plantation system had been organized to accommodate the cotton industry, which required cheap and plentiful labor. Close to a million Africans were enslaved and brought to the land of the free. America's agricultural and human commerce supplied enormous wealth and taxes to both France and England. It was a bonanza for which both sides expended a great effort during the French and Indian War with the goal of dominating the western hemisphere. England was eventually able to oust the French forces and to establish a lasting cultural sphere of influence; its language and customs became rooted in the West.

By the middle of the eighteenth century the New World was showing definite signs of coming of age. The upstart colonies had assimilated settlers from France, Holland, Spain, England, and whatever other countries that included adventurous citizens. From the very first the newcomers adapted their European traditions to the exigencies of the wilderness. They built churches and dwellings in architectural styles that reminded them of home. Many early immigrants had been landless in Europe and were eager for the opportunity to possess their own property and provide their families with the comforts that could be earned from tilling the soil. New skills were learned. New life-styles were experienced. Morality endured side by side with sin, and intelligence persisted along with incompetence, quite like the world they had left behind.

Troubles arose as England attempted to impose unwarranted burdens on the populace. The outcome was that the separate colonies drew together in mutual defense. When the British government tried to extract heavy taxes from merchants, force them to import tea at unfavorable rates, and inflict a dozen more "Intolerable Acts," the citizenry united in their determination to gain control of their own interests. On July 4, 1776, Congress declared the country's independence.

As the century ended, groups of high-spirited men began to move across the Appalachian Mountains in search of fur, freedom, and open land. The American frontier was pushed further and further west as families took to the wastelands, where they established homes and began new lives. Benjamin Franklin thought that centuries would pass before the land would be settled; it hardly took a hundred years. There is comfort in discovering that Franklin didn't know everything.

I. France

The characteristic qualities of French portrait printmaking — reason, intellect, loftiness — which had been brought to their pinnacle in the seventeenth century, were preserved and amplified in the eighteenth. Designs now often included the whole figure, which tended to place the subject farther from the viewer and at the same time suggest maximum authority and prestige. But the concentration on facial expression and the attempt to reveal the sitter's personality in great measure declined. More and more these portraits became universal types, telling us less and less about specific individuals. Larger, accessory-crowded pictures appeared with even greater tonal gradations than had been attempted earlier. We see the sitter's fashionable coat, his lace cuffs, his ornate furnishings, his books, his armor, his furs, his draperies, his silks and satins — everything that is extrinsic to his character. Now the accessories define the man.

The engravers did not invent these models. They hardly designed any of their own work, following paintings that were marvels of ornament, but superficial as likenesses. The originality and subtlety of the seventeenth century engravers were beyond their capabilities or outside their interests. Missing is the sparkling expression of the eyes and the suggestion of skin tones — the pale or luminous complexion, or the aging flush — that was one of the best features of the Nanteuil school. The eighteenth century engravers, however, working after portraitists whose paintings too often resembled exquisite colored marble more than living heads, perfected burin techniques capable of rendering excessively intricate patterns and textures that appealed to the taste of the Louis XV period.

The establishment of an academy for engravers played an important role in fixing approved styles and providing an opportunity to showcase the work of its members. Sound teaching methods and rules laid down by Lebrun replaced the old informal master-apprentice relationship, helped curb exaggerated mannerisms, and yielded high professional standards. However, too often its countless regulations discouraged imagination and forced artistic impulses into prescribed channels. What began as a process of education ended by hardening into a reactionary system that was not able to develop great original printmakers. Nevertheless, reproductive engravers of almost every motif were kept very busy. Beginning in 1704, they were required to submit two high-quality portraits in order to be accepted as members of the Academy. Since inclusion was almost a prerequisite for realizing economically profitable editions, the greatest possible efforts were expended on upgrading techniques.

Fig. 95. Pierre Drevet. *Louis Dauphin*.
Courtesy Rothschild Collection.

Most portrait engravings of this period were based on the paintings of Hyacinthe Rigaud and Nicolas de Largillière. A hundred years before, Mellan had said that he considered it beneath his dignity to portray ordinary people; now de Largillière, for one, found that he could spare a little pride in return for a well-filled pocketbook. He was one of the first painters to specialize in wealthy nobodies; Rigaud catered to bluer blood. Both derived their gestures, elaborate costumes and accessories, as well as poses showing more of the figure than just the head and shoulders, from the Flemish schools of Rubens and Van Dyck. They interpreted those influences in a distinctly French manner, more reticent and less personal. Like Rubens and Van Dyck, Rigaud worked very closely with his reproductive engravers, supervising and correcting their plates; not surprisingly, their prints after his paintings were more successful than those after artists less concerned with printmaking techniques.

Pierre Drevet learned many of his skills from Rigaud. He knew how to model features and how to coax ever more color gradations and texture variations from his plates, but he used too many lines and didn't understand how to arrange them well enough. One of his best engravings after Rigaud was a half-length portrait of Louis Dauphin. By this point in portrait history the face of the child is no longer that of a miniature adult. (Fig. 95) Since very few Frenchmen would ever have the opportunity to see royalty in person, it was only through the wide dissemination of such engravings, in which the prince is represented as the essence of nobility, that public curiosity could be satisfied and majesty made visible. Louis XV knew that there was no better way to convey the meaning of divine right to an illiterate population throughout his realm than to exploit these political posters. (See Fig. 101.) "Occupying, so to speak, the place of God," he said, "we appear to share His knowledge as well as His authority." His naive belief in absolute power seems to have been fully accepted by his subjects.

Drevet's son Pierre Imbert was a better technician than his father. In 1723, at the age of twenty-six, he engraved the portrait of Bishop Jacques Bossuet after Rigaud's posthumous painting of 1705. (Fig. 96) The florid plate is the *pièce de resistance* of the early eighteenth century period and has been called one of the finest engravings ever made. All that shows of

Fig. 96. Pierre Imbert Drevet. *Jacques Bénigne Bossuet*. Courtesy Grunwald Center for the Graphic Arts, UCLA.

Fig. 97. Pierre Imbert Drevet. *Samuel Bernard*. Courtesy Metropolitan Museum of Art, gift of Georgiana W. Sargent, in memory of John Osborne Sargent, 1924 [24.63.29].

the body is the face and hands, and these are rendered with an exacting precision. The avalanche of paraphernalia is wonderfully translated. The stately full-length pose with outstretched right arm may have been the model on which Gilbert Stuart based the "Lansdowne" portrait of *George Washington*, 1796, presented to Lafayette in appreciation of his efforts on behalf of the American Revolution.

The portrait of Bossuet in his lace-trimmed episcopal robe was intended to mark him as an eminent and authoritative figure; its rational, deliberate style, as of a man of reason. He was the tutor of the young dauphin, an inspiring scholar, writer, and speaker who tried, and failed, to force Catholic and Protestant factions into a Christian unity. Rigaud gave the commission his highest priority and worked up a black and white drawing for Drevet to follow, rather than risk any inaccuracies in the tonal balance. The engraving turned out to be finer and more dynamic than the painting. Drevet may have known that it was to be his masterpiece; he labored over it through fifteen states.

In 1729 he engraved the portrait of Samuel Bernard, the banker who loaned an appreciative Louis XIV millions of francs to provide capital for his sinking court. (Fig. 97) Bernard was glad to be able to requite Louis' indulgence to the Jews of France, although he, like other financiers, went bankrupt when Louis could no longer pay his debts. The seventeen-by-twenty-five-inch print, in which Bernard is surrounded by personal effects representing his commercial interests, is likewise after Rigaud, and is technically astonishing, but it lacks clarity and harmony in the arrangement of its abundant details. It appears rather spotty because Drevet was not able to integrate all the trivia into a coherent unity; craftsmanship, rather than interpretation, seems to be the *raison d'être* of the print. Yet there is a sense of power that unquestionably holds the interest. Though Drevet lived on until 1739, he became mentally ill soon after the Bernard portrait and was never able to work again.

François Chereau was a pupil of the Drevets. His *Nicolas de Largillière*, 1715, with the artist's left hand proudly pointing to an unfinished canvas on his easel, is a large engraving after a painted self-portrait, in which Largillière showed off his skill in suggesting deep space. (Fig. 98) He showed it off more than once, repeating the pose in his portrait of the sculptor Pierre Lepautre. Popular artists were often too busy to be original; if a patron wanted a unique pose, he had to pay very generously for the privilege. Chereau modified the design in order to enhance its decorative qualities and concentrate on the head, much as Edelinck and other judicious engravers often did. The plate has grace and beauty in addition to its meticulous workmanship.

The later followers of the Drevets brought the portrait school to its decline and close. George-Friedrich Schmidt, Jean-Georges Wille, and Jean-Gotthard Müller were German engravers who did most of their work in France. Schmidt was at his uninspired best in his engraving after the self-portrait of Pierre Mignard. The face lacks vitality, but the great manual skill almost makes up for the rather dry and monotonous linear system, which incorporated dots and lozenges within the cross-hatching to further differentiate the appearance of textures and fabrics. Mignard had been the outspoken arch-rival of Lebrun and, because of their enmity, was openly antagonistic to the Academy. But at Lebrun's death in 1690, he ate all his derogatory words and was appointed as its head.

Wille did his best prints after Rigaud, who unfortunately died before he could give Wille enough of the solid grounding that he usually provided for his engravers. Wille himself lived for ninety-three years, becoming one

Fig. 98. François Chereau. *Nicolas de Largillière*. Private collection.

of the most sought-after and honored teachers and printmakers of the time. His *Marquis de Marigny*, 1761, after Jean Louis Tocqué, displays the deftness and competence of his burin, but his heads have a stiffness and a metallic effect that could not be overcome in spite of the clever manipulation of his lines. Tocqué was a pupil of Rigaud, a widely respected court painter and a stickler for truthful portraiture, willing to cater to pardonable self-esteem, but not to overweening vanity.

Müller was Wille's pupil, but the student soon outdid the teacher. His engraving of the painter Louis Galloche, after Tocqué, won him admission into the Academy in 1776. (Fig. 99) Most of his work is too methodical, but in this fine print the face and wig are so carefully shaded and impeccably cut that the means are relatively unobtrusive. Müller's son Friedrich was also a well-known engraver. Frederick Keppel in his book *The Golden Age of Engraving* traces the circumstances that too often plagued printmakers:

> Six years before Friedrich's death he was commissioned by Rittner of Dresden to engrave Raphael's *Sistine Madonna*. His very existence

seemed wrapped up in the execution of this plate; he worked upon it day and night with the self-consuming zeal that Mozart expended on the *Requiem*, which proved to be his own. When the plate was finished he took it to Rittner; but the man of business refused it on the ground that the lines were so delicately cut that it would not print a sufficient number of impressions. Every line had to be deepened; and this thankless toil broke the heart of poor Müller. He bore up till his task was finished, and then he sank into the gloom of hopeless insanity, and died the very day that the first proof of his plate was printed. It was hung over his bier as he lay dead.

The human side of history is too often unknown or forgotten.

One more engraver of this school must yet be mentioned. In 1778, another of Wille's pupils, Charles-Clement Bervic, received a commission to engrave a full-length portrait of Louis XVI after a painting by A. F. Callet. (Fig. 100) As T. H. Thomas pointed out in his definitive book *French Portrait Engraving of the Seventeenth and Eighteenth Centuries*, the painting was a servile derivation of Rigaud's *Louis le Grand* (Louis XIV). Bervic's rendering is a servile derivation of Pierre Drevet's engraving. (Fig. 101) However, as a brilliant *tour de force* it demands recognition, although its classical style was well out of date. The king appears in imperial and imperious splendor, but it was his last hurrah; if he intended the portrait to persuade his countrymen that his right was divine, it came to nothing, for his kingdom collapsed the next year with the taking of the Bastille. Bervic, who was a very slow worker, nevertheless kept plodding along on the plate, finally finishing it in 1790, three years before Louis was guillotined for treason. Although he dedicated it to the king, "restorer of liberty," not enough people associated Louis with the cause of freedom.

The story goes that just as Bervic was putting the finishing touches on the large plate, it was snatched from his hands by a Republican sympathizer, broken in half, and thrown into the river. In another version, he was momentarily overcome by a wave of anti-royalist feeling and destroyed it himself. Either way, he retrieved and mended it when no one was looking, but all the impressions still show a faint line across the royal middle. It is well engraved in its sumptuous magnificence, but it lacks animation and expression. Without these attributes, no portrait can succeed.

Side by side with these labored works, the Rococo style, of which Antoine Watteau was the greatest master, evolved as a more graceful and sophisticated phase of Baroque. Although Watteau was not a printmaker himself, his style initiated a move away from the close and overly detailed work of the Drevet school to one of greater breadth and unity. A group of printmakers who adopted Watteau's looser manner also followed Morin's combined use of etching and engraving to create delicate facial tones in order to soften and brighten their prints through the scattering of highlights over the surfaces of their plates. The movement was a reaction to the entrenched academic system, and offered dainty, light-hearted designs in perfect harmony with the pleasure-seeking court of Louis XV.

Fig. 99. Jean-Gotthard Müller. *Louis Galloche.* Private collection.

Jean Daullé, who was employed by Rigaud after the Drevets were no longer able to work, engraved a fine half-length portrait of Louis XV's five-year-old son, *Louis Dauphin,* after a full-length painting by Tocqué. (Fig. 102) It incorporates this lighter quality and is permeated with innocence and the noblesse of royalty. Other portrait engravers of the Watteau school who also combined etching and engraving were Laurent Cars, Nicolas-Henri Tardieu, and Gaspard Duchange.

Medallion designs, about two and a half to four inches in diameter, were another of the many novel styles of portrait engraving identified with the Louis XVI period. They were intended as calling cards or as illustrations for small-sized books, and were executed in a more direct, unaffected, and unembellished manner than the prints of the Louis XV period. The profile was almost exclusively preferred, with the focus entirely on the face. While they appear uncomplicated, considerable technique was required to impart liveliness of expression within the limits of a side view, and with so little attempt at color-values. Their simple and distinct outlines often succeeded with happier results than the more elaborate productions of the Drevet school.

The men who perfected this specialty, often designing their own plates, were Charles Nicolas Cochin the Younger and Augustin de St. Aubin. Many of these medallion prints were based on the methods of the Watteau engravers and were reproduced after Cochin's drawings. A typical example, St. Aubin's *Charles Nicholas Cochin,* 1771, after the subject's own self-portrait, directs all the attention to the sensitive expression of the features. (Fig. 103) It began as a rather insubstantial etching; its salient lines were then added by the burin for emphasis. Great care was taken to maintain the overall cool and delicate effect.

The medallion style emanated from the mid-century "antique" revival, when the ruins of Pompeii and Herculaneum were discovered. These neighboring cities near Naples at the foot of Mt. Vesuvius had been covered by volcanic matter after the mountain erupted in 79 A.D. They lay untouched for almost seventeen hundred years until excavations revealed parts of the towns in remarkably preserved condition with many sculptures and wall paintings intact. The interest generated by this trove of classical art was not only reflected in the clear linearity of the medallion engravers, but in most contemporary French art and decor as well. When Johann Joachim Winckelmann published the first great history of art in 1764, extolling the "noble simplicity and calm grandeur" of Greek order and balance, Neo-Classism became the predictable reaction to the capricious elements of Baroque and Rococo, and was the artistic school that survived the Revolution.

Without question, St. Aubin was the best and most versatile portrait printmaker of this period. Cochin said he could "put life even into the drawing of a wig." His portraits never became as popular as the large, more severe formal work of the Drevet school, but their sympathetic and descriptive modeling was better adapted to decorate the walls of the newly fashionable, more intimate apartments of the upper middle class. In direct contrast to medallion profiles, St. Aubin also executed full-faced images that were light in mood and catered to feminine tastes. Indeed, it was the influence of women in the brilliant salons of the eighteenth century that gave French society its reputation for polished wit and *savoir vivre*. Some of these women, who were neither famous nor members of the nobility, had great sensitivity and resisted exaggerated flattery, welcoming honesty and sincerity in their portraits.

St. Aubin's etching in 1763 after Bernard of Mme. Barbe Louise Nettine, a banker's wife, is noticeably softer and grayer in tone than the typical engraving; the lack of strong black and white highlights, so typical in the Drevet school, gives her a very natural appearance. (Fig. 104) Lady Dilke, in her book *French Engravers and Draughtsmen of the Eighteenth Century*, comments that "in the very folds of her dress there hangs a perfume of faded roses." Her face, though a bit vacuous, expresses an unaffected and native cleverness as well as moderation and refinement; aging is depicted as an agreeable and integral part of life. Pictures of this merchant middle class were more and more welcome; portraits of the royal court were the last things most people wanted to see. The growing sense of republicanism and equality, loosely modeled on the antique Roman citizen-centered government, was making itself felt throughout the social structure, not only in France, but in America as well. Although some critics objected that portraits of commoners debased the talents of the best painters and encouraged vulgar taste, many artists found that not only did the bourgoisie make equally good subjects, but they paid their bills sooner.

Meanwhile, the court was still playing Let's Pretend and living in dissolute magnificence. In its circles, almost nothing was considered beyond the bounds of propriety, and no one in aristocratic Paris seemed to mind that art was becoming salacious. But it was done with such flair that even a fastidious moralist might smile with civilized leniency at the suggestive subjects and exposed feminine charms. French painters and printmakers judiciously hovered at a careful distance from obscenity, but adopted a distinctively licentious manner that has become a time-honored convention. St. Aubin's small plates of a courtier and his mistress, engraved after

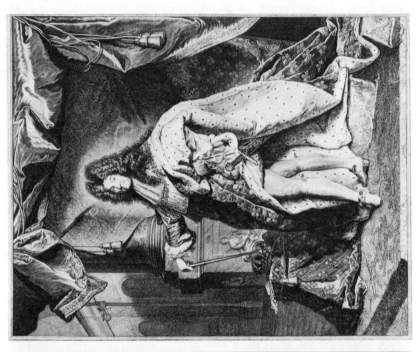

LOUIS XVI
ROI DES FRANÇAIS, RESTAURATEUR DE LA LIBERTÉ

his own design, were modeled by himself and his wife and are examples of how even portraiture was caught up in this fashion. "At least be discreet," she urges (*Au Moins Soyez Discret*). "Count on me," he assures her (*Comptez sur Mes Serments*). (Figs. 105, 106) Such witty and sophisticated pictures hardly represented the taste of the general public, many of whom were already stirred by revolutionary agitation and repelled by the shallowness and dissipation of an elite society. To those who appreciated grace and charm above dignity and intellect, however, this sort of portraiture was the epitome of delightful finish and tender feeling. Although such prints were pervasive among the upper social classes, and St. Aubin and others continued to produce them, the Revolution eventually exhausted the energy and vitality of the market.

Innovators had labored mightily all through the century to tempt their customers with novelties. Jacob Christoph Le Blon, a German printmaker working in France, developed a method that imitated the appearance of paintings and pastel drawings in response to a desire for color prints. Le Blon loosely based his ideas on Newton's discoveries that the primary pigments — blue, yellow and red — when mixed in appropriate proportions, would produce all the shades of the spectrum. Using three separately inked plates, one or more of them mezzotinted, the others etched, he rolled each impression through the printing press, superimposing one color over the other. The method was not consistently successful since the tones didn't always blend or register properly; even in the twentieth century the secret of true fidelity color printing has not yet been cracked. Yet, several of Le Blon's portraits of English and French royalty are quite effective, particularly that of *Louis XV*, 1739, after the English artist Blackey. The king, while not as interested in printmaking as his predecessor, provided Le Blon with a pension, so we may assume that he was pleased with the resemblance.

François Janinet also printed in color, using half a dozen or more separate plates. It has recently been pointed out by John W. Ittmann that these portraits were produced, not in aquatint as has been assumed, but "with rockers and roulettes that have left a distinctive repetitive pattern" similar to the earliest mezzotint method. Janinet's *Marie Antoinette*, 1777, achieved excellent color resolution, but the process inherently lacked sufficient definition to ensure clarity of expression. Although etched work or the burin were often added to overcome this problem, on the whole, most color portraits remain ornamental and superficial in character.

Yet another color process was the crayon method, invented about 1757, in which roulettes were used to produce a grainy appearance in imitation of crayon or chalk drawings. Impressions were usually printed from

Opposite, left: Fig. 100. Charles-Clément Bervic. *Louis XVI*. Courtesy Metropolitan Museum of Art, gift of Miss Adelaide Milton de Groot in memory of her aunt, Miss Emeline Smith Hawley, 1946 [46.95]. *Right*: Fig. 101. Pierre Drevet. *Louis le Grand*. Courtesy Musée Louvre, Rothschild Collection.

Top: Fig. 102. Jean Daullé. *Louis Dauphin*. Private collection. *Center*: Fig. 103. Augustin de St. Aubin. *Charles Nicholas Cochin*. Courtesy Musée Louvre, Rothschild Collection. *Bottom*: Fig. 104. Augustin de St. Aubin. *Mme. Barbe Louise Nettine*. Courtesy Bibliothèque Nationale.

several plates, frequently on pastel colored papers. Louis Marin Bonnet used a number of plates to reproduce drawings in their original pastel colors. He successfully depicted the soft femininity and elegance, but not the vitality, of Countess Du Barry in his crayon engraving of 1769 after a drawing by François Hubert Drouais. (Fig. 107) Du Barry began her professional career as a courtesan, soon becoming one of the mistresses of Louis XV. Depending on who described her, she was either a conniving impediment to the king or a trustworthy asset. It is known that she fled to England to pawn her jewels after his death and was executed by the Tribunal on her return to France in 1793 for plotting against the Revolution. Bonnet's stylish portraits of the royal court, sometimes showing them "sharing" the concerns of the people, were propaganda instruments intended to bring the nation closer to the government.

In a class by itself was the physiognotrace, a device which made silhouette portraits using an optical tracing machine. These life-sized outlines were then rapidly reduced in size and their interior features quickly completed with etching. The instrument was designed by Gilles Louis Chrétien in 1786 and was a popular fad during the following decade. It had once amused the guests at Versailles, and was later brought to America by aristocratic refugees, where it became an affordable substitute for highly finished engravings.

The realities of these troubled times made an end of much that was familiar and traditional. Life-styles that once had seemed the quintessence of good breeding became, in the eyes of the radical leadership, corrupt and decadent. But the brilliance and luster of French culture was too ingrained not to endure, although after the Revolution it did so along new lines and in a new philosophical spirit.

Although two centuries of impeccable portrait artistry had reached — and passed — its peak, Napoleon was sufficiently astute to remember the political advantages of regal portraiture. He tried to preserve those benefits in the early years of the nineteenth century when he commissioned the large engraving *Napoleon le Grand* after François Gérard's painting of 1805. (Fig. 108) Auguste Boucher Desnoyers' print of the emperor in his coronation robes was no better than the painting, facile and weak in facial expression, acknowledging its debts to the Drevets and Bervic. (See figs. 96, 100) The Olympian pose was certainly meant to induce image worship, but the tendency to astound with greater and greater flourishes simply degenerated into an overwrought dead end.

The last gasps of this long school of classical engraving persisted well into the nineteenth century, but they rightly belong within the context of the eighteenth. Claude Ferdinand Gaillard, a Franciscan brother, developed a system of laying lines so close together that they appear to blend unless looked at through a magnifying glass. His original portraits, such as the Benedictine monk, Abbot *Dom Prosper Gueranger*, must be seen to realize the infinite variations of strokes and dots that the burin is capable of. (Fig. 109) While the work no longer suggests the linearity of engraving, as technical wizardry it is absolutely amazing, and as portraiture, it remains effective. Both the proliferation of lines and the strained intensity of Gueranger have appeared excessive to modern critics, but for Gaillard, spiritual qualities, as he understood them, were his first priority. His portraits, mostly done in the mid-century, were the terminal expression of a type of formal engraving that had boasted a coherent unity for over two hundred years. By the time of his death in 1887, the photograph was mocking his manual powers.

But although engraving was a dying profession, other printmaking methods remained very much alive. As the eighteenth century came to a close (with perfect timing for the chronicler who appreciates the neat, but arbitrary, divisions of hundred-year periods), a young German, Aloys Senefelder, invented lithography. It became a distinctly French technique, and, along with the etching revival, reanimated printed portraiture in the nineteenth century; artists never stopped writing biographies in faces — to divert the senses, entertain the inquiring mind, and woo the peacock in every potential sitter.

II. England

Although France and England moved in very different political and

economic worlds, in the arts they shared a common partiality for fashionable and aristocratic portraiture. The French, perhaps, had more discriminating taste, but both produced splendid specimens which were hung on the walls to be envied and admired by one's friends. For the most part, English portraits continued to express stateliness and grandeur. Figures were carefully arranged so that each patrician gesture and glance would certify that blue blood was beyond the reach of the lower orders; the competition between the nouveau and the ancestral rich was clearly understood by artists who labored to make that disparity as obvious as possible. The greatest attention was paid to outward appearance and social position. Sitters vied with each other in the search for a posture, costume, accessory, or romantic garden background that would eclipse yesterday's sensation. Yet these beautiful portraits were not entirely superficial or forgettable, but, in fact, displayed a genuine feeling for the distinctiveness of the clients and the psychology of their time. In spite of sticking to conventional academic methods, painters turned out works that were astute perceptions of a unique society living in a fantasy world.

There was one major exception to this ceremonious style. The maverick was William Hogarth, the first distinguished native-born English artist. He was not only a great painter, but an original engraver in a time of reproductive printmaking; he is less well known as a humanitarian who helped found and support a hospital for orphans. He began his professional career as an armorial engraver on silver plate, but soon discovered that he preferred painting and printmaking. He built a tremendous reputation with his series of sardonic compositions, *The Harlot's Progress*, 1733–4, and *The Rake's Progress*, 1735, which he painted and then engraved to insure their wide circulation. The six or eight pictures in each set were issued serially and were meant to be read as uplifting moral lessons, or, as his friend Henry Fielding said, "to serve the cause of virtue." They were visual short stories that revealed personal character through the eyes of satire, and contained actual portraits of Hogarth's friends, including a fencing master, a prizefighter, and the Vicar of Marylebone. Hogarth painted, but had others engrave, the six plates of his *Marriage à la Mode*, 1745, a case history of greed and corruption. His work was the antithesis of the Rococo style flourishing simultaneously in France.

Portrait painting was not his major interest, yet he was disappointed that it didn't afford him greater professional success. His innate cynicism and unwillingness to curry favor stood between him and a clientele that wished to be flattered. He claimed that portraiture was more popular in England than anywhere else because selfishness and vanity were the "ruling passions" of the country. Although he lacked academic training and suavity,

Opposite, left: Fig. 105. Augustin de St. Aubin. *Au Moins Soyez Discret*. *Right*: Fig. 106. Augustin de St. Aubin. *Comptez Sur Mes Serments*. Both figures courtesy Metropolitan Museum of Art, Harris Brisbane Dick Fund, 1935 [35.100.13 and 35.100.12].

Fig. 107. Louis Marin Bonnet. *Countess Du Barry*. Courtesy Musée Louvre, Rothschild Collection.

his keen observation and genial realism are more highly rated today than many of the showier works of the period.

He issued a group of prints in 1749 with an engraved self-portrait, and etched several other original heads, but the only one of exceptional interest is *Simon, Lord Lovat*, 1746. (Fig. 110) Here Hogarth went back to the open manner of Van Dyck. In addition to using Lovat's face and hands to provide psychological impact, he exploited the casual pose itself to define personality in a way that was well ahead of its time. (Ingres, for instance, in 1832, used a similar composition to delineate character and mood in his famous painting of Louis Bertin, a distinguished and influential journalist.)

Lovat was a morally corrupt individual who had raped and then married the widow of a member of his family in order to inherit her estate. He was a double agent who betrayed both political parties in the intrigues surrounding the Stuart and Hanoverian succession to the throne. The day after he sat for this portrait, he was executed in a carnival atmosphere while crowds jostled for choice seats; he was the last man to be legally beheaded in England. Perhaps he was counting his misdeeds on his fingers; at any rate, despite the upcoming grim proceedings, he looks as though he relished the attention and appears quite cheerful. The demand for this etching was so great that the printer had to work overtime to keep up with the sales. Priced at a shilling, it was a sensation, with more than a thousand copies per week hawked on the streets to satisfy the public's morbid curiosity. Every crafty nuance of the man was captured in this unusually deft image.

Sir Joshua Reynolds, younger than Hogarth by a generation, also portrayed the English character, but from a different perspective. Reynolds painted the romantic illusions of an aristocracy that kept God in his heaven as long as all was right in their world. Hogarth saw the underbelly of that same society and recorded its less decorous and fastidious moments. When he died, it was as a portraitist that he was remembered in the inscription over his remains: ". . . Here death has closed the curious eyes that saw the manners in the face."

Although Hogarth's work was outside the main current, the tendency of most English, as well as French, eighteenth century printmakers was to

Fig. 108. Auguste Boucher Desnoyers. *Napoleon le Grand*. Courtesy Bibliothèque Nationale.

support an orderly continuation of the existing portrait schools. But whereas in France there had been a distinct decline from the finer and more original work of the seventeenth century, in England, after a tentative start in the 1600s, a fully perfected mezzotint style was developed by the second half of the 1700s in a period of experimentation and new approaches to older formulas.

Public response to these prints, most of them portraits, was so positive that commercial enterprises and reciprocal trade laws developed around their production. The government recognized that prints were an economic asset. It provided tax benefits in 1735 to publishers who exported them, while enacting legislation limiting the importation of French prints.

Fig. 109. Claude Ferdinand Gaillard. *Dom Prosper Gueranger.* Courtesy Metropolitan Museum of Art, bequest of Susan Dwight Bliss, 1967 [67. 630.123].

Thirty years later the French retaliated in an effort to protect their own printmaking industry. Modern technologies were adopted to improve the quality of inks and plates. The metal industry upgraded its methods of rolling copper to the necessary hardness and regularity for mezzotint's exacting needs. In addition, smoother European papers, superior to English brands, were regularly imported in large quantities.

Sir Godfrey Kneller's paintings, which spanned the latter seventeenth and early eighteenth centuries, created and sustained a great demand for reproductions, including many of the royal family. His works were translated more often than those of any other artist in the early days of mezzotints. He understood how much his ultimate fame would rest on the work of his printmakers and employed the finest practitioners available. John Smith, who had been one of the best and most refined engravers at the end of the 1600s, worked well into the 1700s, covering the reigns of five English monarchs. His mezzotint after Kneller's self-portrait in 1716 showed his ongoing virtuosity in producing rich and velvety blacks. (Fig. 111; see Fig. 93) John Simon came to England as a Protestant refugee from France and also worked after Kneller, but his reputation is not quite as high as Smith's because, having started out as an engraver, he included hatched lines which sometimes added a rough quality to his otherwise well-balanced plates.

John Faber the Younger reproduced Kneller's forty-eight portraits of the members of the Kit-Cat Club, named for its owner, Christopher Cat. This famous set appeared in 1723 and made a great reputation for Faber, although too many of the plates look alike; trying to make four dozen similar Whigs and wigs each look different was a hopeless job. Faber turned out about five hundred plates, but unfortunately most of them were based on the paintings of second-class artists and have a mass-produced quality.

George White is of particular interest. He etched his plates, until they were almost completed, then used the sharp point of the burin to make noses, mouths, and pupils more distinct; that accomplished, he finally added a mezzotint burr for tone. His portrait of a disreputable bookseller, *Abel Roper*, after a painting by H. Hysing in 1720, successfully used this system, overcoming mezzotint's inherent softness and producing stronger facial characterizations than were previously feasible; most subsequent artists adopted his method. (Fig. 112)

Printmakers had had difficulty finding good paintings to work from in the early years of the century, but they kept the art alive and well—improving on some of the mediocre portraits they reproduced—until the appearance of better artists than Lely and Kneller. While the best mezzotinters always had imagination and skills that went beyond simple craftsmanship, their finest work was indebted to the superior models of painters such as Sir Joshua Reynolds, Thomas Gainsborough, George Romney, and Thomas Lawrence, who worked in a style that was particularly appropriate to the fine gradation,

Fig. 110. William Hogarth. *Simon, Lord Lovat*. Courtesy Fitzwilliam Museum, University of Cambridge.

warm tonalities, and suggestion of color inherent in mezzotint.

Reynolds was the first distinguished native-born English portraitist. During his career, almost the only English art that had any sponsorship was portraiture, most collectors going to Italy for other subjects; "history" paintings had always had a loftier status in the hierarchy of art. The demand for the latter was so great that a flourishing counterfeiting industry grew up on the continent, catering to English enthusiasts. Reynolds almost single-handedly spawned a homegrown industry, upgrading portraiture to a position of equal distinction and consequence. To erase the common perception that portraits required little or no intelligence to paint or appreciate, he included scholarly references that assumed familiarity with mythological or historical themes. Because of him, portrait painting became so fashionable that many of the best artists began to specialize in it.

He preferred titled sitters, occasionally idealizing them to the point where the resemblances were only approximate. The artist "cannot make his hero talk like a great man," Reynolds said, "therefore he must make him look like one." He painted over two thousand well-arranged and quietly poised likenesses, more interesting and varied in composition than his predecessors', but, like theirs, based on the resplendence and affectation of the English aristocracy; some six hundred survive.

Reynolds derived his dramatic landscape backgrounds from Claude Lorraine. Like other artists, he took many of his earlier striking poses from

Left: Fig. 111. John Smith. *Gottfried Kneller*. *Right*: Fig. 112. George White. *Abel Roper*. Both figures courtesy Fitzwilliam Museum, University of Cambridge.

Van Dyck, although his were more varied and seemingly natural. They had an intellectual verve, a refined grace, and a livelier style than Kneller's more monotonous paintings. They took on qualities of congeniality and sympathy, particularly after he visited the Netherlands, where he was influenced by Rubens. Unlike some of his colleagues, he avoided crowding his pictures with superfluous detail, and made an effort to search out subleties of expression.

He was the close friend of the greatest literary men of his period, Samuel Johnson and Oliver Goldsmith, as well as the political leader Edmund Burke, and the finest actor on the boards, David Garrick. The paintings of his men friends were generally stronger and more sincere than those of his women sitters, whom he pictured with more conventional smoothness, but his engravers concentrated on the female portraits, since their softer qualities lent themselves better to the mezzotint technique.

His life spanned much of the eighteenth century, during which he was honored both as an artist and as an exemplary citizen. He was knighted, elected mayor of his home town, and when the Royal Academy was founded in 1768, he became its first president. He was not yet seventy when he died, deaf and almost completely blind.

Gainsborough, Reynolds' slightly younger contemporary, preferred landscapes, but his ability to catch resemblances assured him an endless supply of wealthy clients, a circumstance he could not afford to ignore. His work was somewhat in the style of Van Dyke, but with a more intimate quality. Because he was a great landscape artist as well, the verdant scenery of his paintings is of far more interest than the traditional backdrops. However, his brush work was so personal and unsystematic that few mezzotinters were successful in reproducing it.

Fig. 113. Richard Houston. *Miss Harriet Powell*. Courtesy Fitzwilliam Museum, University of Cambridge.

Romney, while not quite the equal of either Reynolds or Gainsborough, was almost as popular. Lawrence was a boy genius who developed into a showy and clever artist. Both Lawrence and Gainsborough were very interested in printmaking and corrected many of the mezzotint proofs after their works.

It is difficult for today's critics to make fair judgments among these paintings because so many have lost their pristine appearance. Reynolds, for instance, experimented with paints which have already deteriorated. More and more it will become necessary to look at the prints based on their portraits to evaluate and appreciate the skills of these painters.

Many of the best engravers came from Ireland, which could point with pride to the near-flawless quality of their mezzotints. Richard Houston and James McArdell were Dubliners who moved to London in time to collaborate with Gainsborough, Lawrence, Romney, and Reynolds when the reputation of these painters was at its peak.

Houston was a prodigy and might have achieved the highest success, but he was so lazy and dissolute, we are told, that a printseller had him arrested for various bad habits in order to make sure that he completed the prints he had contracted for. His work after Reynolds and others was admired for the mellow brush-like subtlety of the shadows and lights on the faces and costumes, his expertise in this area no doubt enhanced by his study and reproduction of Rembrandt's paintings. One of his finest plates, after Reynolds, is of Miss Harriet Powell, shown performing in a vaudeville theatre in London. (Fig. 113) (She later gave up her career as an actress for that of a countess.) Theatrical portraits were a specialty of eighteenth-century artists throughout Europe and Japan.

Reynolds said that McArdell's engravings would immortalize him. The two began a close association in 1754, ending with the mezzotinter's early death eleven years later. They worked together on thirty-eight plates, but unfortunately this was before Reynolds had undertaken his most mature paintings. The dramatically modulated darks and lights in the print after Reynolds' *Mrs. Bonfoy*, 1755, enhanced the pallor of the subject's face and chest. (Fig. 114) Her elegant outline, gently drawn features, and silky dress are examples of McArdell's special talents. His 1757 portrait, *Mary, Duchess of Ancaster*, was after Thomas Hudson, Reynolds' first teacher, and glowingly recreated every tone. (Fig. 115) Mary was mistress of the robes to Charlotte, queen of George III, who resented her beauty and envied the notice she always attracted. It is a splendid print — the satin gown incomparably brilliant.

The Irish continued to produce and export many of the best mezzotinters. Edward Fisher, James Watson, and John Dixon all were kept busy reproducing portraits. The series of eighteen large-size heads by Thomas Frye showed an even more personal style, since Frye was also an original artist. However, in the last quarter of the century, some English engravers actually surpassed them in depicting overall tonal qualities. But as the demand for these prints was enormous, there was plenty of opportunity for all comers; hundreds were produced after Reynolds alone, and thousands more after many other artists as well.

Valentine Green, a native Londoner, gave up a legal career to become an engraver in 1765, the year that McArdell died. He was distinguished for his ability to produce shimmering tones, but occasionally his vacuous expressions, hair like cotton batting, and unvaried shadings are disappointing. One of his best works, *Duchess of Devonshire*, 1780, after Reynolds, has the softness missing from some of his other mezzotint plates. Here his color-values are faultless and the elaborate wig expertly done. His *Mary Isabella, Duchess of Rutland*, also of 1780, is a graceful vision, although in real life she apparently lacked the refinement and dignity with which Reynolds endowed her; however, he hinted at her occasional unseemly behavior by the suggestion of a mischievous smile. (Fig. 116) In an effort to outshine every other fashion queen, she once made an appearance dressed in an enormous feather. Gawkers usually swarmed around to get a glimpse of her latest nonsense. When the social spotlight moved on, however, Green erased her head and replaced it with the more esteemed Duchess of York. *Sic transit gloria mundi.*

Green's pupils, James Walker and John Dean, fell only a little short of his example; Walker was the finer of the two, less fussy in his manner, but no one approached Dean for evanescent tone. Thomas Watson and William Dickinson were friends and business associates. Their portraits

Opposite, left: Fig. 114. James McArdell. *Mrs. Bonfoy. Right*: Fig. 115. James McArdell. *Mary, Duchess of Ancaster.* Both figures courtesy Fitzwilliam Museum, University of Cambridge.

Fig. 116. Valentine Green. *Mary Isabella, Duchess of Rutland.* Courtesy Fitzwilliam Museum, University of Cambridge.

after Reynolds are among the best ever produced. Watson's work might have been the finest of all, but he died young. They and John Jones also contributed some wonderful male portraits in the tradition of Van Dyck's impeccably good-looking men.

As outstanding as the works of these engravers were, the name of John Raphael Smith signifies the epitome of everything beautiful that gave life to otherwise unremembered gentlemen and ladies. He was an early disappointment to his father, who had hoped to teach him to paint; when he showed no aptitude, his prospects appeared bleak, and it was decided to apprentice him to a linen-draper. He was then ten years old. At fifteen he was in London and took up a serious study of art (and of life, too, for at seventeen he was a husband and father). He had done some portrait painting himself, which gave additional insight to his luminous interpretations of Gainsborough and Reynolds; his prints after Romney were lower in contrast to accord with Romney's simpler style. He brought the latter part of the century to the highest point of many high points of mezzotint engraving, frequently working after his own portraits. A number of his unusually forceful and expressive portraits were of men, that of John Philpot Curran, an Irish politician, after Lawrence, being especially fine and poetic. (Fig. 117) But his most beautiful plate, scraped with the greatest subtlety after Reynolds, is *Mrs. Carnac*, 1778, the wife of a famous general who served in India. (Fig. 118) The portrait is one of the most exquisite of the whole school.

Of all the mezzotint printmakers, Smith was the most consistently artistic and in the greatest demand. In addition to capturing living features in a medium that too often produced only vapid images, his control of glittering tones was second to none. He depicted facial vitality and gossamer material with equal assurance, his facility with fabrics possibly a leftover from his days in the linen-draper's shop.

Most of the sitters of these lovely portraits are of little historical interest; many of them are unknown members of aristocratic families. A notable exception is young Emma Hart, who began her career as a nursemaid and rose to become a semi-naked performer in a theatrical show. She then became the mistress of Charles Greville, who ceded her in exchange for payment of his debts to his uncle Sir William Hamilton, British Minister to the court of Naples. There Lady Hamilton hobnobbed with royalty until she met Horatio Nelson, the naval hero who would eventually lose his life saving England from Napoleon. But in happier days they fell in love and she remained his mistress until his death. John Raphael Smith and others reproduced Emma's portraits after Reynolds and Romney. She had been Romney's favorite model. He was middle-aged and she a teen-ager when they met. He painted her about fifty times in various states of dress and undress. But in spite of her enormous early popularity, in the end she spent a year in jail for unpaid gambling debts and died poor and neglected, having squandered her inheritances from husband and lover.

The clothing fashions of those times were incredibly restrictive. Wigs were so tall that, in order to prevent them from catching fire, it was necessary to remind ladies not to walk or dance under candlelit chandeliers. (The wearing of wigs had originated with Louis XIII of France, who adopted the fashion to hide his balding head, and survives in the formal dress of English judges and barristers.) The harnesses that jammed in every bit of wayward flesh prevented women from bending down and necessitated the gentlemanly custom of picking up handkerchiefs, accidentally or otherwise dropped. Was there ever a class of women and men as elegant, as beautiful, as artificial, as these portraits

Top: Fig. 117. John Raphael Smith. *John Philpot Curran*. *Bottom*: Fig. 118. John Raphael Smith. *Mrs. Carnac*. Both figures courtesy Fitzwilliam Museum, University of Cambridge.

suggest? Did all those celebrated matrons indeed have perfect swan necks, tapered fingers, dainty waistlines, and heightened figures? Probably the painters were simply sharing an idealized and fanciful point of view, when life and political realities permitted a moment of extravagance in the romantic tradition. Rigaud spoke for most society portraitists in acknowledging the great dilemma of his profession: "If I paint women as they are, they do not find themselves beautiful enough; if I flatter them, their portraits are hardly recognizable."

It is true that too often costumes and settings were stressed to the neglect of personality or intellect; trees and foliage were arranged as carefully as the sitters. Too often the approach was adulatory, the technique too mechanical. Faultfinders complained that mezzotint was rarely used as an original medium, and even its spectacular endless tones were criticized for losing the characteristic linearity of printmaking which some purists insisted on. Yet in spite of these perceived weaknesses, mezzotint artists were truly moved by ties of compatibility and understanding for the paintings they reproduced, and they created the closest possible translations of the portraits which the English preferred above all other subjects.

Mezzotint was not the only technique used for portrait reproduction. Another tonal process, stipple engraving, was almost as popular. Its innumerable dots, like grains of sand, were etched and engraved in various combinations over the entire plate to give a characteristic soft appearance. Roulettes and needles, similar to those used for the French crayon manner, impressed the dots which, when printed, simulated expensive chalk drawings and delicate paintings. While stipple was often used on faces alone in seventeenth century portraits, eighteenth century prints differed in that the entire plate was covered. The white of the paper appears luminous between the spatter, giving the impression of flickering light.

Stipple is a less difficult process than mezzotint since it chiefly requires a willingness to incise millions of specks; assistants usually filled in large areas after the master engraver indicated the general outlines. Although the medium did not permit the infinite tonal gradations of mezzotint, it had a light, dainty appearance which was much admired. However, most stipple prints were too fuzzy, even when strengthened by etching or embellished by color. Brownish red or various pastel inks were applied selectively with rags directly onto the metal, in a technique known as *à la poupée*. These plates can print many more impressions than mezzotints before showing wear, and for that reason were a favorite medium of print sellers.

Stipple engraving began its history with two non-Englishmen, but soon became almost an exclusive English specialty. William Wynne Ryland brought the method to England from France, having learned it from François Boucher, who, incidentally had another famous pupil, Mme. Pompadour, the mistress of Louis XV. (As a printmaker, she was mildly talented.) Ryland and Francesco Bartolozzi, an Italian engraver whom he invited to England in 1764, soon gathered together a group of

Fig. 119. Francesco Bartolozzi. *Miss Bingham.* Courtesy Fitzwilliam Museum, University of Cambridge.

engravers and began a lucrative portrait business. Bartolozzi's accomplishments were such that although he was neither English nor even a traditional line engraver, an exception was made in his favor admitting him as a member of the Royal Academy. (The choice was bitterly criticized by English engravers, who were still considered unworthy to exhibit side by side with the best painters.) More than two thousand stipple plates from Bartolozzi's studio alone were turned out, many of them after rather mawkish portraits. His *Miss Bingham*, 1786, after Reynolds, is a good example of the sentimental style that was pretty and tender rather than handsome. (Fig. 119) It has the same classical elements that endow the head of Aphrodite with such delicacy and grace. (See Fig. 5) Although they sometimes had too granular a quality, at their best, stipple prints did what was asked of them, providing delightful wall decorations to accompany sumptuous eighteenth century furnishings. As portraits, they exhibit charm, if not character. Their delicate light-hearted appeal had a relatively short life, collapsing after about 1810.

However, while the technique flourished, John Raphael Smith, his pupil William Ward, and a small number of other printmakers were

Fig. 120. Robert Strange. *Charles I.*
Courtesy Fitzwilliam Museum, University of Cambridge.

versatile enough to build up profitable sidelines doing stipple plates. Caroline Watson, the daughter of the mezzotinter James Watson, was one of the few women who did creditable work. The painter Angelica Kauffman was a great help to these engravers, particularly Ryland, offering them some of her watercolor paintings as models. Many other artists also sought out Ryland, and his success went to his head. Unsatisfied with his modest fortune, he used his engraving skills to forge a large bank note. He hid in a small town, hoping to elude the police, and might have made it, too, had not a shoemaker, who noticed his name inside some boots he took for repair, turned him in. In 1783, Ryland became the last person to be hanged at Tyburn, a spot in London which had been associated with executions for six hundred years.

Traditional engraving, too, still had a few practitioners who kept alive the style of the elder William Faithorne and provided classical portrait prints, chiefly for book illustrations. Sir Robert Strange and William Sharp, who were contemporaries of Wille and Schmidt on the continent, were among the last of this moribund school, but they maintained its high standards. Strange, a Scotsman who fought for the Young Pretender, the grandson of James II, escaped to France after the unsuccessful Stuart attempt to win the British throne for Scotland, the same plot that undid Lord Lovat. He continued his career in Europe for a number of years, buying Van Dyck's *Charles I* in 1770 in order to engrave it. (Fig. 120) The painting had led a peripatetic existence: James II took it to France when he fled England, and it passed through several hands before finding its way to Rome. The engraving is carefully done, although some of the highlights are forced and harsh. Strange routinely etched his basic lines before applying the burin, which give his plates a great richness, especially in the skin tones. Sharp, however, varied his shading with even greater discrimination than Strange when he combined stipple with etching and engraving in his 1788 portrait of a well-known surgeon, John Hunter, after Reynolds. (Fig. 121)

One last English artist should also be cited. Arthur Pond, who etched and also made chiaroscuro woodcuts, revived the drypoint method, hardly used since Rembrandt's day. With his sensitive *Self-Portrait*, 1739, he

Fig. 121. William Sharp. *John Hunter*. Courtesy Metropolitan Museum of Art, Harris Brisbane Dick Fund, 1953 [53.600.1579].

became an able precursor of the technique as it was developed in the nineteenth century. (Fig. 122) In his time he was considered the greatest technician in England.

The English portrait school generated an obsessive interest in collecting. Sir Robert Walpole, son of the one-time prime minister of the country, and an avid art connoisseur like his father, wrote, "We have at present a rage for prints of English portraits. Lately I assisted a clergyman in compiling a catalogue of them. Since this publication, scarce heads in books not worth three pence will sell for five guineas." The clergyman

Fig. 122. Arthur Pond. *Self-Portrait.*
Courtesy British Museum.

referred to was the Reverend James Granger; the catalogue, the *Biographical History of England*, 1769–74. This anthology started the craze of extra-illustration. Books with engraved portrait frontispieces or with portraits accompanying the texts were torn apart, the portraits removed and inserted in the appropriate pages of Granger's biographical histories and other similar publications issued specifically for that purpose. Boswell's *Life of Johnson*, of course, was a natural repository for this sort of thing. These "books" were issued unbound so that the portraits could be placed next to articles relating to them. Single volumes were in this way expanded to enormous size, a dozen or more times the dimensions of the originals. Thousands of books were mutilated for their portraits, some print dealers catering exclusively to this trade. One shopkeeper alone had an overflowing inventory of thirty thousand. "Grangerizing" lasted well into the nineteenth century; no one knows how many engravers were employed in this production, but judging from the amount of material still in existence, there must have been hundreds. Most of this manufacture was totally commercial and made no pretense to artistic merit. The portraits ranged in quality from indifferent to deplorable, and brought about their own demise by surfeit.

By the end of the century the beauty contest between competing pedigreed ladies and gentlemen that had occupied so many artists was over. The aristocracy had played dress-up while the incipient Industrial Revolution marked time in the wings, soon to act out its role in the dissolution of their enchanted world. The growing labor movement shook the self-confidence of the peerage and shifted economic power from the landed gentry to manufacturers and merchants. But, oh, at what a cost to the art of elegant living — ornate, haughty, languid, beautiful, grand, and charmingly absurd.

III. Spain

While both England and France were experiencing significant political and cultural growth in the eighteenth century, Spain was starting a slow and unsteady recuperation from its earlier repressive policies. Beginning in 1700 with the reign of Louis XIV's grandson Philip V, French influences soon dominated the country. Reforms were instituted, and although war marred most of Philip's regency, there was hope that the country would be able to pull itself together.

In 1746 Philip's son Ferdinand VI became king and inaugurated a peaceful period. The Inquisition was greatly modified, intellectual life expanded, and the economic situation dramatically improved. 1746 was also the year that Francisco Goya was born into a lower middle-class family. He was his country's first etcher of any note and is included among the world's great printmakers; in the eighteenth century he was one of the very few important artists doing original rather than reproductive printmaking.

Spain had not been without a great artistic tradition. In the sixteenth century El Greco had opened the Golden Age of Spanish art, and although the political and economic life of the country was disintegrating, José de Ribera, Diego Velazquez, Francisco de Zurbaran, and Bartolomé Murillo provided some of the most brilliant art of the seventeenth century. After Goya, Spain did not produce a major artist until Picasso.

Goya said that he owed his art to Velazquez, Rembrandt, and nature, but he neglected to mention his own enormous resources. In his early years he painted some superficially charming portraits of the aristocracy of Spain, basing poses and costumes on glamorous English mezzotints. His later paintings of the royal family were an indictment of the unsavory Charles IV and Maria Luisa, whom he set down with a biting and ruthless perception. He was rumored to have led a convivial existence crowded with scandal and dissipation, but after 1792, when a severe illness left him totally deaf, he became unsociable and introspective. Like Dürer and Rembrandt, he painted himself many times, searching for authentic insights in his own features.

Aside from Ribera, there were only a few Spanish printmakers from whom Goya could have learned. French-trained engravers provided most of what little printmaking there was. Goya taught himself to etch in 1778 by working after sixteen of Velazquez's portrait paintings. He derived his early etching style from Giovanni Battista Tiepolo and his son Giovanni Domenico, Venetian painters and etchers who worked in Madrid in the 1760s and 1770s. But he suddenly came alive as a printmaker with a wonderfully original set of plates which he called *Los Caprichos* (*Whims*).

It was a series of eighty prints, bitterly attacking the corrupt administration in thinly concealed depictions; Manuel Godoy, the notorious prime minister and the queen's lover, was supposedly represented as an ass, and the king, queen, and church hierarchy as demonic creatures. He removed the prints from sale only a few days after they were published in 1799 because their nightmarish images were clearly heretical or abusive and he feared the Inquisition, which had been reimposed. In 1803 he offered the plates to the king in return for his safety and

Fig. 123. Francisco Goya. *Self-Portrait*. Private collection.

a pension for his son; the government did not publish them until well after Goya's death in 1828, although small editions were printed before then. The *Caprichos* were etched in aquatint, which was invented by Jean Baptiste Le Prince about 1768. Like mezzotint, it is a tonal rather than a linear technique and is a variation of etching. After a powdery ground, such as resin, sand, or other granular mixture, is spread on the metal plate, it is melted so that the flecks stick to the metal. The minute spaces between the particles are then etched away; through successive bitings, tonal variations and intensities can be modulated. When printed, flat tints, resembling wash or watercolor paintings, are produced. Aquatint has neither the blending capacity nor the richness of mezzotint, but Goya admired its graduated shadings. No one has ever used it with greater distinction.

The frontispiece of the *Caprichos* is a forceful self-portrait, executed with short staccato strokes and fluid cross-hatching in a combination of etching and aquatint. (Fig. 123) All Goya's apprehension and suspicion is in his glance; all his stubborn resolution is in his chin. Although he drew himself in a three-quarter pose, his eye challenges the viewer. The superb quality of the face, with its haughty and defiant expression, augured further masterpieces, but unfortunately he was not as interested in printed portraits as in those he painted.

Goya etched *The Disasters of War* from 1810 to 1813, withering indictments of the atrocities of Napoleon's invading armies. He worked in Spain until 1824, when reactionary forces drove him to France, where he remained in voluntary exile until his death. In his latter years he took up lithography, issuing a series of bullfight scenes, and while some of the details were indistinct because of his failing eyesight, they were the first important prints in that medium. His considerable output had an enriching influence on art in the nineteenth and twentieth centuries; although he began as a Rococo artist, he ended up a modern.

IV. America

At the beginning of the eighteenth century there were perhaps a million people clustered along the Atlantic Coast, some of them determined to establish a viable political entity out of a multiplicity of selfish interests. Although at first their differences prevented them from establishing even a semblance of unity, the pervasiveness of English culture and the fear of war eventually brought them together in an effective alliance. Benjamin Franklin's 1754 famous cartoon "Join or Die" depicted the divided colonies as a fragmented snake and epitomized the need for a common defense against French assaults on the American continent.

Within the broader picture of colonial development, there remained the usual ongoing concerns for personal needs and indulgences. Fashions in art closely reflected European taste, portraiture finding a place wherever the ubiquitous itinerant painter could engage a willing sitter. Most were rough limners, but a few, recognizing that their ambitions were limited by their lack of skills, went to Europe to sharpen their techniques.

Printmaking at that time was largely relegated to illustrating children's story books, school texts, business trade cards, and almanacs, almost none of which are of any but archival interest. The first regularly published newspaper appeared in Boston in 1704. Paper currency was printed too, because only small amounts of gold or silver were available for coinage; as early as 1702 attempts were made to create patterns that were difficult to counterfeit, since now and then engravers succumbed to the occupational hazard of forgery.

Printed portraits were chiefly used as frontispieces in books. Benjamin Franklin's brother James was probably the woodcutter of a number of crude likenesses that appeared between 1717 and 1719. However, woodcuts did not find much acceptance, despite the earlier example of John

Fig. 124. Thomas Emmes. *Increase Mather*. Courtesy New York Public Library.

Foster's *Richard Mather* in 1670, because engravings and mezzotints were thought to be of a higher caliber. (See Fig. 94) The first line engraving in America, like the first woodcut, was of the Mather family, in this case, the 1701 portrait of Increase Mather, son of Richard, by Thomas Emmes, an artist about whom nothing is known. (Fig. 124) Mather was president of Harvard and a leading literary and religious figure, intolerant and self-righteous in his Puritan austerity. The Emmes portrait was used in two of his books, *The Blessed Hope* and *Ichabod*. It is a poor, scratchy picture, the pose copied from an English model, and except for its significance as a starting point, it might well be ignored.

Equally stiff and amateurish were engravings by Paul Revere of horseback fame, a silversmith by trade. The harsh lines of his portraits and anti–British cartoons indicate lack of skill rather than want of effort, but are nevertheless memorable because of the celebrity of the artist. He printed everything from money to musical scores. Among the portraits he engraved in 1774 were those of Samuel Adams, a statesman related to the presidential family, and John Hancock, first member of the Continental Congress to sign the Declaration of Independence. (Fig. 125) The following year, during his famous midnight ride, Revere helped both men escape from a house in Lexington, Massachusetts, when the Royal governor ordered their arrest for complicity in revolutionary "offenses." The portrait of Hancock shows a bare-breasted figure of Liberty standing apathetically over the body of an English soldier, her elbow resting on an oval frame containing the patriot's image. We must not expect consummate art from our heroes.

Curiously, the first American mezzotint, 1728, was of yet another member of the Mather family, the Reverend Cotton Mather, son of Increase. (Fig. 126) The artist, Peter Pelham, made the print from his own drawing the year after he arrived in Boston from London, where he had studied with John Simon. He was the first English-trained painter and engraver in the colonies to work in the Grand Manner, an aristocratic style that Americans hardly patronized. Pelham was forced to support himself by teaching stitchery and dancing. However, he helped American art overcome its amateurishness through the competence of his formal, dignified

The Honᵇˡᵉ. **JOHN HANCOCK.** Esqʳ.

Top: Fig. 125. Paul Revere. *John Hancock*. *Bottom*: Fig. 126. Peter Pelham. *Cotton Mather*. Both figures courtesy American Antiquarian Society.

studies. The Mather print was one of fourteen mezzotint portraits by Pelham, all sharpened here and there with a bit of engraving for better clarity, but standardized in their presentation.

Like his father and grandfather, Cotton Mather was a fervent Puritan, although his features suggest more of the gourmand than the abstainer. While he believed in the supernatural and wrote two books on witches, he scrupulously urged the judges of the witchcraft trials of 1692 to distinguish between "genuine" guilt and unsubstantiated accusations. Vain and sanctimonious, he was nevertheless no narow-spirited zealot; he fought for inoculation against smallpox in the face of violent public opinion, led reforms for the welfare of children, the elderly, and prisoners, had a hand in the founding of Yale University in 1701, and was acknowledged by Benjamin Franklin as his mentor. When he died in 1728, this portrait was in great demand; it was the only one from which Pelham made a profit.

While American society did its naive best to emulate English aristocracy, English perceptions of life in the New World may have been a bit distorted after the appearance of John Verelst's painting of four Indian chiefs in full regalia during their visit to London in 1709. A year later, John Simon engraved the picture and it was widely distributed. It is understandable that the colonists hoped that folks back in the Old Country would perceive them as "civilized" and realize that Indian culture did not represent the totality of American life. The portraits they sent home in the following years, they hoped, made them look as grand as any by James McArdell or Richard Houston.

Most of those early mezzotints were printed in London because there weren't enough good presses in New England. (There was almost no printmaking at all in the Southern colonies.) At the time of the American Revolution, European interest in pictures of colonial war heroes and political leaders was high; in America such portraits were among the earliest contributions to national self-esteem. Fashionable English mezzotints were imported into the colonies and served as patterns for poses, backgrounds and even wardrobes for the Americans who were eager to keep up with the latest styles. Printmakers freely copied the silks and satins, marble columns, and gilded furniture, whether or not their clients actually owned such finery or lived in manorial splendor.

John Singleton Copley, born in Massachusetts, was the best mid-century portrait painter in the colonies, probing for individual or personal qualities as well as highlighting costumes and backgrounds. He was the stepson of Peter Pelham, from whom he learned to engrave. He moved to Europe on the advice of Reynolds, who had seen his painting *Boy with Squirrel* and urged him to leave "before your manner and taste were corrupted or fixed by working in your little way at Boston." He also had another incentive. In 1773, his father-in-law had imported the famous tea that was dumped into Boston harbor, and in consequence, the family thought that discretion would be the better part of valor if they all left America.

But long before that, Copley engraved his only portrait, *The Reverend William Welsteed*, 1753, after his own painting. (Fig. 127) It was presented in a straightforward, realistic manner, in what the English would have called a provincial style, but it is unaffected and has the typical direct appeal of native American art; Copley's later European work was more elaborate and aristocratic, but not always as interesting.

After he left, Charles Wilson Peale received most of the best portrait painting commissions, and then went himself to London for two years of study. For almost a century, subsequent artists followed his sophisticated manner. He was an inventor, soldier, scientist, watch-maker, coach-maker, designer of bridges and foun-

Fig. 127. John Singleton Copley. *The Rev. William Welsteed*. Courtesy American Antiquarian Society.

der of the first natural history museum in the New World, as well as a fine artist and member of a distinguished family of scholars and painters. It is not clear where he found the time for all of his activities, for from three wives he had seventeen children, several of whom were successful artists and naturalists in spite of carrying a heavy burden in their given names: Rubens, Rembrandt, Raphaelle, Titian, and so on. He was busy courting the lady he hoped would become his fourth wife when he died at the age of eighty-six from the strain of carrying a trunk to the home of his beloved.

He fashioned a set of false teeth for George Washington and painted his portrait seven times from life. During one of these sittings, Washington wrote, "Inclination having yielded to importunity, I am now contrary to all expectations under the hands of Mr. Peale; but in so grave — so sullen a mood — and now and then under the influence of Morpheus when some critical strokes are making, that I fancy the skill of this Gentleman's Pencil will be put to it, in describing to the World what manner of man I am."

Peale repeated his famous painting *George Washington*, 1779, in mezzotint the following year. The portrait of the commander-in-chief, informally posed with one hand leaning on a cannon, eventually sold twenty thousand copies. (Fig. 128) Peale also engraved a set of very good mezzotints after his own paintings, including *Benjamin Franklin* in 1787, several of Washington, and various other notables from 1787 to 1790. He was not financially successful with this series, possibly because of the

Fig. 128. Charles Wilson Peale. *George Washington*. Courtesy New York Public Library.

economic depression following the Revolutionary War, or perhaps because he stuck to the facts before him, refusing to ingratiate himself with immoderate flattery.

John Norman, an Englishman who came to Philadelphia in 1774, is remembered as the first known engraver to make a portrait of Washington, about 1779. He doubled as an architect and advertised the "lowest terms in the best manner." His book *An Impartial History of the War* appeared in 1782. It contained dull portraits of American military and political leaders and was disdained in its own time: "Surely such extraordinary figures," declared the *Freemen's Journal* in 1795, "are not intended to give the rising generation an improved taste in the arts of design and sculpture." Included was a portrait of Washington, after Benjamin Blyth and Peale. (Fig. 129) Congress, too, got into the act, and passed a resolution that

Washington was to be represented in a statue dressed in Roman armor, the highest accolade they could visualize. An engraving "in the Roman dress," copying the head from Peale and the figure from the English engraver Sir William de la More, was made in 1783, probably by Norman.

There were literally hundreds of portraits of Washington in every type of printed material, including a three-dollar bill by a busy stipple engraver from Connecticut, Amos Doolittle, one of the first American war correspondents, who also sold crude prints of Revolutionary incidents and heroes. It was chiefly through the many prints showing the president as a statesman and military figure that he became a symbol of na-

Fig. 129. John Norman. *George Washington.* Courtesy New York Public Library.

tional national unity. The first known use of the title "Father of his Country" was in a Lancaster, Pennsylvania, German almanac in 1779, showing a winged figure of "Fame" bearing an anonymous portrait of "Das Landes Vater." A portrait of him even appeared on the cover of some sheet music in 1796 engraved by S. Wetherbee. Although etching as a popular medium in America had to wait almost another hundred years, what may have been the first of its kind in America by a well-known painter was a profile portrait of Washington, 1790, by the English artist Joseph Wright. He made the small plate after a crayon drawing surreptitiously sketched during a church service.

Edward Savage was a painter, goldsmith, engraver, and the proprietor of a painting and print gallery, which was later sold to P. T. Barnum. In 1796 he painted a casually posed *The Washington Family* and in 1798 reproduced it in stipple engraving. (Fig. 130) The latter earned him the enormous sum of ten thousand dollars. Group portraits in such informally posed surroundings had become popular in England and were now fashionable in America, too. They were intended to show sitters enjoying the good life, secure enough to appear comfortable and a bit less solemn, well enough informed to take a lively interest in the latest books, pictures, and tasteful objects that were frequently used as props. In the Savage portrait, Washington, his legs crossed and his arm relaxed, is shown with Martha, her two grandchildren, and his manservant, Billy Lee. People who could never hope to see the first family in person eagerly bought the print when it was advertised for sale in the Pennsylvania Gazette:

Philadelphia, March 19. An elegant Engraving, twenty x twenty-six inches, executed by Savage from an original picture, painted by himself, is just published. The Print represents General Washington and his Lady (two capital likenesses), sitting at a table on which lies a plan of the Federal City. A perspective view of the river Potomac and of Mount Vernon, forms an agreeable and appropriate embellishment in the picture. The whole is executed in a style evincive of the rapid progress of an elegant art, which has hitherto been in a very crude state in this country.

Innumerable prints of Washington, in poses ranging from military hero to presidential oracle, helped to establish respect for the office of the presidency. The portraits carefully avoided any suggestion of a royal manner, countering insinuations by his political enemies; it was a fine line that artists rarely crossed. Particularly after he left office, his portraits became objects of pride to the nation, and admiration for him came close to public worship. No parlor wall was complete without his picture. A stipple engraving after Rembrandt Peale, *Apotheosis of Washington*, 1800, was made by David Edwin following Washington's death in 1799, and showed him rising to heaven, an angel in the act of crowning him, Mount Vernon beneath him, and Generals Montgomery and Warren waiting for him above. At his memorial service, Henry Lee, the future father of Robert E. Lee, who led the Confederate Army and married the great-granddaughter of Martha Washington, commemorated him in words that were sincerely felt in his own time: "First in war, first in peace, and first in the hearts of his countrymen, he was second to none...."

Cornelius Tiebout, who was the first American-born print-maker to do high-quality work, and H. H. Houston, who worked in the United States from 1796 to 1798, were active well into the nineteenth century and were among the best stipple engravers in the country, but David Edwin was the most sought after of all the portrait engravers of his period. (See Fig. 178) His stipple engraving of *George Washington*, showed a mouth clearly overburdened with false teeth. (Fig. 131)

Opposite. Fig. 130. Edward Savage. *The Washington Family.* Courtesy the Worcester Art Museum. *Above.* Fig. 131. David Edwin. *George Washington.* Courtesy New York Public Library.

The physiognotrace was brought to America from the Versailles court by Charles de St. Memin and other émigré artists who produced hundreds of profile portraits from 1796 to 1810. Subscribers received the original drawing and twelve impressions of their likenesses from the engraved plate.

As the American borderlands were pushed back, frontier life demanded many forms of creative energy, but not much that was genuinely artistic. The sorry performance of native artists was recognized. In 1791, an editor of an illustrated Bible wrote that he "doubts not but a proper allowance will be made for work engraved by an artist who obtained his knowledge in this country, compared with that done by European engravers who have settled in the United States." Yet it is altogether remarkable that in spite of the stresses and drudgery, shortages, and hard work that were imposed on many colonists, so much interest was allotted to printed portraits. They not only provided important information, but were also authoritative records of the American character that served as role models for generations. They could not boast of the level of European excellence and sophistication, but by the end of the century they had come a very long way, indeed, from the crude and immature efforts at its beginning.

Chapter 6

The Nineteenth Century

Europe changed materially after 1815. The overwhelming power of the Church, the immunities and dispensations of the aristocracy, the lawful inequities and discrimination in social and religious affairs — all were diminished. These reforms were the positive legacies and enduring contributions of the French Revolution and Napoleon. At the Treaty of Paris in 1814 Europe tried to establish "a firm peace, based on a just equilibrium of strength between the Powers." It never happened. The allies took back their territories from France and imposed arbitrary distributions of land and other policy decisions on the smaller countries, ignoring the national wills of the people concerned. France's punishment was the three-year presence of the victor, the Duke of Wellington, ostensibly to oversee the viability of the Louis XVIII government, but in reality to thwart any renewed revolutionary sentiments.

Meanwhile, Klemens von Metternich, who officially ran the foreign affairs of Austria, and unofficially those of most of Europe, came down hard against a movement to liberalize political policies, and insisted on "peace and quiet" as the byword for Europe, a euphemism for the status quo of autocratic monarchy. Attempts to create democratic constituencies based on shared cultures and heritages, patriotism, or self-determination, were forcibly repressed. England alone stood for non-intervention in the legitimate affairs of European nations, while in America, the Monroe Doctrine correspondingly insisted that "controlling in any manner the destiny" of the Americas, particularly the Central and South American states, would be a "manifestation of an unfriendly disposition towards the United States."

Fifteen years elapsed in Europe before a series of revolutions began in 1830. They lasted off and on for two generations and brought about ameliorations such as freedom of the press and extended privileges for the middle classes. Those who believed in the perfectibility of the human race rejected the Reverend Thomas Malthus' pessimistic economic philosophy that poverty and a high death rate were incurable or irreversible; the concept of workers' rights and "Scientific Socialism," enunciated by Karl Marx and Frederick Engels in *The Communist Manifesto* of 1848, soon spread across the continent. "Workers of the world unite," they urged, "you have nothing to lose but your chains." Anarchists — some peaceful and visualizing a stateless society where people voluntarily support an equitable social order, and some violent and encouraging terrorism and assassination to redress economic and political abuses — were responsible for the adoption of many reforms.

All the while Europe was still involved with games of international chess. The sport was nothing new, of course; only the players were rearranged. England and France cooperated more or less effectively in the interests of the Spanish succession, and against Russia in concerns over Turkish rule in the Crimean War. Florence Nightingale, the angel of mercy, confronted the hideous conditions of wounded servicemen and shamed the civilized world into improving health and sanitation measures for the private soldier. Napoleon III proclaimed himself emperor and revived his uncle's dreams of French expansionism, but his meddling in Garibaldi's attempts to unify the Italian states, and his war with Prussia, assured his downfall. In spite of his efforts and those of the pope, but with the accord of England, the people of Italy successfully defended their right to a national identity. In the meantime, the Prussian aristocracy, hoping to prevent the formation of a consolidated liberal government at home, pinned its hopes on Otto von Bismarck, who threatened that "iron and blood" would be the price of German unity, and cynically remarked that "the great questions of the time would not be solved by counting majorities."

Almost continuous war and deception characterized the politics of the century: Spain vs. Portugal; Poland vs. Russia; Prussia and Austria vs. Denmark; Austria vs. Prussia; England, France, and Turkey vs. Russia; France, Austria, and the pope vs. Garibaldi; Russian pogroms vs. Jews; Turkish massacres vs. Bulgarians; Sardinia vs. Austria; France vs. Prussia. The unification of Italy was achieved through internal revolutions and recognition by England. The German states finally got together in an empire which gave them unrivaled power and influence. Alliances, treaties, coalitions, and *ententes cordiales* were made and unmade for expediency or in the hope of peace, because of fears of armed attacks and destructive military machines. England sensibly isolated herself and built up an international commercial and industrial empire exceeding anything on the continent, and led Europe into a scientific and technological era.

New forms of communication, developed in America, permitted the rapid sharing of international news. A host of inventions, improved manufacturing skills, and advanced agricultural methods promised a better future. Labor-saving devices provided leisure to the middle classes. Clothes for both sexes became less artificial and sumptuous, and garments suitable for outdoor recreation and athletic events were copied from sports uniforms. Pajamas replaced nightshirts. Gentlemen's silk breeches were lengthened to the ankles following the example of the French *sans-culottes*;

Revolution or not, Paris still led the fashion world, while French *haute cuisine* changed the culinary habits of the western world. Elegant women gradually gave up their hoop skirts in favor of simpler lines, but although doctors inveighed against corsets that crushed ribcages, the appeal of diminutive waistlines outweighed common sense. Natural hair was seen again after two centuries. Milady's monstrously high wigs disappeared with the lessening of class distinctions and because taxes on deodorizing powders discouraged their use.

Sophisticated investment programs and capital enterprises created enormous personal wealth. For the privileged class, prosperity seemingly knew no limits. It was the Gilded Age.

I. France

The direct effects of the French Revolution were felt for more than a hundred years. Where it had promised to end oppression and an unjust government, it instead abandoned the principles of the Rights of Man. At the end of the eighteenth century, France was in almost total disarray, with much of its traditional social order shattered. Questions of monarchy versus republicanism, aristocracy versus the common man, inequality versus equality before the law, and a propertied bourgeoisie versus the propertyless proletariat haunted the government.

To the great discomfort of the nobility and the Church, their lands began to pass to the control of the middle class. The peasant majority was denied a reasonable share of the spoils and still labored for a pittance under oppressive circumstances, with bitterness between opposing factions continuing well after the end of the extremities of the Reign of Terror. When it seemed as if France had sunk almost too low ever to raise her head among the family of Europe, Napoleon rallied the country to heights never dreamed of at the time of the fall of the Bastille.

He embarked on conquest and by 1810 had stretched France's borders over almost all of Europe; five years later, at Waterloo, his army was destroyed, and the country returned to approximately its former borders. One of the greatest adventures in history failed because its hero never learned to distinguish between his own egocentric ambitions and the higher needs of France in its struggle to become a democratic nation. He had great gifts for leadership, but they were perverted to demagoguery. He was a great general, but he loved making war better than winning peace. He brought his country great victories, but not lasting glory. Yet, he demands a just defense. He rescued France from the disorders and chaos of the Terror. He believed that his enlightened codification of civil law would be his most enduring achievement. He encouraged the sciences and arts (while robbing half the treasure-houses of Europe and Egypt to fill the Louvre). He provided the basis for an improved economy and repaired roads and cities. He followed the earlier lead of Louis XVI and the Constitution of

1791 in extending all rights of citizenship and freedom to Protestants, Jews, and actors. He was the great anomaly of his time.

To his sorrow, he lived long enough to watch his empire overpowered and discredited. After his fall the demoralized nation floundered through almost as many phases as the moon—from the restored monarchies of Louis XVIII and the reactionary Charles X to the oppressive citizen-king Louis-Philippe, to the more temperate Second Republic, to the Second Empire and ultimate humiliation under Bonaparte's nephew Louis Napoleon, to the Third Republic—all in not much over half a century.

In 1870 France began a disastrous struggle with Prussia for power and prestige, surrendering only when German soldiers marched into the streets of Paris. Much like the situation that existed between the capital and the rest of the country at the time of Louis XVI, the quarrels between the citizens of Paris and the rest of France resulted in civil war. Leftist Commune interests, anxious to continue the fighting, hoped to decentralize the government, but were repressed in a slaughter that took twenty thousand lives. Not until 1878 was order restored with the establishment of the Third Republic and the institution of some reforms in the bureaucracy, although the underlying animosities continued to persist and fester.

Most elements of the Church and the army, and the conservative members of the government, remained opposed to liberal interests. Church-State discord, labor unrest, and political and social conflicts all contributed to the alienation which found a scapegoat in Alfred Dreyfus, a Jewish army captain falsely accused of treason in 1894. Forged evidence and prejudice led to a guilty verdict. Neither the powerful pen of Emile Zola nor the persuasive logic of the statesman Georges Clemenceau was able to control the fury of anti–Semitism, which even Pissarro experienced from Degas, Forain, and Renoir because of his Jewish heritage.

The real issue, of course, was military and government prerogatives versus broader individual rights and a true representative government. One result of the Dreyfus case was that it helped effect the definitive blow to Monarchism and the final separation of Church and State, although as early as 1890 the pope had already begun to move in that direction.

When Dreyfus was at last exonerated and that struggle defused, the nation, despite everything it had suffered for so long, strengthened its democratic instincts, instituted social legislation and economic policies, and began to resolve some of its most persistent problems. A sense of hope, infused by the promises of the Revolution and never entirely lost, was propelled by optimism and escapism, and gradually began to lift the spirit of France.

Social realism, adopted in the works of Millet and Courbet, acknowledged both the dignity and burdens of the working man. Some popular newspapers took up the liberal cause in which Daumier's political caricatures played an important role. Great railways were built which permitted the Impressionist painters to visit and immortalize the outskirts of Paris. New boulevards replaced much of the medieval city and permanently changed its appearance. Banking systems proliferated and supported the prosperity created by increased foreign trade. In literature, science, music and painting, the country reached an efflorescence of intellectual and imaginative energy.

By the end of the century, France, if not as splendid as it once had been, was certainly *à la mode.*

At the beginning of the nineteenth century things were relatively quiet in the world of printmaking. Artists were no longer receiving the support from the royal academies that had once fueled their vast output. The traditional patrons, Church, royalty, and aristocracy, were worn out or involved with more pressing interests. Portraits were still produced and the public still acquired them, but they were far less pervasive, possibly because they were associated with unpleasant memories of the recently overthrown leaders. Rich people, who were building mansions ready-made for wall-sized portrait paintings, occasionally hired engravers to make copies of their portraits for distribution to friends.

New attitudes and a fresh vocabulary of cultural and artistic isms — Neo-Classicism, Romanticism, Realism, Impressionism, Post-Impressionism, Symbolism — had to be invented to encompass the changing priorities of the nineteenth century. As academies lost their stranglehold on creativity, artists began to express personal rather than traditional viewpoints. Even though it sometimes meant partial or full starvation, some artists, willing to give up sinecures and make tentative efforts in new directions, abandoned academic training and sharpened their knowledge and skills in museums and galleries, or in the studios of their colleagues. In their eagerness to explore original rather than reproductive techniques and approaches, they made rapid and dramatic innovations, so that where previously, new styles had appeared from time to time and were modified gradually from century to century, now they began to tumble over each other decade by decade.

These moves away from stereotypes and conventional disciplines turned out to be a very good thing for portraiture, particularly in prints. No longer forced to churn out stately images on commission, artists began to concentrate on the human face with extraordinary and unparalleled inventiveness. Not only did they analyze features for what they told about the psychology, appearance, and times of their sitters, but they also interpreted unique visions with refreshing inspiration. Shapes, surfaces, planes — the formal elements that constitute art for its own sake — became significant reference points on which artists, in the latter part of the century, based highly individual styles, often misunderstood or repudiated in their own time.

Two discoveries radically affected their work. One was lithography. In 1799 a struggling young writer named Alois Senefelder received a patent for a cheap method of reproducing scripts and musical scores; it probably never occurred to him that he was about to expand the world of art. Had he lived anywhere but Bavaria, he might never have accomplished his purpose, but luckily for a thousand artists, the requisite limestone, with just the right combination of porosity and texture, was quarried there almost exclusively. He had bought a piece on which to grind his greasy ink and experiment with relief printing, and used its surface, for want of something handier, to jot down a laundry list for his mother. Although he removed the marks, when the stone was inked, the writing reappeared. It was one of those rare moments when all the necessary ingredients were present for the gift of good luck.

The word lithography literally means stone drawing. It is the graphic medium that is most capable of producing very dark rich blacks with a glossiness or vibrancy that not even mezzotint gives. First, the stone (or, nowadays, possibly a treated metal plate) is marked with a greasy pencil or liquid, then dampened, and a layer of greasy ink rolled over it, the ink clinging to the oily drawing, but nowhere else; the moist stone rejects the ink since grease and water repel each other. A sheet of paper is then pressed onto the stone and the original image is transferred. In this way, lithography, a *planar* or *surface* printing method, differs from the *incised* or *intaglio* method of etching and engraving, or the *relief* method of the woodcut.

Lithography preserves the artist's notations with great fidelity and is the quickest printmaking method as well as the easiest to learn, since the print can be done freely, without the interjection of burin, acid, or gouge. Because of this autographic feature, and because of its ability to render almost any shade of black through selective dilution of the greasy ink, lithography was increasingly popular, particularly in France, although it didn't begin to prosper until the end of the century. The hardness of the stones permitted an almost unlimited number of equally good impressions; their considerable size made large prints possible. Lithography had the additional advantage that artists could work directly on specially treated papers, and at their convenience, transfer their designs to stones, eliminating the necessity of drawing in reverse or coping with cumbersome and heavy weights. Almost every method of transmitting an image — brush, crayon, chalk, spatter, fine pen — could be used in combinations ranging from the sparsest lines to the densest and fullest tones.

Lithography attracted a few enterprising artists almost immediately, but it was far more commonly used for the printing of labels, posters, maps and other commercial items. Because of these mercantile associations, with the exception of its use by Goya and Daumier, it languished as a major creative tool in the first half of the nineteenth century. Ironically, Daumier himself unwittingly lent the process a poor reputation because he was considered a mere illustrator rather than a serious artist. It was perceived as low class and its initial artistic trials were short-lived.

Lithography developed simultaneously with a new fashion that conformed to Napoleon's theories of art. The emperor, hoping that France would sense in him a reincarnation of imperial Roman civilization, supported a Classical revival. It was a welcome relief from often over-wrought Baroque and Rococo forms, typically refraining from deep emotion or inner tension. Evolving from Winckelmann's earlier studies of antiquity, it providentially corresponded with Napoleon's propagandistic instincts and yearnings for glory. Jacques David, who had originally been a great partisan of the Revolution, recanted in zealous service to the emperor and was Neo-Classicism's principal advocate in the field of painting. But in the graphic medium, its greatest exponent was David's pupil, Jean-Auguste-Dominique Ingres. He had studied in Paris before going to Italy where he earned an uncertain livelihood drawing wonder-fully deft portraits of friends and tourists who came his way. Influenced both by classical art and by Raphael's orderly linear patterns, he was a master of clear draftsmanship, compressed compositions, and har-monious proportions. In a minor lithograthic experiment, he sketched a set of four portraits of the North family. His only venture into etching was an elegant portrait, done in 1816 in a formal engraving style, of Mon-signore Gabriel Cortois de Pressigny, Ambassador to Rome. (Fig. 132) Prcssigny's commanding likeness is typically French in its self-assurance, insinuating glance, and arrogant half-smile, every line precisely thought out and exquisitely placed. Although Ingres' allegorical paintings were frequently over-pompous and academic, in his portraits at least there was no taint of tired mechanical clichés.

Ingres turned away from his own troubled times, looking back to a period of idealized perfection. He rejected spontaneity and an outward show of feeling, preferring an austere coolness in his drawings. No one ever showed greater skill in the art of lucid delineation than Ingres; he equated his stringent outline with beauty and truth in the tradition of Holbein, the early Renaissance artists, and later, Van Dyck. Like them, his every line defined the image it shaped. He refrained from chiaroscuro, but the observer accepts this convention and automatically clothes the wiry lines with volume. Degas later took him as a role model, developing some of Ingres' principles into even more remarkable conceptions.

When Ingres returned to Paris in 1841, it was to do battle with the increasingly popular Romantic school which had appeared at the end of the Napoleonic era and was to last until the Franco-Prussian War of 1870. Romanticism, in the sense of emotional fervor, free handling, and personal references, completely rejected Neo-Classic rationality. Its high priest was Eugène Delacroix, born in 1798, Ingres' junior by eighteen years, and supposedly the natural son of the French statesman Talleyrand. Where Ingres expressed line and form in graceful sinuosity, Delacroix stressed color and movement, in a vibrant painterly style, unprecedented in French art and looking forward to Impressionism. The extreme views of the two artists made them natural antagonists, but Ingres perhaps understood that a new style had inexorably taken root. Walking a group of his students through a gallery in which a Delacroix painting was hung, he ordered them to "take off your hats, but do not look at it."

Fig. 132. Jean-Auguste-Dominique Ingres. *Gabriel Cortois de Pressigny.* Courtesy Metropolitan Museum of Art, Rogers Fund, 1921 [21.83.3].

Delacroix tried his hand at printmaking at the age of sixteen, etching a lightly finished profile of Napoleon in 1814 and an introspective self-portrait in 1819. His lithographs endowed the medium with artistic credibility and promoted a wider interest in its use, particularly his illustrations for the German poem *Faust* in 1828. They were rather melodramatic in treatment, but the poet admired their "disorderly manner," and they made a handsome contribution to one of the most beautiful books ever produced. A vivid portrait of Goethe, who was an enthusiastic print collector and amateur etcher, was included as its frontispiece.

It was partly through Delacroix's and Goethe's efforts that the imagination of Europe was caught up in the Romantic spirit, in what Wordsworth had called the "spontaneous overflow of powerful feelings." The heightened quality of sensitivity and awareness with which Delacroix infused the lithograph of his twenty-one year old pupil Louis Auguste Schwiter, 1826, typifies that movement. (Fig. 133)

Lithography's greatest genius was a painter of middle class French society, Honoré Daumier, who also produced a body of political and social cartoons that flouted every academic prescription. There is hardly a satirical draftsman today who doesn't owe an enormous debt to Daumier's eloquent pen and courageous independence; he influenced every nineteenth century artist from Delacroix to Toulouse-Lautrec. At the beginning of his career, he studied printmaking with a lithographic portraitist, and from 1831 to 1872 produced four thousand topical lithographs for the French periodicals *La Caricature* and *Le Charivari*. Through a half dozen political administrations he mocked every bloated hypocrite in sight. No other modern artist has had a wider audience. In spite of his immense output, however, he lived in poverty, ending his life blind, helpless but for the generosity of Corot.

His prints were a feared weapon with which he devastatingly lampooned Louis-Philippe, among others. His demands for justice and reform were occasionally presented with a scatological audacity. In 1832 he published a caricature of the king as Gargantua, stuffing his mouth with the wealth of the country, and transmitting the spoils to his cronies via the end product of his digestive system. His political work was censored for this affront and he spent the next four months in jail. In another depiction of Louis-Philippe, 1834, *Le Passé, le Présent, l'Avenir (Past, Present, Future)*, he developed the theme of past disappointments, present dissatisfaction, and flagging expectations. (Fig. 134)

The European revolutions of 1848 helped to bring about a school of Realism which repudiated both the idealism of Neo-Classicism and the lyricism of Romanticism, and reflected the general unrest. Young pragmatists followed Daumier's dictum that "one must be one's own time." They examined the world critically, and systematically

Fig. 133. Eugène Delacroix. *Louis Auguste Schwiter.* Courtesy Metropolitan Museum of Art, Derald H. and Janet Ruttenberg Gift and the Elisha Whittelsey Collection, the Elisha Whittelsey Fund, 1983 [1983.1170].

stripped it of illusion, looking objectively at their contemporary environments as though through the dispassionate lens of the newly invented camera—the second dramatic discovery that would affect the artists of the nineteenth century. Everything, regardless of how commonplace, arrested their attention; everything was a resource for their art.

The basic technical information about photography had been known for a long time. It was consolidated and hurried into commercial development largely in response to the demand for inexpensive portraits. Now that a picture containing marvels of detail could be had in a matter of minutes, it was no wonder that most people flocked to photographers' studios or posed outdoors, even though protracted lens exposures were unavoidable, necessitating head clamps to insure immobility. After photography was invented by Louis Daguerre in 1837, it created a technological revolution on a par with that of printmaking in the fifteenth century. It is difficult to imagine the time when people got their pictorial information exclusively from paintings, drawings, or prints. A radical change took place not only in the way people saw, but in what they saw as well. The unselective lens, arbitrary in its recording of everything within the viewfinder, fixed on chance backgrounds and accidental arrangements, suggesting new theories of composition to artists. As time went on they began to include cut-off images, casual groupings, and the blurred visions made possible by controlled focusing.

Among other things, photography launched a new industry—art history—and almost finished off the familiar art form of printmaking. Until the invention of the camera, an art critic either had to memorize

Fig. 134. Honoré Daumier. *Le Passé, le Présent, l'Avenir (Past, Present, Future)*. Courtesy Armand Hammer Foundation.

every work and hold its details in his head, or be dependent on a drawing or print which interpreted or distorted the original according to the artist's skill or point of view. In addition, such information was deceptive because neither drawings nor prints are able to indicate tactile qualities such as the painter's brush strokes or the sculptor's chisel marks. Winckelmann and other experts had relied in great measure on engravings of objects they had never seen; once the accuracy of the photograph was available for comparison and evaluation, the specialist had a better scholarly tool, while the reproductive engraver, unhappily, found himself technologically vulnerable—in many cases his job disappeared.

The latter part of the century witnessed a tremendous burst of art-historical research, since almost everything that had been written based on the second-hand reporting of drawings and prints had to be reconsidered and revised. Books filled with photographic illustrations became important learning tools, helping the public understand, appreciate, and buy art with discrimination.

Almost everyone could afford the exciting new substitute for prints; it was a repetition of the time when engraving emerged as a cheaper alternative to painting. No longer was it necessary to envy the aristocrat his painted or engraved likeness. Stock backgrounds provided instant elegant settings, and even fine clothes and expensive accessories could be borrowed from the photographer's supplies.

Once printmakers were emancipated from their basic role as suppliers of information, they began to explore more interesting approaches. Fresh and imaginative styles were inadvertently forced into being by competition from the camera. The printmaker had to prove that he was not superfluous — that he could read character, suggest a telling expression, and compose a picture with greater selectivity and analytic power than the photographer; the print, therefore, had to become more "artistic" and more capable of significant interpretation than the literal or objective camera. It should not be inferred, of course, that prints are necessarily finer works of art than photographs or that the camera is unable to record hidden meanings or even abstract concepts. Certainly the soft-focus portraits of early photographers such as Julia Margaret Cameron and the distinguished twentieth century contributions of Edward Steichen, Alfred Stieglitz, and others are filled with sensitivity, creativity, and skill. However, the print, with its own characteristic tints and surface qualities, ranked higher as a hand-made work of art, and often conferred a unique distinction on the sitter.

One of the first artists to respond to these crosscurrents was the Realist Gustave Courbet. Like Daumier and Degas, Courbet borrowed the relaxed pose popularized by the photograph. His own life, however, was anything but placid. He was a fervid iconoclast, and his non-conformist attitude became his undoing. At one time he deeply offended many people with a painting of drunken priests; the picture was destroyed by its Catholic purchaser. In the civil disturbances of 1871 he was accused of leading the group that tore down the Napoleonic victory column in the Place Vendôme, which had been designed as a replica of Trajan's column in Rome. For this escapade he was jailed and fined the cost of its rebuilding — four hundred thousand francs. Not having that kind of money handy, he fled France for Switzerland and died there four years later in 1877, only fifty-eight years old. He helped originate the image of the artist as a revolutionary Bohemian type who shocked and dismayed the public.

One of his rare lithographs is a portrait made in 1850 of his friend, the "apostle" Jean Journet, starting out on his "conquest of universal harmony." (Fig. 135) The image seems harmless enough today, but it had political overtones, since Journet was a student of the Fourier school of Socialism, as was young Courbet himself; the elevation of rude working class figures as subjects of art was controversial. The portrait was appropriate to Courbet's democratic tastes, but unfortunately, liberalism was being suppressed at the time the print was made, with the government reverting to authoritarian rule. Radical sympathies were an unhealthy enthusiasm in the conservative climate of France after the Revolution of 1848.

Fig. 135. Gustave Courbet. *The Apostle Jean Journet.* Courtesy Metropolitan of Art, Harris Brisbane Dick Fund, 1932 [32.7.68].

In addition to the rather ungraceful figure, it was printed with twenty-two verses of "complaints" which surround the portrait on three sides. The informal appearance of the subject suggests the candid snapshot and illustrated how photography was changing posing styles. Journet walks casually along a road, hat and stick identifying him as a peasant, knapsack filled with Fourier pamphlets slung across his shoulder, workpants rolled up, his coat shabby and worn. Who in the world had ever seen such a portrait? Yet unconventional clothing was gaining some familiarity through gossip about George Sand's wearing of pants and the dress codes that progressive thinkers like Walt Whitman in America were popularizing. Whitman described himself as "rough" and boasted, "I cock my hat as I please." For the portrait frontispiece of *Leaves of Grass*, 1855, Whitman wore an open-necked shirt, hat tilted to one side, one hand at his hip, the other nonchalantly in his pocket. "I lean and loafe at my ease," he wrote. It was the declaration of a new faith.

Although most printmakers were having a hard time, book illustration still kept some engravers busy, but it was only a short reprieve. Reproductive engraving became virtually obsolete after the invention of the dotted halftone screen in the 1880s for pictures used in books, magazines, and the daily newspapers. This process transfers sensitized photographs or negatives to a cylindrical plate for machine-powered, high-speed printing. It is the same method that supplies our newspapers, and this book, with tonal illustrations that appear under magnification, not as lines, but as minute dots.

However, original etching, having lain mostly dormant for a century and a half, unexpectedly came back to life with Charles Meryon, who in the 1850s produced superb visions of old Paris, a series almost completely ignored by the public during his unhappy lifetime. Soon etching was taken up as a vehicle for poetic landscapes and peasant scenes by the Barbizon school of artists, including Charles Jacque, who produced in 1866 a sensitive half-length portrait of M. Luquet, an associate of Alfred Cadart, the founder of the Société des Aquafortistes (Etching Society) in 1862. (Fig. 136) Slowly the etching revival, which lasted in France until about

Fig. 136. Charles Jacque. *M. Luquet*. Courtesy Metropolitan Museum of Art, the Elisha Whittelsey Collection, the Elisha Whittelsey Fund, 1965 [64.605.38].

1880, became all the rage. Although lecherous gentlemen were reputed to inveigle innocent maidens to view their collections, the main concern of the etching society was to rally interest in original etching and to take the field against photography and lithography. A number of critics, such as Charles Baudelaire and Philippe Burty, championed its cause in various magazine articles. Their efforts revived etching as a non-reproductive art form based on intuitive perceptions and a natural drawing style. Portrait etching received an additional impetus when the Louvre began to sell late impressions pulled from Van Dyck's *Iconography*. While these restrikes were fairly worn, they stimulated a renewed enthusiasm for printed portraiture in both France and England.

Cadart published folios of prints which included works by the best

Fig. 137. Edouard Manet. *Lola de Valence*. Courtesy Grunwald Center for the Graphic Arts, UCLA, gift of Mr. and Mrs. Fred Grunwald.

artists and amateurs of the time: Jean Baptiste Corot, Edouard Manet, Alphonse Legros, Félix Bracquemond, and the King of Sweden were among the contributors. In the second folio in 1863, Cadart included Manet's figure of a popular exotic Spanish Dancer, Lola de Valence. (Fig. 137) Beneath the portrait appeared Baudelaire's comment that she scintillated like a red and black jewel. Manet, who made the etching after his own painting and also repeated the composition in a lithograph, gives no hint of her celebrated vivacity, but rather presents her in a quiet mood. Her mantilla provides a soft contrast to the background and to her dark skirt and hair. Following Goya's example, Manet employed a wide range of tones in the aquatinted lights and shadows, but he lacked that master's wonderful sense of movement.

Manet was not a great etcher, but he was a major force in Realism. Like Courbet, he believed that any subject matter was appropriate and he was instrumental in furthering attitudes that emphasized truth to nature. His erotic painting *Olympia*, and the equally notorious *Luncheon on the Grass*, 1863, both portraits of his model Victorine Meurent, made him the talk of the town in advanced art circles, but the public thought he was past praying for. The latter painting had been taken directly from a sixteenth century engraving by Marcantonio Raimondi after a lost drawing by Raphael, *Judgment of Paris*. Raphael's three figures were nude since the gods of mythology did not wear Renaissance attire, but Manet dressed his gentlemen in contemporary clothing, leaving their female companion in the altogether. Salon jurors, appalled by its modernity and frank sexuality, rejected the painting. *Olympia*, which he also produced as an etching, was grudgingly accepted in effort to be *au courant*, but the censors felt vindicated when it was critically damned. It took another generation before the public learned to shrug an indifferent shoulder at up-to-date nudes; by then Manet was dead from complications following the amputation of his leg.

He was less adventurous in his etching of Baudelaire, 1869, and in a haunting lithograph, about 1873, after his painting of his sister-in-law Berthe Morisot, herself a painter and printmaker. (Fig. 138; see Fig. 147) Neither portrait had the peacock beauty or abundant details that were generally admired, but his economical use of cross-hatching and his apparently inspired and spontaneous treatments provided a refreshing sparkle. His lithographs have a freer and less traditional quality than his more contrived etchings, as is evident in the de Valence and Morisot portraits. The latter image has an unfinished quality, as though the final touches have not yet been added. The black pyramid, lit by the white of the subject's face, is echoed by the small triangle of flowers at her chest. By scraping the stone here and there so that the paper showed through, Manet achieved an atmospheric effect that relieved the somberness of the large hat, neckpiece, and cape. Later artists adopted Manet's manner, but not always as successfully. His lithographs were hardly known until that medium was popularized at the end of the century.

Félix Bracquemond was a pivotal figure in the revival of etching. He was a great technician and knew the medium's strengths and limitations as well as anyone. He taught its methods to Manet, Degas and others, and was an important printmaker himself, spanning the period from Neo-Classicism to Impressionism. In the 1882 portrait of the writer and critic Edmond de Goncourt, he even attempted to reproduce cigarette smoke, and rival photography's perfect ability to convey vaporous fumes. (Fig. 139) The decorative background details shown in an early state of this portrait, provide a glimpse of typical late nineteenth century interior design.

Goncourt and his brother Jules wrote appreciatively about etching, the profession of the hero of their novel *Manette Salomon*. Bracquemond's etchings of artists are among his finest works and include striking portraits of Meryon, Delacroix, Legros, and Corot. His faces sometimes fall short of psychological insight, but they were all considered excellent likenesses and good personality studies.

After relatively short flirtations with Neo-Classicism, Romanticism and Realism, the art world began a permanent love affair with Impressionism. At first there were the usual spats and misunderstandings that attend all infatuations, particularly since the radical new style was at the mercy of reactionary critics, but a warm relationship developed once people learned to judge for themselves. There are now vast numbers of reproductions and imitations of Impressionist art all over the world. And why not? They offer delightful bouquets of pure fresh colors, bevies of charming ladies, and the enchantment of Parisian streets and the French countryside, where all troubles are banished. For many, the latter nineteenth century was a period of easy circumstances which they were determined to enjoy.

The term Impressionism (originally used pejoratively) derives from one of Claude Monet's paintings of light on water called *Impression — Soleil Levant (An Impression — Sunrise)*, exhibited in 1874 (and stolen in 1985). Impressionistic elements had already been introduced by Manet in the 1860s, when he and a number of other artists had become interested in outdoor painting, attempting to catch, as Courbet had done, the true appearance of objects at the moment they are seen, rather than as they are later remembered in the studio. But in 1870 when the onset of the Franco-Prussian War interrupted their studies, Monet and Camille Pissarro, who had been practicing landscape painting and penury, decided to go to England to avoid army conscription. There, in the paintings of Constable and Turner, they discovered new ways to treat color and light. Perhaps at the time they also saw Rubens' portrait of his sister-in-law, entitled *Le Chapeau de Paille (The Straw Hat)*. Completed about 1630, it is the only seventeenth century portrait apparently painted in the open air, using the natural glow of sunlight to effect lush skin tones.

Upon returning home after a year's absence, the artists were horrified to find that Pissarro's house had been ransacked by German soldiers, and that hundreds of his paintings had been used to line and waterproof trenches dug around the grounds. However, they resolved to try out what they had learned and began to incorporate incandescent light and flitting particles of shadow in their informal scenes of daily life.

In the spring of 1874, along with Renoir, Degas, Cézanne, and some two dozen other artists, Monet and Pissarro decided to bring their work to public notice and applied to the official Salon, where all art had to be

Opposite, left: Fig. 138. Edouard Manet. *Berthe Morisot*. Courtesy Metropolitan Museum of Art, Harris Brisbane Dick Fund, 1923 [23.21.22]. *Right*: Fig. 139. Félix Bracquemond. *Edmond de Goncourt*. Courtesy Art Institute of Chicago.

accepted by a jury in order to be exhibited. Like most innovative work, it was refused; perhaps the prismatic patches of color were perceived as threats to the panel's own traditional styles. This exclusion understandably created a great deal of anxiety, since, as Renoir said, "There are in Paris scarcely fifteen art lovers capable of liking a painting without Salon approval. There are eighty thousand who won't buy an inch of canvas if the painter is not in the Salon." However, because at least four thousand avant-garde paintings, Impressionistic and otherwise, had also been rejected, Napoleon III agreed in 1863 to the formation of an independent association, the Salon des Refusés (Salon of Refused Works), where the controversial paintings of Renoir, Monet, Pissarro, and Cézanne were first shown.

Art history was made at these exhibitions. They were the *coup de grâce* to the Salon and the birthday of Impressionism. The press hooted, but the exuberance of feeling and the ravishing colors of the spectrum soon overcame all the negative judgments. The artistic revolution that followed left old-fashioned conservative tastes far behind. Impressionism turned out to be the herald of modern art.

Most of the Impressionist painters put a great deal of effort into print-making, learning to simulate natural daylight effects by the skillful placement of their lines against the white of the paper. They frequently used soft-ground etching, a technique popularized in the late eighteenth century, in which the design is drawn with a pencil on thin paper laid over a waxy etching ground. When the paper is lifted off, the ground sticks to its underside, leaving on the plate the pattern of the grain of the paper and the pressure marks made by the pencil. After the metal is etched in the usual way, the design appears in soft outlines, resembling chalk or crayon drawings. Color lithography, in which prints are serially taken from separately inked stones, was also adopted to provide a suffused atmosphere and an intense coloration.

As with Impressionist paintings, the public at first ignored or disparaged the loose, unrealistic appearance of these prints, not believing that these unfinished qualities lent themselves to portraiture. Those interested in having conventional or formal prints of themselves turned instead to photography or to the few stubborn traditional engravers who were still eking out an existence. Printmakers, therefore, had to sit for each other, impose on their friends, or look in the mirror. This turned out to be fortunate for posterity; freed from the obligation of producing flattering commissioned images, they created imaginative and inspired portraits, and left behind a gallery of the best artists and literary figures.

At one time these prints were thought to be simple and somewhat slapdash in style. They were, on the contrary, quite complex and carefully organized, and have maintained their appeal because they offered new ways of looking at the human face. Painstaking resemblance and evocation of character were not the first priorities; the primary concern was to work quickly in order to capture what Pissarro called the "spontaneity of sensation"—impulsive notations hinting at effects rather than spelling them out in detail. The play of light across the features was an equally important element, but that alone was hardly original. What was special and new was that the fundamental subject matter of art now was light itself as it decomposed the objects which it touched; Monet called it the principal person in a picture and believed it was more important than form.

Pissarro was the eldest of the Impressionists, and by all reports, the best loved. He acted as peacemaker and sympathetic confidant, was especially helpful to Cézanne, who called him the master of the Impressionists, and gave a hand as well to Degas, Gauguin, and Van Gogh. He was born in the West Indies of Jewish parents and ran away from home at a young age because they opposed his artistic career. When he later won their reluctant consent, he went to Paris, where he came under Corot's influence. He was the most prolific, but not the best, graphic artist in the group, although Mary Cassatt said he could teach a stone how to draw. He produced over two hundred atmospheric and inventive prints, mostly turned out for his own pleasure, but never published by himself.

His few portraits are well-defined and imbued with sincerity. His first print, completed in a single sitting, was etched on a cold day in 1874, catching the self-confident and vigorous figure of Cézanne. The strength of the image is evident in the steady gaze and assured posture, although the beard covers everything below the nose, and the hat everything above the eyes. (Fig. 140) It has a boldness and conviction not always found in his sometimes overly sweet genre paintings. Cézanne apparently cherished this rendition, since he included it twenty years later in a catalogue of his own work, but when he etched his own self-portrait, he gave himself a straighter nose. (See Fig. 157) His sensitivity about his baldness at the age of thirty-five accounts for the cap, which he frequently wore to cover his receding hairline.

Pissarro's *Self-Portrait*, etched about 1890, when he was almost sixty, is a far cry from the way he depicted Cézanne. (Fig. 141) Although by then a recognized master, he represented himself as a humble peasant. He utilized a grainy aquatint with dissolving tonalities ranging from very light to dark grey, and with typical unconcern never bothered to remove accidental scratches from the plate. The white hat contrasts sharply with the background as does the white beard above the black coat. Again, very little of the face is visible, but the solemn eyes have a watchful look behind the half-glasses. Those eyes were already failing him, and he died blind thirteen years later.

The best draftsman among the Impressionist artists, and the one most interested in facial expressiveness, was Edgar Degas. After studying law, he took up academic drawing, painting, and sculpture, gradually moving away from Ingres' orthodoxy to the graphic style of Daumier and Japanese prints. Although his partiality for subdued color and light took him somewhat outside the scope of the Impressionists, his flickering surfaces and unexpected poses confirmed his affiliation, and he exhibited with them

Top: Fig. 140. Camille Pissarro. *Paul Cézanne*. Courtesy Philadelphia Museum of Art, the Louis E. Stern Collection. *Bottom*: Fig. 141. Camille Pissarro. *Self-Portrait*. Courtesy Museum of Fine Arts, Boston.

beginning in 1874. He preferred to control his light effects arbitrarily and therefore painted more indoor than outdoor scenes. For the last thirty years of his life he was a recluse, and although he continued to be productive, he no longer showed his work, publishing only four prints in his lifetime. Like Manet and Toulouse-Lautrec, his wealth permitted him to remain aloof from the vexations of the art marketplace.

In his youth he etched a few portraits, mostly of his family; after his death, they came as a surprise to all but his closest friends. In his *Self-Portrait*, 1855, at the age of twenty-one, he used the traditional method of cross-hatching to achieve his modulated tones, but the etching has a modern look because of the variety and free handling of his lines and the openness and objectivity with which he permits the viewer to share his vulnerability. (Fig. 142) The portrait went through five states; Degas typically tested various inking processes and worked and reworked his plates, altering their character and seeking chiaroscuro effects with the diversity and sensitivity of Rembrandt. In 1856 he was studying in Rome, and in his etching *The Engraver Joseph Tourny* put into practice Ingres' words of advice: "Draw lines, young man, many lines and you will become a good painter."

He based his later etched portraits on early family daguerreotypes. Several years after his self-portrait, he made an affectionate study of his younger sister, *Marguerite de Gas*, 1860–1862. (Fig. 143) (He adopted an alternate form of the family name as a democratic gesture, since the original spelling indicated nobility.) Not even Whistler surpassed this depiction of pensive young womanhood, which neither idealizes nor gushes over the phenomenon of youth. Marguerite seems to be looking out from darkness at an uncertain world.

Degas' enthusiasm for Japanese woodcut prints followed the example of Bracquemond, Manet, and the Goncourt brothers. Japan had been "opened" a dozen years before by the American commodore Matthew Perry when various countries were demanding reciprocal trade relations. For over two hundred years its ports had been closed to Western influences, although oriental designs were occasionally seen in the drawings and prints of Rembrandt and Rubens. However, these were rare and had no major impact. Once Japan began to export porcelains, fans, and other decorative items, all kinds of oriental-style tableware and household articles appeared in French shops and were eagerly snapped up—according to the Goncourts, by "idiots and middle class women."

Japanese prints had been used as stuffing material in the shipment of fragile objects and would have been routinely discarded at their destinations had not a batch been rescued by the master-printer Auguste Delâtre. After Degas became familiar with them, he adjusted his experimental style to their flat, simplified forms, off-balance postures, and asymmetrical designs. In 1879–80 he returned to portraiture with an unusual image of his artist friend, *Mary Cassatt in the Paintings Gallery of the Louvre*, a place where many artists trained in lieu of formal art schools. (Fig. 144)

Top: Fig. 142. Edgar Degas. *Self-Portrait*. Courtesy Los Angeles County Museum of Art, purchased with funds provided by the Garrett Corporation. *Bottom*: Fig. 143. Edgar Degas. *Marguerite de Gas*. Private collection.

He borrowed a number of elements from Japanese prototypes and the camera—the tall narrow format, the vertical strip of wall on the left, the almost too-large figures of Cassatt and a woman reading, and the informality of the poses. He changed the lighting and indefatigably modified the composition through twenty states, adding aquatint, drypoint, and other techniques to give it a painterly quality and make sure that only the most vital details were retained. When friends commented that his work appeared unpremeditated, he insisted that no one's art was less spontaneous than his.

The theme, women concerned with works of art, was distinctly new. The women are conventional types, rather than court or courtesan figures, and were conceived from a dramatically striking viewpoint, facing away from the artist and the audience, apparently unaware of either. The long diagonal reaching from Cassatt's hat to the tip of her umbrella forms a subtle

Fig. 144. Edgar Degas. *Mary Cassatt in the Paintings Gallery of the Louvre.* Private collection.

contrast with the verticals and horizontals; the area enclosed is in itself a well-designed shape.

Cassatt was a printmaker as well as America's best woman painter. She exhibited with the Impressionists although she did not share their preoccupation with kaleidoscopic light. She grew up in a Philadelphia banking family that provided an art education but did its unsuccessful best to discourage her from pursuing a professional career; women who were serious about art faced dim prospects in post–Civil War America. She moved to Europe instead at the age of twenty-three and studied in Italy before going on to Paris, where Degas became her friend and mentor. She was an exceptionally fine draftsman, much admired by her colleagues, but Degas thought it was intolerable that a woman could draw so well!

She published a set of drypoints between 1889 and 1891 of an unusual sensitivity and exquisite range of tones, but the public wasn't much interested. Of this group *The Parrot*, 1891, was a deeply felt portrait of Matthilda, her servant, friend, and occasional model. (Fig. 145) The

Fig. 145. Mary Cassatt. *The Parrot.*
Courtesy Metropolitan Museum of
Art, gift of Arthur Sachs, 1916 [16.3.5].

delicate surface qualities in the print are carefully indicated, with equal attention paid to feathers, fabric and skin, but it is the character of the face that interested her most. The skirt is barely suggested below the dark bodice, an idea she may have borrowed from Whistler's *Weary.* (See Fig. 173)

From 1890 on, Cassatt adopted the flat, bold format of Japanese woodblocks. Her ten colored etchings from this period were the high point of her graphic work. Mostly she portrayed women and children with an energetic, open, and clean-cut line, generally without over-idealization. In 1904 she drew a solidly modeled portrait of a youngster, thought to be the granddaughter of the president of France, *Sara Wearing Her Bonnet and Coat.* (Fig. 146) The charm of this print lies in the ingenuousness of childhood and the rapport between artist and sitter. It is one of only two lithographs that Cassatt made.

She did her graphic work at night when the light wasn't good enough for painting, and her eyesight may have suffered; for the last twelve years of her life she was essentially blind. It was through her efforts to help the Impressionists find patrons that American connoisseurs began to collect Impressionist paintings, many of which are now in the major museums of the United States.

Berthe Morisot, Manet's sister-in-law and occasionally his model (see Fig. 138), was, like Cassatt, one of the first women to be associated with the Impressionists. Although she never had the power or incisive drawing ability of Cassatt, she had a warmth and ease that Cassatt lacked. She was likewise interested in mother-child relationships, but the unstrained love and security evident in the enfolding triangle of *Leçon de Dessin* (*The Drawing Lesson*), 1889, a self-portrait with her daughter, was in her own manner. (Fig. 147) It is one of only eight prints that she made. She skillfully indicated the distinctions between adolescence and maturity in the two similar faces. The facial shadows, feathery drypoint modeling, and the cross-hatching behind her figure to avoid the appearance of flatness, all separate her work from Cassatt's and the Japanese woodblock style.

Pierre-Auguste Renoir grew up in a poor tailor's home, but unlike the unsympathetic families of many would-be artists, his father helped him get his first job decorating porcelain and his mother subsidized him as much as

Top: Fig. 146. Mary Cassatt. *Sara Wearing Her Bonnet and Coat*. Courtesy Metropolitan Museum of Art, Rogers Fund, 1916 [19.1.7]. *Bottom*: Fig. 147. Berthe Morisot. *Leçon de Dessin* (*The Drawing Lesson*). Courtesy Library of Congress, Washington, D.C.

she was able during his student years. Later he and Monet became friends and shared art lessons and the camaraderie of outdoor painting. In time he slowly established himself as a portrait painter, and although he continued along those lines on and off all of his life, he considered portraiture an unappealing, if necessary, means of making a very good living.

He loved the ambiance of dance halls, cafés, and boating parties, where he painted young people having a good time. Later he chose generously proportioned rosy nudes based on his study of Rubens. Who would guess from these voluptuous figures that they were made by an artist whose hands were frozen by arthritis and whose body no longer served him? He worked for years in a wheelchair with brushes awkwardly clutched in his twisted fingers. When he died in 1919 he left about six thousand pictures, testifying to a spirit that refused to concede disability or accept the ugly.

In his forties Renoir moved away from strict Impressionism after becoming uneasy that in his concentration on light and atmosphere, he was neglecting fundamental drawing skills. In 1881 he visited Italy, where he painted Richard Wagner's portrait; four years later he reinterpreted it with loose, free strokes in a lithograph. His studies of Raphael and Ingres helped tighten his ability to describe form through linear means, and he incorporated those lessons in his few prints. Although as a graphic artist he was never exceptionally creative – his lithographs being close translations of his paintings – he produced twenty-five delightful prints, many of which were portraits of his friends and family.

La Dance à la Campagne (*Country Dance*), 1890, in soft ground etching, also the subject of an oil painting and drawings, represented his brother Edmond and the artist Suzanne Valadon at the popular resort of Bougival (Fig. 148). Valadon was a painter herself, having received Degas' highest accolade, "You are one of us." She shared her charms as model or mistress with half the art colony of Paris. The presentation is in a sensuous mood, unlike the analytic style of most Impressionistic art. The black accents lend richness, the short strokes and broken lines give it movement.

In 1893 Renoir painted *Le Chapeau Epinglé* (*The Pinned Hat*), portraits of the daughter and niece of Berthe Morisot, and repeated the composition in several lithographic editions, 1897–1898. (Fig. 149; see Fig. 147) Time is almost stopped in this evocation of youth. The softness of the skin was accomplished by a painterly blurring of strokes. One of these editions is in lovely color, a technical *tour de force* involving eleven different stones. Renoir first made the drawing on transfer paper, then indicated the required colors in pastels for Auguste Clot, a master printer, who prepared stones for him as well as for other artists.

Such partnerships in printmaking are as old as printmaking. Most early woodcuts, including those of Dürer and Holbein, were drawn on the block by the artists and cut by enormously skilled technicians. Many etchers had professional printers who supervised the acid biting and printing process after the composition was drawn on the grounded plates.

Fig. 148. Pierre-Auguste Renoir. *Country Dance*. Private collection.

Delâtre, for example, printed some of Meryon's etchings, while Bracque-mond did the same for Corot. Japanese woodcuts were always a three-way collaboration between the designer, the cutter, and the printer. As long as the original artist controlled the production, the definition of what consti-tuted an original print remained fairly static. The intricacies and controver-sial issues involved in the technology of contemporary printmaking have forced a rethinking of the precise meaning of "original" work.

Exploration of different techniques and styles crowded the last years of the nineteenth century. Auguste Rodin, the most famous sculptor of his time, was deeply affected by the unfinished statues of Michelangelo, and likewise left many of his own works without a smooth polish. His rough, fragmented planes, modeled with superb perception and intensity, catch the broken light with the lambent qualities of the Impressionists.

After he learned printmaking from Alphonse Legros, Rodin made eleven drypoints, including three of Victor Hugo, about 1885, that have an exceptional vitality. (Fig. 150) There are in these prints a solidity and power that established Rodin as a master of graphic as well as sculptural art, and one whose knowledge of portraiture was comprehensive in whatever medium he chose. Hugo was a high priest of the Romantic move-ment in France and author of the novel *Les Misérables*; his other books are among the best unread works of France. He was a man of enormous ego, but not of profound philosophy. Rodin gave the heads great convic-tion, every hollow or projection as plastic and palpable as if they had been molded in clay. His monumental sculptures of the mature Hugo, based on these etchings, represent Rodin's ironic theory of aging: "Nothing can equal the splendor of this opposition between our desire for eternal beauty and the actual fact of atrocious disintegration."

An innovative lithographic technique emerged in the prints of Eugène Carrière. "Emerge" is as good a description as any for the haunting images that float before us. His method has points in common with mezzotint, but its black magic was created on a stone, its surface scraped so that white highlights appear in the shadows. The faces seem to be night-time or seance apparitions hovering in space. Like mezzotint, his work is not defined by line, but by a tone that combines smudge and sparkle. But evanescent as Carrière's extraordinary portraits were, his modeling was solid and his heads well structured. Among his many subjects were writers and artists, but the portrait of his wife, *Marguerite Carrière*, c. 1890, has a particularly unearthly quality that disturbs the imagination. (Fig. 151)

One theme that artists never seem to tire of is beautiful women; gentlemen admire them, and ladies compare themselves with satisfaction or despair. Dashing portraits of elegant *femmes fatales* reflected the super-ficial life style of the first years of *La Belle Epoque*. Never mind that most of these pictures lacked human qualities; they were incredibly glamorous and depicted high life on Easy Street. Never mind that too many of them were insipid and intellectually unburdened; their sex appeal and vapid charm cast a spell over a wide audience.

Fig. 149. Pierre-Auguste Renoir. *Le Chapeau Epinglé* (*The Pinned Hat*). Private collection.

James Tissot, who lived and worked in England during the 1870s, knew exactly what fashionable women hoped they looked like. His etchings and rich drypoints of sirens in their fur hats and scarves were romantic fantasies. The very popular *Mavourneen*, 1877, is empty of character, but full of amorous suggestion. (Fig. 152) The title, an Irish version of "my darling," refers to his mistress Kathleen Newton, who had a short and tragic life. Only sixteen years old, she was married off to a family friend, although she really cared for another man, by whom she had a child. Tissot met her after that lover deserted her, and they lived happily until she died of tuberculosis at the age of twenty-eight. F. L. Leipnik in

in his *History of French Etching* mentions the "rather noisy success of *Mavourneen* as a portrait in which a large picture hat and a boa seem more important than the person portrayed." However, the profuse burr, contrasting with the delicate linework, perfectly expresses the enchantment and affectation of the era.

Most of Tissot's designs, very skillfully etched and printed, were based on his oil paintings and were intended to create a market for them. Unfortunately, they lost spontaneity in translation. They were cut from the same cloth as those of his countryman Paul Helleu, whose seemingly effortless virtuosity was accomplished with even greater elegance and good breeding. His drypoint of Mrs. Walter Lewisohn, a noted beauty of the day, combines refinement with a touch of provocation, as well as tonal variation and sensitive line quality. (Fig. 153) Alphonse Mucha was a clever illustrator who represented women of the world through the sinuous and decorative calligraphy of the Art Nouveau movement in the late 1890s. Edgar Chahine, Louis Legrand, Manuel Robbe, and others brought to life the gamut of femininity, from gentle maternity to erotic nudity, from the underworld streets of Montmartre to the chic avenues of the Bois de Boulogne.

One of the most remarkable portrait painters and etchers of this genre was Anders Zorn, born in Sweden, but French in spirit. His etchings, consistently more interesting than his paintings, are made up of innumerable strokes and little cross-hatchings which dance magically across the sheet. His shimmering portraits are the essence of Impressionism; light twinkles in his flashing lines. His etching *Miss Emma Rassmussen*, caught with a vital spontaneity, is one of his brilliant examples of the type of woman who is aware of her beauty and projects it with candor. (Fig. 154) He was not, however, one-dimensional, as is evident in his etching of the theologian and philosopher Ernest Renan, 1892. (Fig. 155) Renan was ill at the time and the artist was limited to a one-hour sitting, during which he indicated the main features, completing the plate later from memory. He was an excellent draftsman, capturing the tired but still-alert expression along with the heaviness of the body slumped in a chair. The slashing lines on the black coat contrast with the delicate work on the scholar's head and on the strewn books and papers.

Interesting as these portraitists are, none was as successful in exploring intimate and sensual moods as Paul-Albert Besnard in his many prints of both men and women. The instruction he received from Legros and Bracquemond shows up in the strength of his characterizations; from Zorn came his emphasis on light. His etching of his wife, *Mme. Besnard*, 1884, portrays her with an inward-looking spirit, the dense cross-hatching contributing to the expressive and purposeful treatment. (Fig. 156)

Many of the subjects of these pictures were high-born and affluent;

Opposite, left: Fig. 150. Auguste Rodin. *Victor Hugo*. Courtesy Art Institute of Chicago. *Right*: Fig. 151. Eugène Carrière. *Marguerite Carrière*. Private collection.

their portraits reinforced their celebrity, in addition to preserving their individuality. Society artists, from Rubens to Reynolds and their descendants, were all members of an honorable craft whose success depended on their ability to minister to the social appetites of their clientele. They have been accused of a skin-deep understanding of character, but their surfaces were brilliant, and how lovely was the skin!

Disappointment over early public opposition to Impressionism, dissatisfaction with its emphasis on naturalism, apprehension that photography would replace hand-made portraits, and alienation from fashionable themes, stimulated another group of artists to search for alternative forms. Although the term Post-Impressionism wasn't coined until 1911 when the paintings of Gauguin, Cézanne, and Van Gogh were exhibited, the style began about 1880, emphasizing psychological insights, a renewed interest in linear design, and the mathematical relationships of space. Abstract or structural elements which appeared in these works emanated from heated imaginations and the desire for innovative subject matter and compositions.

The first of the Post-Impressionists was Paul Cézanne. He began as a wrought-up Romantic, developed as an Impressionist closely associated with Pissarro, and evolved into the greatest master of analytic painting of the century. Color was his keystone to pictorial illusion, but he used it to depict mass rather than surface decoration. The Renaissance tradition, which had remained reasonably intact until his transitional work, had represented distance by means of chiaroscuro and receding planes; Cézanne achieved perspective in a single plane of changing color harmonies. He recognized that Impressionism lacked solidity and order in its handling of surface lighting, and he wanted to return to a more authentic manner, something that would be "like the art of museums." His pictures were therefore carefully planned and developed rather than instinctively designed. In this effort he looked back to the abstract classicism of Ingres.

Cubism claims him as its leader although he didn't include that shape in his theory of painting. He believed that the cone, sphere, and cylinder were the basic structures in nature, and that painting should be built up around geometric configurations rather than lifelike forms. After his seminal experiments artists began to make dramatic changes in the depiction of natural objects.

Cézanne's family was in the banking business and he originally intended to go into law. But his inclination was for painting, particularly after he met Pissarro, and he devoted the rest of his life to art, although

Opposite, top left: Fig. 152. James Tissot. *Mavourneen*. Private collection. *Top right*: Fig. 153. Paul Helleu. *Mrs. Walter Lewisohn*. Courtesy Metropolitan Museum of Art, gift of Charles S. White, 1941 [41.33.52]. *Bottom*: Fig. 154. Anders Zorn. *Miss Emma Rasmussen*. Courtesy Metropolitan Museum of Art, bequest of Blanche S. Guggenheimer, 1953 [53.628.7].

Fig. 155. Anders Zorn. *Ernest Renan*. Courtesy Art Institute of Chicago.

the public never appreciated or understood his work. Printmaking was a casual hobby in which he was encouraged by Edouard Vuillard, but he never felt much enthusiasm for it, completing only five etchings and three lithographs. In his pensive *Self-Portrait*, 1898–1900, a lithograph done in a traditional style, he controlled his lights carefully and achieved a sense of composure with very few facial lines. (Fig. 157) There is, however, a hesitant or tentative quality to it; Pissarro's portrait of him outstrips his own modest effort. (See Fig. 140)

   A wave of tortured geniuses who fascinated and repelled their country-men now moved onto center stage. Gauguin, Van Gogh, Toulouse-Lautrec—the stories of these neurotic Post-Impressionists are the stuff of novels and movies. They answered to nothing but their own standards of art and morality, conditioned by lives of pain and small hopes. Their *fin de siècle* works exemplified the schizophrenic extremes of angst and hedonism, terminating many older traditions and opening new outlets for expressive feelings. If it had ever seemed that art had gone about as far as it could go, these inspired prodigies not only challenged that notion, but revolutionized all of aesthetics and freed it from conventional rules and pictorial accuracy. Suddenly the scandalous Impressionists appeared quite tame.

Fig. 156. Paul-Albert Besnard. *Mme. Besnard*. Courtesy Metropolitan Museum of Art, Rogers Fund, 1920 [20.27.2].

Paul Gauguin began his career as a bourgeois, but soon opted for an unfettered life style. After working as a successful stockbroker, marrying, and fathering five children, he decided to give up western civilization. He abandoned his family and moved from place to place, eventually settling for long periods among the primitive natives of Tahiti, where he remained in poverty and acrimony, syphilitic and suicidal until his death at the age of fifty-two. While there, he made crude woodcuts which had their origins in the flattened space of Japanese prints, Courbet's interest in folk characterization, the Tahitian life style, and above all, his own dreams.

In 1891, after his work with Van Gogh and Cézanne, but before he moved to the South Seas, Gauguin made one of his few etchings, a portrait of Stéphane Mallarmé, the young poet who had recently translated Edgar Allan Poe's *The Raven*. (Fig. 158) This likeness, with the mysterious bird Nevermore perched in the background, is an example, within the Post-Impressionist movement, of the Symbolist style which included supernatural "dreams no mortal ever dared to dream before." Heavy lines alternate with delicate strokes, creating a balanced, strong image. The sharply angled eyebrow, nose, and ear, as well as the bird's bill, give the print a particular intensity and power.

Fig. 157. Paul Cézanne. *Self-Portrait.*
Courtesy Grunwald Center for the
Graphic Arts, UCLA, the Fred Grun-
wald Bequest.

Vincent Van Gogh's life story was as harrowing and troubled as Gauguin's. He was born in Holland and worked as a poor missionary among coal miners in Belgium. When he was thirty-three he moved to Paris where he became familiar with the Impressionists' sunlit dabs of color. His own brushstrokes were subjected to a powerful staccato rhythm, not in imitation of realistic nature, but rather in its agitated re-creation. He struggled along virtually unknown, selling almost nothing during his life; in his last two years — he died at thirty-seven — he was intermittently insane. All the world knows the story of how he cut off his ear and sent it to a young prostitute who playfully requested it for Christmas. In 1890, at the suggestion of Pissarro, he became the patient of Dr. Paul Gachet, a physician who had treated another disturbed artist, Charles Meryon. Gachet himself was an amateur printmaker and encouraged Van Gogh to use the materials he had in his home. Mutual friendship and sympathy might have stabilized the artist. Unhappily it did not. After two months of care, he shot himself.

Van Gogh's extremely intense art was the antithesis of Impressionism. Like Gauguin, he was an early Expressionist, reacting against the objectivity of the camera and inventing a new system of painting. In his last days, his writhing lines expressed the chaos of his mind, but his canvases remained carefully organized and rationally composed. His only etching, which he produced with great forcefulness and vitality, was an 1890 portrait of Dr. Gachet. (Fig. 159) His limited experience with printmaking, however, resulted in a design that seems to flow in the wrong direction, looking more stable when viewed in a mirror which, of course, is the way it appeared to him as he worked. (He also painted a portrait of the doctor which likewise slants from left to right.) It is possible that he didn't consider that the etching would print in reverse. In any event, he never saw it on paper, since the few impressions that were taken were made by Gachet after his death. Van Gogh consciously tried to get away from a photographic resemblance; his distortions symbolized the "broken-hearted expression of our time," a reference to the doctor's troubled emotions as well as his own. Shortly before he died, he wrote to his brother Theo that he considered portraiture the most exciting of all subjects; his

Fig. 158. Paul Gauguin. *Stéphane Mallarmé*. Courtesy Grunwald Center for the Graphic Arts, UCLA, gift of Mr. and Mrs. Fred Grunwald.

ambition, he said, was to "induce impassioned expression and exaltation of character."

By the end of the century many artists were no longer spending much time in the playgrounds of Paris, but to the young scion of a noble French family, Henri Marie Raymond de Toulouse-Lautrec-Monfa, the son of Count Alphonse the Second, its brothels, cafés, and theaters had a tremendous attraction. He was only twenty-one in 1885 and already an habitué of the Montmartre district. His first signed lithographs appeared in 1892 when he linked up all that he had learned from Japanese woodblocks, the works of Degas, and the old masters, and began a serious career in printmaking. The few years he had left until his death at thirty-seven—the same age at which Van Gogh shot himself—were spent in dissipation and drawing.

Fig. 159. Vincent Van Gogh. *Dr. Gachet*. Private collection.

His legs had been crippled in boyhood so that he remained dwarf-sized, but however bitter his personal life, he did not let it affect his series of rhythmical and provocative visions of Paris by night.

His style was strictly linear with seemingly simple outlines enclosing flat, unshaded blocks of bold, contrasting colors. He was a great draftsman, constantly inventing new angles of vision and creative design elements. Everything was startling in his work, from the studies of prostitutes and theatrical performers, which shocked his aristocratic family and offended almost everyone else, to his satirical facial expressions, exaggerated gestures, and seductive color harmonies. Each portrait had grandeur and vigor, and spontaneously acquired a personality of its own. Although the life he portrayed was not as glamorous as it appeared — too often it was a world of frailties and degradation — he offered neither psychological introspection nor moral judgments.

Many of his prints were colored lithographic posters for which special printing techniques had to be devised. They were pasted on kiosk billboards around Paris to advertise nightclub attractions, but were removed by collectors almost as soon as they were put up. Their jarring viewpoints, unusual long shots, and vivid close-ups were suggested in part by the versatility of the new portable cameras, and indeed he, like other artists of the day, did not hesitate to use photographs as starting points in his work. His influence extended to Picasso, particularly in the latter's early period of simplified forms, flat bright colors, and sophisticated themes.

Lautrec's good friend Jane Avril appeared with music critic Edouard Dujardin in the print *Divan Japonais* (*Japanese Divan*), 1893, as a café audience for Yvette Guilbert (a music-hall singer; headless in this portrait, she can be recognized by her affectation of long black gloves.) (Fig. 160) Avril, who was also a dancer and entertainer and the subject of numerous prints, is silhouetted in an elaborate hat reminiscent of geishas' headdresses in Japanese woodcuts; as in all Lautrec's portraits, the resemblances are free rather than literal. In this thirty-two- by twenty-five-inch, four-color lithograph poster, in which every curve is harmoniously related to another, the cropped outlines of the bass fiddles and the

Fig. 160. Henri de Toulouse-Lautrec. *Divan Japonais (Japanese Divan).* Courtesy Art Institute of Chicago.

arms make a stunning composition. The emphasis on designs with only a limited reference to natural objects points the way to twentieth century abstraction.

In a more complete image, *Yvette Guilbert*, 1894, the stage-lighting from below dramatically accentuates the performer's long neck and the tilt of her chin. (Fig. 161) There is an almost palpable tension in the contrast between the black gloves and the white of the paper. Lautrec said that in his sixteen portraits of her he stressed total essence rather than any transitory elements. Her melancholy theme song, which she recited to music rather than sang—"the gay world unmasks itself and becomes a tragedy"—not only reflected her own and Lautrec's life, but was a concise account of the not-always-gay Gay Nineties.

Fig. 161. Henri de Toulouse-Lautrec. *Yvette Guilbert*. Private collection

Lautrec reversed the composition, this time emphasizing black-stockinged legs, in *La Clownesse Assise* (*The Seated Clown*), an 1896 portrait of Mlle. Cha-U-Kau from the portfolio *Elles*, a series about the brothel where he lived for a time. (Fig. 162) Lautrec drew long-legged women with a grace that denied his own deformed body. Mlle. Cha-U-Kau herself was not one of the prostitutes, although her cynical half-smile, expressively French in its manner, is too seasoned for her years. The floor, slightly pitched upward, and the nickname, lend an oriental flavor to the four-color lithograph, although the face has an individuality seen only rarely in Japanese art. Lautrec's frequent additions of a stamped monogram and the calligraphy on some of his prints are further Japanese influences. The spatter technique, taken from the dotted flecks of Neo-Impressionist paintings, is a change from his usual strong outline and flat colors.

Although most of his portraits were of women (which by far outsold those of men), he created a superb masterpiece in his color lithograph of a song writer and vocalist advertising his club, *Aristide Bruant dans son Cabaret*, 1893. (Fig. 163) Lautrec successfully established an authoritative identity for Bruant, despite the limited view of his face and the elimination of almost all detail. Actually Bruant was a rather nasty hell-raiser, but Lautrec's recreation of him in great swirling lines and a flat shape gave him a heroic appearance. The composition itself, with its flamboyant bravura style, becomes the medium through which personality and character are evoked. Likewise, the diagonal arrangement and unrestrained exuberance of the singer Mlle. Marcelle Lender, an eight-color lithograph, were highly expressive (Fig. 164). The print was considered too French in manner when it appeared in a German magazine in 1895, and because of the persistent acrimonious rivalry between the recently belligerent nations, the editor was fired for lack of discretion.

It is necessary to visualize these portraits with a nineteenth century eye in order to appreciate their originality. Their style has been imitated so often that the novelty has been weakened, but at the time they were made, the poses, expressive distortions, innuendos, and even the placing of the figures in public settings, were fresh and exhilarating. No artist ever had

Fig. 162. Henri de Toulouse-Lautrec. *La Clownesse Assise* (*The Seated Clown*). Courtesy Metropolitan Museum of Art, Alfred Stieglitz collection, 1949 [49.55.50].

a more fecund imagination or exhibited such diversity in portrait design, although the direction that portraiture took in the next century emanated not from Lautrec's glamorous colors and shapes, but from the primitivism of Gauguin and the rationality of Cézanne.

Yet another group of Post-Impressionist painters called themselves Nabis, the Hebrew word for prophets. Although they exhibited with the Impressionists during the decade of the 1880s, they favored a subjective rather than objective examination of nature, with less emphasis on technique and working out of doors, and more on painting from memory. They chose flat, ornamental patterns, simplified forms, sinuous lines, a deeper color palette, and a wider latitude in their themes, following stylistic principles derived from Gauguin's Symbolism and Japanese prints; they adopted his decorative elements, but eschewed his intensity. For about ten years, from 1889 to 1899, Pierre Bonnard and Edouard Vuillard, who were associated with the Nabis, created off-center designs and two dimensional perspective, setting their middle class figures in intimate poetical

environments. Soft muted tones and the omission of the black boundary line highlight Bonnard's color lithograph, *Family Scene*, 1893, a decorative rather than representational portrait of his sister, her husband, and their infant. (Fig. 165) Faithful resemblance was not a very important consideration; Bonnard's interest clearly lay in the irregular contours, atmospheric spatial qualities, and emotional relationships. He cropped the forms, forcing the spectator to complete the design and thereby share in the creative experience. When the Nabi movement broke up after 1900, Bonnard and Vuillard reverted to the greater naturalism of the old masters and Impressionists. Bonnard's portrait of Renoir, with its crippled hand and disheartened face, evokes a Rembrandtian pathos, and envisages the shadow of death; the etching was made about 1916, three years before Renoir died. (Fig. 166)

Vuillard, who shared Bonnard's painting studio, absorbed something of the latter's drawing style in *The Seamstress*, c. 1893. (Fig. 167) This depiction of his mother no doubt was borrowed from the portrait of Bonnard's sister; as Colta Feller Ives has pointed out in *The Great Wave*, their profiles and dress patterns have more than a passing similarity. (See Fig. 165) The colors were chosen to enhance the emotional impact of the composition, rather than to produce Impressionistic light effects. The print, stressing quiet domesticity, was executed in a combination of color lithography and woodcutting. Woodcuts, absent from art history for almost three hundred years, were resurrected in the late nineteenth century and firmly reestablished in the early twentieth, thanks to Vuillard, Gauguin, and others who introduced Japanese and primitive treatments into their own works.

The century had produced many important artists in France, each with his own unconventional style, each deciding what were appropriate subjects, each participating in the evolution of great art. In almost every case they were not primarily printmakers; etching and lithography were only one aspect of their work. None slavishly followed his predecessors as had most of the seventeenth and eighteenth century portrait engravers; instead, they handed down to the twentieth century a tradition of independence in both classical and expressionist art, where the depiction of abstract forms or inner feelings took precedence over the world of appearances.

II. England

French adventurism under Napoleon, British resistance under Nelson.

Opposite, left: Fig. 163. Henri de Toulouse-Lautrec. *Aristide Bruant dans son Cabaret*. Courtesy Metropolitan Museum of Art, the Harris Brisbane Dick Fund, 1932 [32.88.17]. *Right*: Fig. 164. Henri de Toulouse-Lautrec. *Mlle. Marcelle Lender*. Courtesy Art Institute of Chicago.

Fig. 165. Pierre Bonnard. *Family Scene*. Private collection.

Top: Fig. 166. Pierre Bonnard. *Renoir*. Courtesy Grunwald Center for the Graphic Arts, UCLA, gift of Mr. and Mrs. Fred Grunwald. *Bottom*: Fig. 167. Edouard Vuillard. *The Seamstress*. Courtesy Metropolitan Museum of Art, Elisha Whittelsey Fund, 1973 [1973.615].

France on land, Britain on the seas. Never before in history had two powers achieved such a frightful capacity to inflict personal and economic dislocation through blockades and trade restrictions. Both countries suffered unemployment, hunger, and fear. England's troubles were aggravated by the American entry into war in 1812 in protest over illegal searches of her shipping vessels. But when Germany, Russia, and Spain turned against France, victory for England became a near certainty. A hundred days after Napoleon's return from Elba, he was defeated by England's greatest hero, the Duke of Wellington. When the painter and etcher Alphonse Legros was asked why he deserted France for English citizenship, he lightheartedly replied, *"J'ai gagné Waterloo."*

But perhaps what no one realized was that the partitioning of Europe after the downfall of Napoleon assured future trouble because the arbitrary imposition of boundaries disregarded nationalistic aspirations of much of the continent. However, England's unquestioned supremacy and prestige enabled her to enforce peace in Europe for a time and to protect her commercial interests around the world. British prosperity exceeded the most generous predictions.

The Industrial Revolution brought about a shift from hand tools to machine power in the early years of the century and changed forever the manufacture of goods. The factory system took production out of the confines of the family, causing abrupt upheavals in social, political, and economic life. Manufacturers, operating in fourteen-hour days, employed large numbers of people, including very young children. Small farmers migrated to bulging cities because they lost their property when grazing lands were enclosed to improve crop development. Shabbily built housing quickly turned into overcrowded slums.

To the credit of the English social system, many of these shocking conditions were recognized. Armies of reformers, their consciences spurred by the novels of Charles Dickens, undertook improvements through volunteer philanthropic organizations. Well-to-do ladies distributed food baskets and worked together to protect the rights of women and children. Legislation shortened daily working hours, broadened voting and educational opportunities, and permitted businessmen, and later, labor leaders, to play greater roles in promoting civil rights under constitutional guarantees, while the rising workers' movement found its expression in *The Communist Manifesto* of Karl Marx. The political "isms"—nationalism, communism, anarchism, socialism, capitalism, conservatism, liberalism—were mostly nineteenth century designations, although their concepts are as old as history.

In 1859 Charles Darwin published his *Origin of Species* and revolutionized doctrines of biological development and the way in which human beings thought of themselves. Some people angrily inferred that the Bible had been repudiated and bitterly opposed Darwin's conclusions. Along with its scientific implications, his theory of the survival of the strong over the weak generated attitudes of national superiority or fitness. Perhaps those ideas influenced two of the country's greatest literary figures, who may have exacerbated religious and social prejudices. Rudyard Kipling's patronizing reference to the "sullen peoples, half-devil and half-child" in *The White Man's Burden* called attention to American colonial aggrandizement in the Philipines, but most Englishmen saw imperialism as the patriotic expression of a legitimate national idea. Alfred Tennyson's celebrated poem *Locksley Hall* contained not only such famous lines as "In the Spring a young man's fancy lightly turns to thoughts of love," and "knowledge comes but wisdom lingers," but also "I count the gray barbarian lower than the Christian child," and "Better fifty years of Europe than a cycle of Cathay [China]."

Moral attitudes changed dramatically in the course of the century. The conspicuous display of mistresses — royal, high-born, or not worth speaking to — was no longer socially acceptable; the open liaison of Lord Nelson and Lady Hamilton in the early years of the century would have been unthinkable in the reign of Queen Victoria. Husbands were expected to be models of the straight and narrow, and no doubt some of them were.

When Victoria celebrated her Diamond Jubilee in 1897, she was the ruler over about twenty million square miles of territory, almost a quarter of the world's total. Yet economic and political advantage slowly began to move away from England as other countries competed for foreign markets and international leadership. Trade unions threatened traditional labor operations, democratic fervor mounted as power was transferred from the aristocracy to the working people, the Irish question intensified, war broke out in South Africa. The tightly knit fabric of Victoria's empire, still cohesive and resilient at her death in 1901, came apart at the seams after the convulsive reversals of two world wars.

Etching really caught on after the 1850s, although inventive printmaking of various kinds had already been undertaken in the earlier years of the century. The visionary poet William Blake had created obscure and mystical engravings; J. M. W. Turner and John Constable provided models for lyrical etched and mezzotint landscapes; George Cruikshank and Thomas Rowlandson regaled their audiences with sardonic prints pickled in brine. Illustrated books of all kinds continued to be very popular, many enlivened with highly detailed little vignettes produced by Thomas Bewick's eighteenth century invention, wood engraving. He hit upon the idea of using the burin on the very hard cross-section slices of wood instead of cutting on the softer planks along the side grain. The density and hardness permitted exceedingly fine lines and allowed for an almost unlimited number of impressions. Wood engraving is a relief process, as is wood cutting, in that both print from the surface of the block, but in the former the lines which constitute the design are incised and lie below the inked surface and therefore appear as white against a black background.

Books with such engravings were reasonably priced because the wood blocks and the metal type of the text, both being in relief, could be printed simultaneously in a letter-press. Improved bookbinding machinery and steam-powered presses were also bringing down prices and speeding up output, but volumes with copper engravings were still quite costly because two separate presses were required and hand-coloring was frequently applied. They were usually superior in quality and were necessarily printed in small editions, since their plates wore down relatively quickly under pressure. What was needed for the middle class market was a combination of the best features of each — inexpensive, mass-produced books illustrated with high-caliber engravings.

The publishing industry turned to steel plates, which, although more expensive than copper, had the capacity for printing tremendous numbers of impressions, but while some of the dreary manual labor could be eliminated by first etching in the basic design, they had been considered too hard for general use. Therefore it was good news when in 1822 specially made steel plates were developed that could be chemically softened for the engraver. This invention made it possible to produce an avalanche of fine illustrated books at a low cost for the increasingly art-conscious market. Like wood engraving, steel plates are capable of printing very fine lines with incredibly small details hardly visible to the unaided eye; the lines are cut so close together that the prints often have a tonal rather than a linear character, and are greyer in appearance than engravings on copper.

Artists such as Thomas Phillips negotiated handsome fees with publishers for reproduction rights to their paintings. William Finden, one of the best steel engravers, executed a portrait of Lord Byron in Albanian dress, after a painting by Phillips, as the frontispiece to the 1841 edition of the poem *Childe Harold's Pilgrimage*. (Fig. 168) Byron was the handsomest and most romantic man in Europe; like his spiritual heir, Rudolph Valentino, who appeared publicly in similar exotic costumes, he melted the hearts of a generation of ladies. On the other hand, such volumes as the *Portraits of the Illustrious Personages of Great Britain* consisted of coarse commercial hack work and were deplored in their own time. They were cooperatively manufactured by several craftsmen, each skilled in his own specialty — backgrounds, faces, or clothing — until shortly after mid-century, when photography and photomechanical printmaking all but eliminated steel engraving.

With the exception of Wenzel Hollar in the seventeenth century and Hogarth and Bewick in the eighteenth, non-reproductive printmaking had been almost entirely neglected in England. In the early nineteenth century Andrew Geddes, a Scotsman who was inspired by Rembrandt and Van Dyck, made a number of original prints, the finest being *Artist's Mother*, about 1820, after his own painting. (Fig. 169) His rich drypoint burr was enhanced by etching, engraving, and mezzotint. Although his plates were sensitive and well done, they had a tendency to be overworked and are most pleasing when seen in their early states before he got carried away.

Here and there a few other printmakers took up etching, trying to make a dent in the vast proliferation of reproductive engravings that were

Left: Fig. 168. William Finden. *Lord Byron*. Courtesy East Sussex County Library, Brighton Reference Library. *Right*: Fig. 169. Andrew Geddes. *Artist's Mother*. Metropolitan Museum of Art, Rogers Fund, 1918 [18.55.25].

flooding the market; some artists made more money from the prints after their paintings than from the original works themselves. In 1838 a small group of painter-etchers, as they called themselves, established a print-making club and barely managed to keep etching alive, but it wasn't until 1858 that a true renaissance began. In that year, a process was invented that extended the life of copper plates by electroplating a microscopically thin layer of steel to protect their surfaces, detectable only by the most discriminating and discerning eye. When the plating wore, it could be removed and replaced. Another support for the revival was the production of excellent scholarly handbooks to guide and educate potential print buyers. In addition, public exhibitions were becoming popular social affairs, encouraging a wider interest in art. In just a few years etching gained a sure foothold in England, with even Victoria and Albert executing some modest plates. By the end of the century it was fashionable and even lucrative.

The single most important element in the genesis of this success story was the work of Francis Seymour Haden and James Abbott McNeill Whistler. During most of Haden's ninety-two years he was better known as a physician than as an artist. As a young medical student in Paris he met the etchers Charles Meryon and Charles Jacque and took up the etching needle with the idea that the manual dexterity acquired through print-making would improve his surgical skills. On his return to England he became an amateur artist, in the literal meaning of the word "amateur" — all his life he was a lover of etchings. He worked entirely according to his own tastes, more conscious of expressive technique than concerned with grandiose subject matter. He became an avid and exacting collector, particularly of Rembrandt's prints, which he took as his model, as had Geddes. Haden taught himself to say more with less in his serene land-scapes, using only the most necessary and expressive lines and giving empty space equal priority. He was an impressionist before the Impres-sionists, observing his subjects carefully, and setting down each thought quickly and freely, so as not to "weaken its concentration," he said, "or bury its inspiration." Like many English artists, he produced intimate and deeply felt compositions, far different from the cooler intellectual elegance of the traditional French school. Haden struggled to overcome the restric-tions against printmaking at the Royal Academy, which, until he submit-ted his own work in 1860, had only accepted a few engravers for admission. When his demands for greater recognition of etchers and creative etching were not granted, he founded the Society of Painter-Etchers in 1880, for which he was knighted in appreciation of his services to the arts.

Haden's junior by sixteen years, Whistler was born in Massachusetts, although, like Mary Cassatt, America can claim him only by birth, not by custody. He studied briefly at West Point, where he excelled in drawing but failed in chemistry, and at the United States Coast Survey Office, where he learned to etch maps. In 1855 he went to France to become an artist, concentrating on principles of Realism and descriptions of light learned from Courbet, Legros, and Degas. Three years later he was in London living with Haden, whose wife was Whistler's half-sister. The two etchers often worked together depicting scenes around the Thames River, and each etched a portrait of Mrs. Haden reading by lamplight. It is presumed that Haden, comparing his effort with that of Whistler's, wisely decided to stick with landscape subjects, of which he was an outstanding master. However, his 1862 *Self-Portrait*, showing himself at work with his etching materials, is a fine analytic study, set down without artifice or mannerisms. (Fig. 170) More than in most self-portraits, he is unmistakably looking in a mirror, carefully scrutinizing his face for its most characteristic traits.

Whistler began experimenting with drypoint in 1859 after admiring some of Haden's early prints in that medium. He took unusual care during every stage of his printmaking, from the grounding of his plates to the judicious application of the ink. He continually checked his designs, adding or subtracting lines, concentrating on the salient forms, and just barely suggesting the others. Although many of his earlier plates were clean-wiped, he later preferred to manipulate shadowy films of ink that printed as moody atmospheric hazes, a technique pioneered by Rem-brandt. No two of his impressions were exactly alike; collectors consider

Top: Fig. 170. Sir Francis Seymour Haden. *Self-Portrait*. Courtesy Boston Public Library. *Bottom*: Fig. 171. James Abbot McNeill Whistler. *Drouet*. Courtesy Grunwald Center for the Graphic Arts, UCLA.

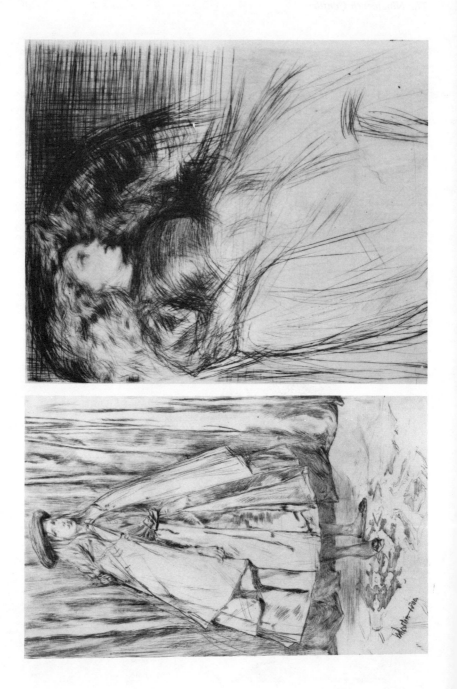

each a unique rendering. He often printed his own work, particularly after 1879, and was as competent a printer as any skilled professional.

His drypoint of the French sculptor Charles Drouet, 1859, with its broad forehead and brooding expression, is a more powerful and energetic likeness than most of his other male subjects. (Fig. 171) The portrait, like so much nineteenth century work, was influenced by Van Dyck's *Iconography*, which Whistler had seen in his brother-in-law's collection. He also made a number of charming plates of the Haden children and believed that the full-length drypoint portrait of his twelve-year-old niece Annie Haden, 1860, was his best work; he said that he would stake his reputation on it. (Fig. 172) Her engaging but unidealized pose was perhaps derived from Holbein, and the shallow area behind her figure borrowed from Velazquez, whose paintings had recently been exhibited in England, but most of all, it expresses Whistler's interest in Realism. Self-absorbed, Annie stands patiently arranged before a curtained background which serves to bring out her costume and push her forward into the spectator's arena; at the same time, the space beneath her feet tends to move her figure back, suggesting the ambivalence and irresolution of adolescence.

The 1863 drypoint of Whistler's Irish mistress, Joanna Hiffernan, his frequent model for both his paintings and prints, is an eloquent example of understatement in line. (Fig. 173) Her listless pose is indebted to Dante Gabriel Rossetti's drawing of *his* mistress, Fanny Cornforth. Although he and Rossetti shared an admiration for dreamy-souled imagery, Whistler's version has a pensive swooning quality that makes it one of his most extraordinary compositions. Her heavy-lidded eyes, half open mouth, and undone blond hair contribute to the smouldering sensuality. The chief emphasis is on the head; the area below her waist is tentatively sketched with a few provocative, dissolving lines. He called the picture *Weary*. Because he never mastered all the niceties of figure drawing, he had difficulty with hands and legs and, as with many of his other portraits, was glad when his suggestive style let him eliminate what he couldn't do well.

Although Whistler preferred etching, he made close to a hundred lithographs after he helped to reintroduce that medium in 1878. It had been used most often in England for topographical views, but under his influence other artists soon adopted it for more personal subjects. His first lithographs were portraits: Cézanne, Mallarmé, and his best pupil, the painter-etcher Walter Sickert. Sensibility and refinement (perhaps over-refinement) are especially evident in the lithograph of Count Robert de Montesquieu, 1895, as he emerges from an indeterminate background into a flickering light, almost as though seen through a veil. (Fig. 174) A comparison between the portraits of the count and Drouet (see Fig. 170)

Opposite, left: Fig. 172. James Abbott McNeill Whistler. *Annie Haden*. Courtesy National Gallery of Canada, Ottawa. *Right*: Fig. 173. James Abbott McNeill Whistler. *Weary*. Courtesy Metropolitan Museum of Art, gift of William Loring Andrews, 1883 [83.1.28].

Fig. 174. James Abbott McNeill
Whistler. *Count Robert de Montes-
quieu.* Courtesy Metropolitan
Museum of Art, Harris Brisbane Dick
Fund, 1917 [17.3.251].

illustrates Whistler's wide range—
self-consciously theatrical, aesthetic, and dandified with an
economic use of line in one; unpre-
tentious, virile, and fuller in tone
in the other.

Most of his portraits were personality rather than character
studies, less deliberate and
documentary than his earlier
etchings. He believed that his
smudgy or misty "unfinished"
works were among his most artistic
inventions, but they didn't always
strike his detractors in the same
way. The critic John Ruskin,
steeped in the styles of Turner and
the Rossetti school, couldn't
accommodate himself to Whistler's
advanced ideas. When he wrote, "I
have seen and heard much of
Cockney impudence before now,
but never expected to hear a cox-
comb ask two hundred guineas for
flinging a pot of paint in the
public's face," Whistler sued for
libel and won—a farthing. The
painting referred to was *Nocturne
in Black and Gold: The Falling
Rocket*, 1877. The trial cost
Whistler his savings; in order to
earn money, he went to Venice in
1879–80, back to his paint pots and printmaking. He etched a series of
fragmentary and haunting city views which were as evocative as the landscapes of Rembrandt.

He had as many idiosyncrasies as he had points of genius. He prided
himself, perhaps in a false show of bravado, as being among the "rare few,
who early in life, have rid themselves of the friendship of many." He was
left with few intimates, one of them Drouet. Predictably he and Haden fell
out. Actually Haden fell through a glass door, pushed by the not-so-gentle
Whistler. They were both arrogant, vain, contentious, and after that
fracas, never spoke to each other again. More in anger than in sorrow,
Haden refused to exhibit Whistler's etchings in the Society of Painter-
Etchers. Whistler retaliated by suggesting that the organization would "die
the death of the absurd." His acerbic tongue was intimidating to his
numerous enemies. Yet he had other sides: He was unstinting in his efforts

to help fellow artists, and he provided the press with an endless string of wisecracks. He and Oscar Wilde were the greatest wits of their day, marvelous foils for each other's waggery. (Wilde, after hearing a *bon mot*: "I wish I'd said that." Whistler: "You will, Oscar, you will.")

Whistler summed up a lifetime of knowledge and spleen in his book *The Gentle Art of Making Enemies*. "The imitator is a poor kind of creature," he wrote. "If the man who paints only the tree, or flower, or other surface he sees before him were an artist, the king of artists would be the photographer. It is for the artist to do something beyond this: in portrait painting to put on canvas something more than the face the model wears for that one day; to paint the man, in short, as well as his features."

What was experimental and original with him was later emulated by other printmakers, as well as by early photographers. Like all great artists, he reported the world differently from anyone else and, along with Haden, believed that the way one saw was infinitely more important than what was seen. His poetic qualities as well as many of his eccentricities became models which were parroted well into the twentieth century: the use of vignettes; a penchant for small editions on high quality old papers; compositions on a small scale; and a sparse use of lines that somehow seem to omit nothing. He usually trimmed off the blank margins, leaving just a small tab with his butterfly signature, a cipher derived from his initials. He and Haden hand-signed their prints, ostensibly to establish genuineness and approval. But, like the custom of numbering impressions in sequence and edition size (begun in the late nineteenth century), these practices had, and still have, as much to do with exploiting the public's credulity as with reliable information.

Whistler constantly involved himself in the lives of other artists. In the late 1850s, with the etching revival under way in Paris, Alphonse Legros had begun to exhibit prints of stoical peasant life in which he was strongly influenced by Jean François Millet and Courbet. The prints attracted the notice of Whistler, at whose urging (and because there were more etchers in France than in England) Legros decided to move to London in 1863. There he contributed significantly to the promotion and advancement of portrait etching. Although Legros was naturalized in England, he never learned to speak the language well. Like Hollar, he only had the normal use of one eye. His academic style reflected the sensitivity and firm classical line of Ingres and the fastidiousness of Holbein, although his manner was a good deal more solemn. He depicted his artist friends and other sitters with distinction, but without sentimentality, and, like Van Dyck, concentrated on the head alone. His prints have a simple grace that few draftsmen can match. Among his subjects were Hugo (See Fig. 150), Darwin, and the painters and sculptors G. F. Watts, Alfred Stevens, and Edward Poynter.

Legros' pyramidal drypoint of Cardinal Manning, 1876–77, has an otherworldly quality, with hollow melodramatic eyes, sunken cheeks, and compressed lips. (Fig. 175) Manning became a convert to Catholicism and then a priest after a distinguished career in the Church of England. He was

Fig. 175. Alphonse Legros. *Cardinal Manning.* Courtesy Boston Public Library.

recognized as a compassionate labor and social reformer, for which he was branded a socialist, a nasty insult in the nineteenth century. It was largely through his efforts that the doctrine of papal infallibility was promulgated; had he been more of a politician, he might have become the next pope, but he chose to support another candidate. Fitzroy Carrington, the editor of *The Print Collector's Quarterly,* called Manning's portrait a "triumph of spirit over flesh," and it is certainly a masterpiece of sensibility and fervor. Legros was the most effective teacher of the time at the prestigious Slade School, where he trained a generation of young etchers. His friendship with Whistler broke up after a series of petty, but almost obligatory, quarrels. But it was because of their work that the popularity of printed portraiture was reestablished.

Legros' best pupil was William Strang, a prolific printmaker whose hundred and sixty portraits were vigorously and expertly drawn. Among his sitters were popular writers such as Rudyard Kipling, George Bernard Shaw, and Robert Louis Stevenson, and artists such as Legros and himself (whom he depicted nineteen times.) The designs, however, were somewhat stiff and lacking in the elegance and humanity with which Legros endowed his own works, perhaps because Strang was more interested in the technical side of etching than in its aesthetic qualities. There is an austerity to the profile etching of author Thomas Hardy, 1894, a strong image in the tradition of Legros' impeccably clean lines; its untouched background gives the portrait significance and dignity. (Fig. 176) Hardy, the "last of the great Victorians," was trained as an architect, but his stories of fatalism and sex, which were rooted in his beloved "Wessex," were by far his greatest satisfaction.

Mortimer Menpes, a native of Australia, began as Whistler's pupil and soon joined his entourage of satellite artists. However, he had the temerity to arrive at some of his own decisions, such as whether or not to visit Japan, and that was the end of their friendship; as he and others were willing to testify, Whistler's bite was considerably worse than his bark. Nevertheless, Menpes described the enormous influence that Whistler had on his followers: "If we etched a plate, we had to etch it almost exactly on

Whistlerian lines. If Whistler kept his plates fair, ours were so fair that they could scarcely be seen." Menpes was, however, no mere sycophant. His prints have greater precision than Whistler's and his clientele was drawn from a wider social and theatrical circle. Both the Duchess of Sutherland and Sarah Bernhardt sat to him. His etchings and drypoints of Whistler have an offhand style that tell an unvarnished tale of the cantankerous genius and shrewd foppishness of their subject. (Fig. 177)

There were some dozens of other etchers who, one way or another, were involved in the Whistler mystique. Many of them turned out portraits, almost three hundred of which were of the master himself. Competent artists who were once highly praised, they are mostly unknown today; in their time they suffered or succeeded according to Whistler's whims.

Fig. 176. William Strang. *Thomas Hardy*. Courtesy Metropolitan Museum of Art, Rogers Fund, 1918 [18.45.14].

III. America

George Washington died in 1799. Thomas Jefferson took office on the new Republican ticket in 1801 after Alexander Hamilton swung the tied vote away from Aaron Burr. The election was a triumph of the Declaration of Independence and the rights of the working man over government by the privileged class. The capital moved from Philadelphia to the District of Columbia, which was still in an inchoate situation, beset with yellow fever and cholera; amenities were lacking, and members of Congress had to scramble to find housing. The push towards the western frontier began as families, preceded by adventurers such as Lewis and Clark and Daniel Boone, overcame tremendous physical hardships, turning forests into cities. Some of the settlers prospered and built homes filled with gracious, imported furnishings; more lost everything to an unyielding nature or Indian attacks. Although he was a revered figure, Boone himself ended his career with fifty cents because of unfortunate land investments. (See Fig. 181)

Jefferson bought the Louisiana Territory from France, doubling the country's size. For Napoleon it meant fifteen million dollars; for America, it was the best bargain since Manhattan. Relations with England, however,

Fig. 177. Mortimer Menpes. *Whistler*. Courtesy St. Louis Art Museum.

were getting more unpleasant. British naval officers had taken to boarding American ships to search for deserters who, because of terrible English shipboard conditions, had signed up with United States merchant vessels. Thousands of sailors and many ships were kidnapped along with tons of merchandise. Negotiations failing, America declared war in 1812. The hostilities proved the competence of American shipbuilders; the famous frigate *Constitution* received the nickname "Old Ironsides" because she proved invulnerable to British cannon.

Some of the English forces, however, managed to reach Washington, and set fire to the White House. Dolly Madison lost her ball gowns, but managed to save her parrot and Gilbert Stuart's portrait of Washington. The invaders got as far as Baltimore, but were driven back after a desperate fight in which bombs burst in air, giving proof through the night that our flag was still there. Whatever internal political differences had troubled the young country, national pride in the final victory of 1815 pulled citizens together, ushering in the presidency of James Monroe (1817) as a temporary Era of Good Feelings. President Monroe warned Europe, and Spain in particular, that the "American Continents... are not to be considered as subjects for future colonization by any European powers."

The success of the cotton gin permitted slaves to prepare enormous quantities of cotton for export to England, and provided a graceful standard of living for slaveholders, who were convinced that their economic good fortune was good for the country. In 1831 William Lloyd Garrison published an ardent appeal for abolition in his Boston newspaper. Impassioned speeches, mobs, and murders attempted to sway those who stood either for or against the private ownership of human beings.

Meanwhile, the Congressional regulation of patents was encouraging the inventions of a thousand useful articles which changed the ways in which men grew their food and manufactured their necessities. A national bank was chartered and a system of national defense was undertaken. In 1847–48 two young officers, Ulysses S. Grant and Robert E. Lee, distinguished themselves in the war with Mexico for control of California; the following year gold was discovered there and a quarter of a million enterprising men headed west to hack out boom-or-bust mining towns. In the 1850s liberated ladies in New York cut off their skirts below the knee and scandalized the neighborhood with bloomers that hinted at, but still concealed, a wicked ankle. It was a time of vicious anti–Catholic politics, and the first stirrings of the temperance movement were felt.

But beneath the making and shaping of events, the separation between pro- and anti-slavery interests was widening. Although Congress had outlawed the African slave trade in 1807, the Supreme Court decided that Dred Scott, a slave who made a bid for freedom, was an "article of merchandise" and had no rights under the American Constitution. To Abraham Lincoln, it was an unacceptable decision. He ran for the Senate, rallying the North around his declaration that a "house divided against itself cannot stand. I believe," he said, "this government cannot endure permanently half slave and half free." Issues of national authority versus state sovereignty finally led to the Civil War, the cost of which was beyond reckoning. When it was over, General Grant announced that the "rebels are our countrymen again," but it took the rest of the century before his enlightened sentiments were understood and appreciated.

The South rose again after a generation of bitter accommodation, but the Negro problem remained. Racist societies such as the Ku Klux Klan were a blight, as were other embarrassments—the political corruption of the Tweed Ring, frauds perpetrated in tax collections, exploitation of the Indian population, and the sale of Congressional votes for railway grants. Reforms were begun; some were successful. Labor movements were founded with radical doctrines, but they eventually moved into the mainstream. Enormous changes in finance and industry brought about an undreamed-of prosperity, though at the price of sweat shops and slums. The development of mining towns and the building of railroads linking up the Atlantic and Pacific coasts encouraged the rambunctious West to settle down. New style Americans were born of the industrial expansion that followed—the robber-barons and the tycoons. Families like the Vanderbilts, Astors,

Huntingtons, and many others established themselves as American royalty and built appropriate palaces in which to display their wealth.

After 1890, military campaigns between Indians and the white man ceased, and the frontier reached its outer boundaries. "Whether they will or no, Americans must now begin to look outward," proclaimed the influential president of the Naval War College. Annexation of Hawaii soon followed, as well as the losing guerrilla battle that the Philippines fought against overwhelming United States forces. William Randolf Hearst and Joseph Pulitzer flagrantly egged America into hostilities with Spain after the sinking of the battleship *Maine*, in which some two hundred and sixty men were killed. Theodore Roosevelt thought it was a "splendid little war"; to the losers it was a sudden and unexpected act of imperialism.

Vast numbers of Europeans, fleeing hunger and religious persecution, came to the United States after 1880. The New World was no longer very new, but to millions of refugees the Statue of Liberty symbolized everything that was still free and sheltering. A contest was held to find a suitable inscription for this gift from France to the American people. Almost every prominent writer, including Walt Whitman and Mark Twain, participated but it was won by a little-known Jewish poet, Emma Lazarus:

> Give me your tired, your poor,
> Your huddled masses yearning to breathe free,
> The wretched refuse of your teeming shore;
> Send these, the homeless, tempest-tossed, to me,
> I lift my lamp beside the golden door!

Throughout a good part of the nineteenth century, the United States was too busy with its political and economic development to be heavily involved in the fine arts. A settled society being a prerequisite for such participation, interest in pictures was still fairly minimal except for portraits, which occupied an important place in American life both as family records and as statements of upward mobility. Their artistic merits had advanced only slowly in the previous century; local limners were still not well trained, although many of their works were charming and even moving. They reflected a way of life and an artistic viewpoint that was developing by trial and error outside of official European academies, but indirectly under their influence.

After the War of 1812, the English aristocratic tradition with its surface polish and elegance began to fade, especially near the frontiers where regional characteristics encouraged a more natural and robust artistic style. Andrew Jackson's presidency set a new kind of national agenda, appealing to a growing democratic and patriotic spirit as the country moved west. Americans wanted pictures of political figures, theatrical personalities, and whatever celebrity was conspicuous at the moment. But while there was no shortage of portraits, aesthetic judgment was slow to develop. James Audubon's exquisite watercolors of birds had to be engraved in England because the only competent printer in America refused the job on the grounds that the birds were poorly drawn. Except in the major cities, some kinds of equipment were still hard to come by. Van Wyck Brooks in *The World of Washington Irving* gives an account of an early engraver, Alexander Anderson, who taught himself his trade by reading an encyclopedia. Lacking professional-quality instruments, Anderson had to have a set of tools forged by a blacksmith, and his plates manufactured by rolling together copper coins.

Cornelius Tiebout was an American-born printmaker who, dissatisfied with opportunities at home, spent three years studying and working in England before returning to New York. His stipple engraving of Thomas Jefferson, 1801, after Rembrandt Peale, is typical of the better American portraits. (Fig. 178) In addition to serving as president and authoring the Declaration of Independence, Jefferson was the founder and architect of the University of Virginia, the designer of Monticello, an inventor, violinist, singer, scholar, and perhaps most agreeably to himself, "the most ardent farmer in the state." He was known as an unusually hospitable and decent man, and was probably the most intellectually gifted person of his time. After he died, his home and all its furnishings had to be sold to pay the debts incurred by his generosity.

Asher Brown Durand was one of the few American artists to complete his training at home. As a beginner, he made his own tools and copper plates. In 1820 he engraved John Trumbull's famous painting of the signatories of *The Declaration of Independence*; its very large size necessitated bringing a printer over from England. Durand gave up printmaking because he couldn't make a living at it, although he was the best engraver in the country. He later became a prominent landscape and genre painter and the president of the National Academy of Design, which he helped found. Much of his fame rests on a group of steel engravings depicting Washington, Hamilton, and other statesmen. Durand's portrait of Chief Justice John Marshall was after a painting by Henry Inman, New York's most celebrated portraitist. (Fig. 179) It was Marshall's farsighted decisions that gave the Court its prestige and authority, established the judiciary as the ultimate definer of the Constitution, and provided future Courts with the precedents necessary to broaden the interpretation of federal laws.

The head-and-shoulders format was used most frequently in this period, eliminating the problem of how to represent the arms and hands; the personality of the sitter, however, can often be rendered more descriptively if he holds a book, paint palette, legal document, or other object that represents his position or interests. There was an inhibiting stiffness in many of the portraits of national leaders, which perhaps was intentional at a time when the dignity and status of public servants had not yet entirely been established.

Top left: Fig. 178. Cornelius Tiebout. *Thomas Jefferson*. Courtesy Worcester Art Museum, Worcester, Mass. *Top right*: Fig. 179. Asher B. Durand. *Chief Justice John Marshall*. Courtesy American Antiquarian Society, Worcester, Mass. *Bottom left*: Fig. 180. John Sartain. *Self-Portrait*. Courtesy National Portrait Gallery, Smithsonian Institution, Washington, D.C., gift of Marvin Sadik. *Bottom right*: Fig. 181. Albert Newsam. *Daniel Boone*. Courtesy National Portrait Gallery, Smithsonian Institution, Washington, D.C.

Another important engraver was John Sartain, who trained in London as a mezzotinter and then worked in Philadelphia, turning out about fifteen hundred portraits. Most of them managed to avoid a mass-produced quality through Sartain's ability to personalize his treatments with a rather delicate and loose touch. Although they had a pleasant appearance, they lacked the strength and richness of English mezzotints. Their popularity was such that the copper plates eventually became worn from continuous use; instead of disposing of them, they were reworked and reworked until they were completely ruined. Leading painters and prominent sitters commissioned Sartain's work; he engraved the portraits of two presidents, *Andrew Jackson*, 1832, after William J. Hubbard, and *Martin van Buren*, 1834–35, after Inman. For his own mezzotint *Self-Portrait*, about 1848, he depended on a daguerreotype after one of the most outstanding photographers of the time, Marcus Aurelius Root. (Fig. 180) Sartain was one of the first to recognize the linkage between printmaking and the daguerreotype, which came into general use after 1839, once it overcame its designation as the "devil's work."

Lithography was introduced to America about 1819 by the Philadelphian Bass Otis with two small landscapes. A likeness by Otis of the *Reverend Abner Kneeland* (1818), which served as a frontispiece for a collection of Kneeland's sermons, has been commonly accepted as the first portrait lithograph in the United States, but it is probably a combination of linework, stipple, and aquatint. Max Rosenthal, a capable mezzotinter, and his son Albert located a lithographic business in Philadelphia and published about eight hundred portraits. Hundreds more were executed by Albert Newsam, a deaf-mute artist whose talents secured him commissions from Inman and the best portrait painters and publishing houses. His portrait of *Daniel Boone*, after Y. W. Berry, though carefully done, is more interesting as reference material than as an art object, but it provided a hero's image for a patriotic audience. (Fig. 181) Boone was also the subject of the first engraving in the western territories beyond the Mississippi River. That portrait, by J. O. Lewis after the 1819 painting by Chester Harding, supposedly is the best likeness of the Kentucky rifleman.

The Currier and Ives lithographic firm, established in the 1850s, published over seven thousand hand-colored Americana scenes and portraits, which were reproduced by the millions and are still treasured by a nostalgic public. William Sharp, having recently arrived from England, introduced chromo or color lithography in 1839, in which stones inked in a variety of colors are run consecutively through a press. Sharp's stylish portrait of the *Reverend F. W. P. Greenwood*, 1840, drawn from life, was presented free of charge to Greenwood's church in order to attract clients for the artist, a stratagem that worked well, for, with his attractive English manner of working, he became a popular and successful printmaker. (Fig. 182) The great Civil War photographer Matthew Brady turned over some of his mid-century daguerreotype portraits from his *Gallery of Illustrious Americans* to lithographers, who reproduced them for wide circulation.

Fig. 182. William Sharp. *Rev. F. W. P.*
Greenwood. Courtesy American Antiquarian Society, Worcester, Mass.

Biographical histories became
very popular in the Era of Good
Feelings when readers were
inspired by stories of honored
Americans. English publishers had
already found an enthusiastic
American market for illustrated
biographical dictionaries, and now
enterprising Americans hoped to
create and capture a similar native
demand. Publications such as
Joseph Delaplaine's *Repository of*
the Lives and Portraits of
Distinguished American Charac-
ters, issued about 1815, were widely
admired for a more spirited treatment than had been evident in
earlier work. Engraved stipple portraits of famous citizens, accompanied by laudatory testimonials,
appeared in multiple volumes. As
the call for these portrait-gallery
books increased, the quality of
their pictures and prose declined,
although one engraver-publisher optimistically, if unrealistically, set as his
standard the French seventeenth century portraitist Robert Nanteuil.

In 1839, an organization that later became known as the American
Art-Union commissioned and sold prints based on paintings by artists such
as Thomas Cole, George Caleb Bingham, and Asher B. Durand. For thirteen years these paintings were raffled off to lucky club members until the
courts ruled that lotteries were illegal. By then over twenty thousand people had participated in the program, and an immense number of landscape
and genre prints of all kinds and qualities had been published. Although
the pictures had very few artistic pretensions, the union served as a source
for the appreciation and dissemination of American art.

A significant event occurred in 1866. Alfred Cadart, the man who had
organized the French Etching Society in 1862, came to New York to promote etching as a fine art among printmakers who had recently begun to
make picturesque plates of landscapes and country life. The club he started
was a very small beginning since it turned out to be mostly social in nature,
but it was followed by the more serious New York Etching Club, which
lasted from 1877 to 1893, and held annual exhibitions for the last eleven
years of its existence. In 1882 Seymour Haden paid a visit to the United
States. Whistler, whose prints had been exhibited in New York and other
cities, also thought about coming—"One cannot continually disappoint
a continent, " he said—but he never came. Haden lectured on the

beauties of etching and loudly asserted its superiority over engraving. His authoritarian manner and English bearing evidently impressed a good many artists in the East and Midwest, with the result that etching clubs were formed in half a dozen cities. Local exhibitions and handbooks on the subject by Philip Gilbert Hamerton and others offered important instruction in art history and technique as well as in connoisseurship.

Julian Alden Weir, an original portraitist and one of the very few truly perceptive etchers of the period, started out in Paris, where he studied Impressionist art. His work, almost alone, pointed to the level of excellence that would be reached in America in the coming generations. He was at first unaffected by Whistler's "incomplete" style, but later came under his influence. Weir's drypoint of his surgeon brother, Dr. Robert F. Weir, 1891, shows its debt to both Whistler and Legros in its descriptive and lucid style. (Fig. 183) Weir's father, by coincidence, had been Whistler's drawing teacher at West Point.

Photography had begun to encroach on the engravers' livelihood as early as mid-century. Matthew Brady, to whom we owe our first photographs of Lincoln, began as a portrait painter, but discovered that he could make more money behind a camera than in front of an easel. His early work in daguerreotype portraiture made itself felt in print and painting styles through his tasteful and realistic approaches to sitters, his treatment of dark values and strong contrasts, and even the rigid poses which were necessitated by long exposures to the lens.

Throughout much of the nineteenth century, steel engraved portraits and views hung in every office, school, or home that claimed an interest in culture. Their tonality was derived from the closeness of their exceedingly fine lines, which made them resemble photographs. Generally, they appealed to a middle class market. For upper class sitters, it was another story; steel engravings had little or no attraction. For formal portraiture, neither the nouveau-riche nor the social climbing nouveau-not-so-riche cared to pose for the engraver or the camera. Large, imposing portrait paintings, which had been out of style during the democratic post-Revolutionary days, became *de rigueur* with the prosperous economy of the Gilded Age. Their glossy blandishments were berated by Nathaniel Hawthorne, who complained of their "unChristian flattery." He said that photography was more truthful, but, of course, when fashion dictated and money commanded, artists responded.

Styles in portraiture shifted perceptibly from an indigenous realism to one with a more fashionable European appeal. Americans could now point with pride to their own society painters, some of whom were also print-makers: William Merritt Chase, who made a few portrait etchings, the best of which, perhaps, is that of the lawyer and author Daniel M. Tredwell, (c. 1880) his right side concealed in a heavy shadow; (Fig. 184) Samuel F. B. Morse, who invented the telegraph as well as introducing the daguerreotype to America; Thomas Eakins, who used photographs and prints as aids in his portrait paintings; and John Singer Sargent, who dabbled a bit with

Fig. 183. Julian Alden Weir. *Dr. Robert Weir.* Courtesy Metropolitan Museum of Art, Rogers Fund, 1918 [18.59.17].

lithography in addition to his portrait paintings, and produced six prints, four of which were portraits, the other two, studies of unidentified young men. They were all trained in Europe, where the best teachers were to be found, and where original famous paintings, unknown to them except through engravings or photographs, could be seen. Much of their later work was done in America, thus helping to foster and accelerate a closer cultural interaction between the United States and Europe.

Before he began his distinguished painting career, Winslow Homer made some lithographic portraits, but it was for his wood engravings of sentimental country scenes and Civil War campaigns that he became famous in the print world. Thomas Nast's political cartoons and George Caleb Bingham's frontier paintings were reproduced as wood engravings. Other American artists, such as Benjamin West, who made the first English lithograph of high quality in 1801, and later, Whistler and Cassatt, went to Europe and became expatriates.

Although portraiture retained an important place in American art, it too often lacked the sensitivity, penetration, and self-expression that was necessary for the best results, particularly after 1860, when crass commercialism reduced engraving to a trivial level. Marketplace psychology met the demand for portraits of Civil War heroes with a glut of empty, though technically competent, likenesses. The trouble may have been that the requisite interpersonal relationship between artist and sitter was not yet thoroughly understood. Among others, a nineteenth century essayist, Alexander Smith, spotted this weakness: "A good portrait is a kind of biography," he wrote, "and neither painter nor biographer can carry out his task satisfactorily unless he be admitted behind the scenes."

Nevertheless, Americans admired and imported portrait prints, buying and selling them with almost the avidity of English collectors. Not even the proliferation of mediocre or indifferent work that appeared in newspapers and magazines saturated the market. James Claghorn, a prominent nineteenth century businessman and a founder of the Philadelphia Academy of Fine Arts, amassed a group of over forty thousand prints, many of which were portraits, and he enjoyed showing them to friends and fellow

Fig. 184. William Merritt Chase. *Daniel M. Tredwell.* Courtesy Metropolitan Museum of Art, Harris Brisbane Dick Fund, 1917 [17.3.756-2002].

enthusiasts. Samuel Avery, who was an engraver on metal and wood in addition to working as an art dealer, contributed an enormous collection of French Impressionist and other prints, including a large number of portraits, to the New York Public Library. Frederick R. Halsey collected thousands of American and English portrait prints at the end of the nineteenth and beginning of the twentieth centuries. During the second half of the nineteenth century museums were founded and university print departments established with donations by generous artists, dealers, and other devotees. The first public print collection was begun in 1872 at the Boston Museum of Fine Arts with an inventory of one. Seven years later, the museum hosted a print show which included four hundred forty-one etchings, eight of which were by contemporary American artists.

Patronage and interest in art was accomplished despite the earlier pessimistic view of Alexis de Tocqueville, a young French aristocrat who arrived in 1831 and stayed for nine months. In his book *Democracy in America,* he observed that the country's artistic experience was too brief to sharpen its critical judgments or refine its culture. He offered his reasons for the disparity between the modest standards of American crafts and the excellent levels of achievement in the Old World. In addition to crediting its long-established systems of guilds, he believed that Europe's aesthetic tastes were synonymous with a high degree of civilization. In the States, while many artworks were produced, they were generally not made very well, he wrote, not only because the country was young, but because democracy encourages conformity and compromises with quality. Tocqueville was partly correct. American work did not compare with the best being done in Europe. What he could not foresee, of course, was that rugged individualism and the desire for competition and preeminence would soon make America not only the leader of the industrialized world, but also a primary and significant achiever in the arts.

Chapter 7

The Twentieth Century

At the beginning of the twentieth century Europe was still the leading political entity in the Western world. For a very long time it had dominated almost every phase of culture, religious experience, and technical and economic development. Its general well-being and prosperity were all but taken for granted. Peace was thought to be almost inevitable, because great controlling financial interests were supposedly imposing the necessary ingredients for the expansion of wealth and would not permit a major war; indeed, there had been none since 1870. It therefore came as a tremendous shock to those who were unable to read beneath the surface when a conflagration erupted in 1914.

Loyalties were assigned within the narrow borders of individual countries; gone was the fragile allegiance to overriding international sovereignties such as a universal church or interconnected diplomatic and aristocratic families. The war was supposed to be short, but the sides were too evenly matched, and men are capable of sustained agony. When it ended four years later, Europe was in eclipse, with the cost in manpower over twelve million dead and twenty million wounded. The world had never before seen the like of this war. It bred illness and near starvation, triggered the Russian Bolshevik Revolution, and eventually led to World War II. The imperishable monarchies were weakened or destroyed, and generations of preeminence in creative artistic expression declined.

The production of goods began again. Labor movements moved forward and politicians mended their fences. Cities grew at an alarming rate; rapid long-distance travel became commonplace. Modern technologies appeared, old class-lines tended to blur, and a fresh democratic spirit arose, almost obliterating the former aristocracy. Yet, the post-war recovery failed, precipitating a devastating depression. High rates of unemployment, reduction of trade, and the fear of poverty, brought about by the near collapse of the banking system, generated tensions that provided the breeding ground for excessive nationalism. A search for radical solutions permitted the rise of totalitarian governments.

The theory of exclusive allegiance to one's country led with horrible logic to exaggerated loyalty to one's language, origin, and finally, "race"; the writings of Sigmund Freud, by coincidence, gave credence to one aspect of Fascist ideology, through the suggestions that violence was unavoidable and even healthy. Ironically, Freud himself was the target of the anti–Semitism that forced him to escape to England in 1938, the year before his death at the age of eighty-three.

War began again when Germany invaded Poland. The world shivered at the first photographs of the German army marching triumphantly under the Arc de Triomphe in Paris in 1940, but Stalingrad in 1943, and D-Day the following year on the Normandy beaches, signaled the end of the adventures of the Axis powers. When pictures of concentration camp victims and tortured survivors appeared in newspapers, civilized society wept. American reconstruction helped to alleviate the desperation of millions of demoralized people, both friends and former enemies. The free world turned to the United States for leadership, while Europe strained to keep its influence alive as a junior partner of Russia and America.

Between 1945 and 1960 most of Europe's empires in Asia and Africa were dismantled, although only occasionally through peaceful means. Colonial jurisdiction, which had begun with sixteenth century explorers, gradually ran its course. The countries of the world chose up new sets of allies and adversaries and continue to threaten their own survival. Terrorism has become a substitute for diplomacy. As the twenty-first century approaches, recurring battles between nations appear unescapable, while concerns over armaments and outer space intensify the struggle between the two great superpowers jousting for a razor's edge of supremacy.

Twentieth century history has been as unhappy as any; it was born with great hopes, but grew up in anxiety and the shadow of nuclear annihilation. We may yet hope that there is time to jump from the fire back into the frying pan.

I. France

France had reason to feel optimistic in 1900. A great world's fair opened in Paris, parading achievements in the arts, sciences, and technology that represented the best Europe had to offer. There was no question that Paris was the cultural capital of the world. French was still the language of well-bred Europeans. Music, art, literature, science, the theater, all contributed to French glory and rejuvenation. Debussy and Saint-Saens, Picasso and Matisse, Anatole France and Stéphane Mallarmé, Marie and Pierre Curie, Sarah Bernhardt and Leon Bakst, all worked their magic well into the twentieth century.

In addition, the world of politics appeared to be improving. Elections in the early years of the century spotlighted a dramatic shift away from Church and army influences, following the scandals of the Dreyful affair.

Separation of Church and State became the law, and complete freedom of worship was allowed. Church interference in politics ended, control of the army and navy passed from a small clique of officers into more competent hands and permitted a more democratic and effective organization. But by 1914, unstable financial and political leadership brought the country close to anarchy. As one nation after another went to war, France, partly because of her military preparedness, was able to field a strong army. Its populace, drawn together by the crisis, carried the brunt of the suffering for two years until England was fully able to mobilize its armies and America could send reinforcements.

At war's end France had lost almost three million men killed or wounded, and large areas of its land were devastated. The nation continued to endure hardships that almost divided it between Fascism and Socialism; only a grand scheme of reforms overcame ominous rioting and strikes. But once the essentials of the recovery program were looked after, many Frenchmen simply wanted to escape from unhappy reality as best they could. While German post-war temperament was preoccupied with destruction and death, France was caught up in conviviality, hedonism, decoration, and the illusion of stability. Artists from all over continued to migrate to its centers promoting defiant and whimsical styles, such as Dadaism and Surrealism, that scorned all logical analysis and naturalistic representation.

The 1930s disenchanted even the most optimistic souls in Europe. During the economic misfortunes that demanded aggressive leadership, dictators assumed control with shocking ease and rapidity. After barely twenty years, Europe was mired in another world war. When Adolf Hitler invaded the Rhineland in 1936, France found herself facing a growing military machine in Germany. Although her own situation was precarious, had she and Britain combined their forces, Hitler could probably have been stopped at that point, but neither country made the effort. Germany attacked Czechoslovakia in 1938 and France two years later, but the French apparently lacked the power and the will to defend themselves. The country fell after only six weeks of fighting; the eighty-four year old Marshal Pétain, with his premier, Pierre Laval, arranged an armistice and began a collaboration with the Nazi regime. Humiliation was complete when even the national slogan of "Liberty, Equality, Fraternity" could no longer be expressed. When the German army occupied Paris, France was numb with grief, but her spirit survived in the resistance movement under the exiled government of Charles de Gaulle — Charles of France. He brought the country from oppression and chaos to liberation and hope, and restored it to prestige in the European family.

In 1954 France's colonial empire began to come to an end. After years of war, Vietnam was finally divided into northern and southern territories. Arab and African states achieved independent status. Only Algeria continued its struggle until, in 1962, de Gaulle's diplomacy assured its freedom.

Political ferment and social unrest, persistent legacies of revolutionary times, have mostly subsided. Like the rest of the world, France faces the problems of survival, the environment, and new definitions of traditional values. Perhaps someday she will renew her cultural supremacy. It is her divine right.

Much of early twentieth century art, as it developed in France, looked fundamentally different from what had been the prevailing taste. It was generally less polite, more non-representational and experimental, and occasionally outrageous. It reflected the psychological and material environment in which it grew, yet it shocked and challenged the public, many of whom hardly knew whether to cheer or sneer at these radical new designs. The style unfolded in Paris simultaneously with Expressionism in Germany, and while very unlike in appearance, they both evolved out of a number of common roots: rejection of Impressionism; the utilization of flamboyant colors for expressive purposes; an interest in primitive art; and the use of subject matter and techniques reflecting personal preferences rather than inherited traditional systems. Paul Cézanne, the father of modern art, wished to move on from Impressionist "weaknesses," and substituted firm, weighty, explicit shapes for fuzzy-looking surfaces and indistinct outlines.

French art had traditionally been based on analytical and rational organization, clearly modeled within a stable, classical framework. Cézanne reestablished that order, yet freed it from some orthodox rules of drawing and composition and the narrower goals of Impressionism. Shortly before the turn of the century he had considered a series of questions: Was it possible to create patterns out of swatches of colors and tones that would produce a solider structure than Impressionist paintings? Could he avoid the flat appearance of Toulouse-Lautrec's and Gauguin's works and yet not revert to the deep space of Renaissance art? Can forms be analyzed intellectually and then represented so as to avoid photographic realism?

Cézanne developed his famous theories that the shapes of spheres, cones, and cylinders tend to establish stability, and that the eye can become accustomed to visualizing colored forms modeled, not by shadows or one-point perspective, but in receding planes through varying flat tonal effects. His block-like configurations restored a weight and substance that had been absent for a decade or two. But since he was relatively unknown even after 1895 when Ambroise Vollard, the legendary publisher and dealer, began to show his works, it really was not until a retrospective exhibition in 1906, shortly after his death, that the above questions were substantively dealt with by younger artists beginning to absorb his lessons. He died too soon to know that his paintings, with their subtle color medleys, would pioneer a dramatic change away from Impressionism and spawn much of twentieth century art.

However, the rejection of Impressionism and the invention of planar perspective were not the only starting points on the road to modernism. Van Gogh and Gauguin had already introduced jarring complex color relationships. African art was on display in Paris, and both Matisse and Picasso had seen primitive masks and sculpture in local collections. In 1905, having assimilated some of these influences, a half-dozen young painters, including Matisse, Maurice Vlaminck, and Georges Rouault, decided to exhibit their revolutionary works under the auspices of the Salon des Indépendents. The critic Louis Vauxelles declared himself outraged that every familiar and tasteful formula had been capriciously and summarily dumped. He labeled the artists *Les Fauves* (Wild Beasts) because, without any apparent qualms, they slapped together violent colors that bore no relationship to what the eye actually saw. Vitality, freedom, and intensity were what the new fashion was all about, and distortion and shock were its tools; Vlaminck called the colors "sticks of dynamite."

Henri Matisse was the leader of this disorderly bunch. He was hardly out of his teens when he took up painting to while away the time during an illness. Perhaps he decided that he could starve equally well with art as with his intended legal career. At any rate, he taught himself quite a bit during the time he was employed by the Louvre painting official replicas. When he broke with past artistic movements, startling combinations of elegant lines and dissonant color juxtapositions flowed from his brushes; he systematically took draftsmanship and design long steps away from the imitation of natural appearances.

Although the Fauves resembled the German Expressionists in their disavowal of strict representation and their psychological references to color and line, what really separated the two styles was that Expressionism introduced a personal and socially conscious approach to art, whereas the Fauves concentrated on ornament and pattern. French artists, unlike the Germans, were generally apolitical; for them, art was valid for art's sake alone — *l'art pour l'art*. Matisse believed that "composition is the art of arrangement in a decorative manner . . . for the expression of what the painter wants." In his early years he was influenced by Impressionism, and later, by Cézanne's strong modeling. Along with the Cubists, he was fascinated by Cézanne's ability to block out and organize space so that it seems to slip back and forth between foreground and distance. His extension of Cézanne's theories and his handling of brilliant color arrangements started the agitated Fauves on their way.

In his print style Matisse moved closer to the French tradition of "balance, purity, and serenity, devoid of any troubling subject matter." One of his great interests was portraiture, which by its nature suited those who preferred their images comfortably legible. His work encouraged a toleration of irregular, unfamiliar images which, while not exact facial renderings, nevertheless met his guidelines of design and purpose; where he used distortion, it was to express rhythm of line and form rather than introspection. "Expression to my way of thinking," he said, "does not consist in the passion mirrored upon a human face or betrayed by a violent gesture. The whole arrangement of my pictures is expressive. The space occupied by figures or subjects, the empty spaces around them, the proportions, every-thing plays a part."

Matisse began a unique series of etchings and lithographs in 1903 which are models of descriptive calligraphy. His likenesses are unconventional, yet vivacious and suggestive. Without any interior shading, his heads magically take on volume and light in an unprecedented way, exploiting the natural asymmetry of the face and accentuating only its most distinctive features. His etching of Mme. Derain, 1914–15, wife of the Fauve artist André Derain, comes close to caricature, but in its few lean strokes, it "condenses the essen-tial character" and embodies all the *je ne sais quoi* of French sophistication. His most trenchant portrait is that of the nineteenth century Romantic poet and critic *Charles Baudelaire*, whose additional claim to history is that he acquainted France with the poetry and mystical tales of Edgar Allan Poe, on whom he partially modeled his own Symbolist writings. (Fig. 185) Although Baudelaire had died from drugs and dissipation in 1867, and the etching wasn't done until 1930–1932, there is an energizing force about it that gives it the impulse of life and rivets the attention. The spare simplicity of the design and the kinetic, broken flow of its lines delineating the bony struc-ture of the face make this study a masterpiece of dynamic characterization and dimensional form. Every touch epitomizes Plato's comment that "beauty of style and grace and good rhythm depend on simplicity."

In his last years, Matisse's hands were crippled and he had difficulty holding a brush. He literally drew with his scissors when they were almost all that he could manage; the patterns he cut from colored papers were translated into stencil prints and influenced the American hard-edge style of the 1950s and 1960s. He was past eighty when he made his only color aqua-tint with a verve and sweep of line that belied both his age and infirmity. *Marie José en Robe Jaune* (*Marie José in a Yellow Dress*), c. 1950, demonstrates that while his precision and control were not what they had been, his ability to establish figures in arbitrary space had not diminished. (Fig. 186) He always succeeded in giving his works a free and easy appearance, what he called "the light joyousness of springtime," although his sitters reported that many weary hours of posing and dozens of trial drawings preceded his apparent spontaneity.

Most of the important painters of this period recognized that print-making offered them a wider public recognition than their paintings alone. Some developed highly innovative combinations of printing and photo-engraving that are still difficult to unscramble because of the unorthodox processes employed; perhaps Georges Rouault's are the most creative in their mixed technical treatment and crashing harmonies. Vollard arranged for photomechanical reproduction of Rouault's drawings onto metal plates, hoping to obtain an intense visual quality comparable to that of his can-vases. The artist then added etching, drypoint, and aquatint, laboring to "preserve their original rhythm." His thick black contours outlining brilliant dabs of color resembled stained-glass leading, a carry-over from his early training restoring windows in the Chartres Cathedral.

Left: Fig. 185. Henri Matisse. *Charles Baudelaire*. Courtesy Collection, Museum of Modern Art, New York, Abby Aldrich Rockefeller Fund. *Right*: Fig. 186. Henri Matisse. *Marie José en Robe Jaune* (*Marie José in a Yellow Dress*). Private collection.

Although Rouault was associated with the Fauve movement for two of its three-year existence, he rejected its decorative character, infusing his images instead with a universal moral appeal. His works carry strong links to both Rembrandt and German Expressionism in their concern with human anguish. Rouault believed that social inequities were largely responsible for the abject and shabby lives of the prostitutes and circus people whom he admired and frequently portrayed. In his series of fifty-eight prints known as *Miserere* (*Pity*), he expressed his anxieties and hopes for mankind. He brought together subjects as diverse as barbarous street life and the solemnity of Christian mysticism, sensing tragedy and the martyrdom of suffering in both themes. The eighth and most famous plate from the set, *Qui Ne Se Grime Pas?* (*Who Does Not Paint a Face for Himself?*), 1922, is actually a self-portrait, illuminated with strong lights and darkened with deep shadows, in which the clown represents the sorrowing spirit behind a window-dressing of buffoonery; to him it symbolized the "dereliction of man without God." (Fig. 187) The wide, reproachful eyes sum up his estrangement from a hostile or indifferent world.

Top: Fig. 187. Georges Rouault. *Qui Ne Se Grime Pas*? (*Who Does Not Paint a Face for Himself*?) Courtesy Brooklyn Museum. *Bottom*: Fig. 188. Georges Rouault. *Paul Verlaine*. Courtesy Collection, Museum of Modern Art, New York, gift of the Artist.

His dramatic lithograph of *Paul Verlaine*, 1933, was based on a death mask. (Fig. 188) The white paper seems to light up the skull, while the prominent forehead suggests intellectual power. The portrait revived interest in the romantic adventures of Verlaine, a French Symbolist man of letters and one of the more sensational personalities of the late nineteenth century. Symbolism, which uses intangible or spiritual elements to create esoteric meanings, had its day in the 1880s. Verlaine, one of its leading figures, was a well-known Bohemian writer when he met Arthur Rimbaud, a profligate poet ten years his junior, with whom he had what was delicately called an "extravagant" relationship. Their turbulent affair ended when Verlaine almost succeeded in murdering his eighteen-year-old companion. For that crime he served a two-year sentence in prison, during which he converted to Catholicism and wrote lyrical religious verses. After his release, he lived as irrepressibly as poverty and illness would allow. His poetry was eventually acclaimed and to everyone's surprise he ended up with a distinguished and honored name.

In the meantime, Rimbaud had tramped and starved around Europe, dropping out of sight for years at a time, soldiering and gunrunning in far-off places, and living with semi–Westernized tribes in Africa. He finally emerged from mysterious obscurity, having acquired along the way a palace in Ethiopia and a record of clandestine diplomatic missions for France. He never found out that Verlaine, assuming he was dead, had arranged to have his beautiful early poems published, and that he had earned a fine literary reputation. (Their adventures have not been forgotten. After almost one hundred years, Rimbaud's image was recently summoned up in a series of portraits by the American artist Jim Dine.)

Classical analytic principles, persisting in France notwithstanding the brief interruption by the Fauvist experiments, made a dramatic comeback in another of the artists befriended by Vollard—the Spanish prodigy Pablo Picasso. He was already a competent artist by his early twenties when he moved to Paris in 1904. He spent long hours in the Louvre studying Post-Impressionism and, like Rouault and Toulouse-Lautrec, was attracted to the street life of Montmartre, where he struggled for a living.

He depicted his precarious life style in one of the most popular prints in modern art, the 1904 *Le Repas Frugal* (*The Frugal Repast*). (Fig. 189) A young man (thought by some to be Picasso) and his companion, destitute and meagre to the point of emaciation, sit at a table. Their wretched circumstances draw them together in physical contact, but they stare away from each other in psychological isolation and loneliness. The wonderful interplay of their spidery hands creates a rhythmic movement that by itself is of extraordinary interest. The etching lay forgotten for forty years, possibly because Picasso didn't think it had a wide appeal, although he gave impressions of it to a few of his friends. It was only his second plate, made at the end of his Blue Period, when he was painting melancholy and emotional portraits. The print reflects his Spanish tradition—Velazquez's direct approach and El Greco's elongated figures

Fig. 189. Pablo Picasso. *Le Repas Frugal* (*The Frugal Repast*). Courtesy Brooklyn Museum.

and expressive hands and faces — as well as the simplified clear outlines of Gauguin and the solid tones of Toulouse-Lautrec.

By 1905 things were looking up a bit and Picasso was no longer overwhelmed by financial problems. He began an exploration of spatial tensions and dimensional modeling. Having seen some exotic African art as well as the work of the "primitive" painter Henri Rousseau, who was flattening out shapes in an inconsistent, unnatural fashion, he invented a way of representing objects in a unique visual system. His landmark painting *Les Demoiselles d' Avignon* (*Young Women of Avignon*), 1907, in which the figures were drawn with stark angularity and fragmented by overlapping planes, was the first Cubist work of art and the definitive break with the classical norm for the human body. It proposed a new aesthetic standard dedicated to powerful and energetic images in which light, shade, and space were used arbitrarily. But when the public first saw the painting it was repelled by the distortion, violence, and ambiguity of the design. The picture of a group of prostitutes, explicitly renouncing Matisse's "decorative manner," was conceived in geometric terms that forced traditional shapes into a bewildering and disconcerting pattern.

The initial direction for Cubism had come from Cézanne's formal ground plans in which abstract elements were as important as subject matter. Picasso took those ideas a step further and broke up each entity so that objects no longer retained their original organic relationships; he then cleverly reassembled them in an interlocking harmony so that front, back, and sides materialized simultaneously to the view. He painted what he "knew" was there, rather than what he saw, and based his images not on conventional likenesses hostage to Renaissance perspective, but on his own optical frame of reference. It was a streamlined process of communication.

The first Cubist prints date from 1911, a pair of portrait-type etchings, which Picasso used as illustrations for the book *Saint Matorel* by his good friend Max Jacob. These prints broadened the scope of linear composition and encouraged other artists to climb on the Cubist bandwagon. In the first etching, the standing nude figure of the hero's mistress, *Mademoiselle Léonie*, is still fairly recognizable, not yet disintegrated to the extent of the more complicated *Mademoiselle Léonie on a Chaise Lounge*, where the search for clues to the jigsaw puzzle is more difficult. (Figs. 190, 191) (The back of the chair appears in the upper right, the shaded arm rest is below and the leg support is drawn in the lower left.)

The "portraits," although based loosely on an acrobat acquaintance, were obviously not intended to resemble real life figures, nor to rival traditional academic nudes in beauty. Picasso manipulated the forms, removed their boundary lines and placed them in an arbitrary space, but shaded various areas to add a warmth and cohesion that kept them from appearing totally schematic. His scintillating planes made short work of common logic and denied the role of art as a tool of straightforward representation.

Daniel Henry Kahnweiler, who commissioned and published *Saint Matorel*, described Cubism as "the *essence* rather than the appearance of objects." But the public did not understand what Picasso was trying to do, nor did they much like what they saw. Newspaper reporters and art critics continued to poke fun. Even Matisse, who gave the style its name, thought of it in disparaging terms. Nevertheless, Cubists persisted in taking apart objects and examining their structures angle by angle. The prints they produced for illustrated books strengthened the bond between modern art and literature.

Picasso never became completely abstract; although sometimes hidden, a subject is always present in his work. While his experiments moved too far from the familiar and recognizable for most people, he certainly wasn't the first to see grace and elegance in the manipulation of

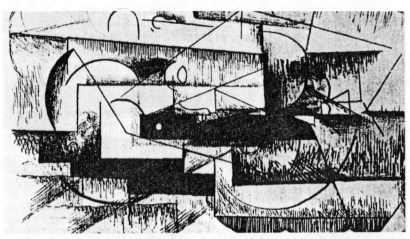

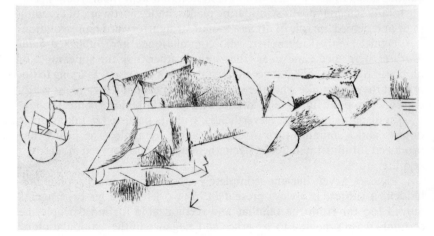

angles and arcs. Almost two thousand years earlier Plato, another radical theoretician, wrote:

> I will try to speak of the beauty of shapes and I do not mean what most people would expect, such as that of living figures, but I mean straight lines and curves, and the plane or solid figures which are formed out of them; for these I affirm to be not only relatively beautiful, like other things, but they are externally beautiful ...

Quite probably Picasso was unaware of his distinguished ally; he usually arrived at his ideas independently. The role of the artist, he said, is to provide new concepts and definitions, even though people cling to old-fashioned or worn out assumptions.

In 1913 Picasso etched a portrait of Guillaume Apollinaire. (Fig. 192) One of the most influential Surrealist poets and art pundits of his time, Apollinaire's admiration of Cubism was instrumental in winning acceptance for the new look. He defined it as the creation of totally new artistic building blocks existing in a non-visual reality. However, Braque once sneered that Apollinaire, for all his aesthetic pretentions, couldn't tell a Rubens from a Rembrandt.

The painter that Apollinaire could tell, and would never forget, was Leonardo da Vinci. In 1907 he had permitted a scapegrace friend, one Géry Pieret, to stay in his apartment. Boasting of his light fingers, Pieret swiped three Iberian sculptured heads from the Louvre, and at Apollinaire's suggestion, sold two of them to Picasso, knowing of the latter's interest in primitive art. When the *Mona Lisa* disappeared from the museum in 1911, the police followed an anonymous tip that led to Apollinaire's apartment where letters from Pieret were found, written after he had taken off for parts unknown. Apollinaire was arrested as a possible accomplice and for harboring Pieret, wanted for questioning in connection with the missing painting. Picasso was summoned as a character witness but, terrified because of his own involvement, denied knowing Apollinaire or anything about the statuettes; apparently no one recognized the oversize ears of the little sculptures on the central ladies of his *Les Demoiselles d'Avignon*.

The true story didn't come out until 1913, when a former custodial worker at the Louvre was discovered attempting to sell the most famous portrait in the world to an art dealer in Florence; he had stolen it for a team of swindlers who planned to have it copied and sell the forgeries, but when he discovered that his partners were two-timing him, he patriotically decided to return the masterpiece to his, and its, original home in Italy. Apollinaire and Picasso apparently patched up their differences; perhaps

Opposite, left: Fig. 190. Pablo Picasso. *Mademoiselle Léonie.* Courtesy Collection, Museum of Modern Art, New York, Purchase Fund. *Center*: Fig. 191. Pablo Picasso. *Mademoiselle Léonie on a Chaise Lounge.* Courtesy Collection, Museum of Modern Art, New York, Purchase Fund. *Right*: Fig. 192. Pablo Picasso. *Guillaume Apollinaire.* Private collection.

the portrait was etched as a peace offering. It was used as the frontispiece for *Alcools*, a volume of poems written while Apollinaire was in the Santé prison. For many years Picasso refused to discuss the affair, but in 1959 he confided to an interviewer that he had been ashamed all his life of his unwillingness to acknowledge his friendship with the poet who, as a result, had spent four very unpleasant days in jail.

It wasn't until after World War I that "modern" art finally became respectable and even fashionable, as people began to recognize and accept new motifs. In the meantime, Picasso went about his business, continuing his printmaking on and off; except for a visit to Rome, he stayed in Paris during and after the war. Eventually his partiality for Cubism gave way to other options in design. In about 1926 he focused on a different form of distortion, painting both eyes on the same side of the face and flinging bodily parts around with the abandon of a blind juggler. Some thought his eyesight or his sanity was impaired, but his hand was constantly turned to fresh conceptions — this one partly in violent reaction to the vapid insipidity popularized by the "Gibson Girl." He was determined to inject cerebral energy into art and purge it of both the softness of Impressionism and the emotional agitation of Expressionism. For a good part of the century, portraiture would emphasize design rather than representation, with the sitter basically an excuse for the artist to hang his ideas on. Harmony, color, or structure were frequently no longer by-products of a portrait, but *were* the portrait.

Occasionally Picasso returned to a representational style when Realism staged something of a comeback. His aquatint of Ambroise Vollard, 1937, was a tribute to the man who discovered, encouraged, and sustained two generations of artists. (Fig. 193) Without Vollard's generosity and friendship, Bonnard, Matisse, Rouault, and a dozen others might never have been able to overcome the burdens of poverty and neglect. Vollard's enthusiasm for Picasso dated back to 1901, well before the young artist settled permanently in Paris. The portrait is a penetrating analysis and demonstrates the painterly aspects of Picasso's enormous range of genius.

When World War II came, the German occupation laid a heavy hand on the art scene. While many of his colleagues fled from Europe, he quietly remained in Paris and went on with his work. The story is told that, in the cold winter of 1945, one of the few well-heated houses in the city belonged to the master printer Fernand Mourlot. Picasso moved into his home for the duration and together they developed lithographic techniques that yielded unusually rich impressions. Once he had renewed his interest in lithography, after a fifteen-year hiatus, he again showed his diversity with a stunning portrait of his current mistress, Françoise Gilot. Great embroidered sleeves symmetrically flank her nude figure in the elegant *Femme au Fauteuil*, (*Woman in an Armchair*), 1949, one of a series of lithographic studies in which she was featured. (Fig. 194) Gilot inspired a gentler and exceptionally sensitive style. Her portraits have a subtle tone and tranquility not always found in Picasso's works.

His scope was phenomenal. Whether conventional or scandalous, tremblingly intuitive or coldly analytical, he recreated and restructured the face and body with authority and imagination. In addition to ceramics, paintings, sculptures, and plays, he produced over two thousand prints. He was the most innovative force in twentieth century art, influencing not only other artists, but writers as well. James Joyce and Gertrude Stein certainly are among his literary analogues. Above all, he had style, that mysterious quality that the British poet Stephen Spender defined as "three parts natural grace, one part sense of period and two parts eccentricity."

Fig. 193. Pablo Picasso. *Ambroise Vollard*. Courtesy British Museum.

In general, French painters preferred still-life subjects to introspective portraiture and, since they did not have the same commitment to printmaking as their peers in Germany, their portrait prints are fewer in number, although skillful and revealing as ever. The most prolific and successful Cubist printmaker was Jacques Villon, born Gaston Duchamp, one of six children, four of whom became artists. He changed his name at about the age of twenty, although his well-regulated life hardly accorded with the extraordinary image of his hero, François Villon, born in 1431. The fifteenth century lyric poet was a hotheaded outlaw, roving and brawling in and out of prison with a band of thieves, as well as writing poetry and making love to as many young maidens as were willing or available. He inspired generations of French intellects, including the Duchamp family.

One brother was the sculptor Raymond Duchamp-Villon, who died at the age of twenty-one shortly after being gassed in the first World War. Another was Marcel Duchamp, whose depiction of movement in the painting *Nude Descending the Staircase* in the famous New York Armory Show in 1913 left art lovers gasping. The highly gifted family was particularly close and shared an interest in philosophy as well as Cubism.

Villon began his career as a newspaper cartoonist and illustrator, a training-ground which undoubtedly helped him catch idiosyncratic qualities in his portraits. He was still drawing pretty ladies and well-dressed gentlemen in the typical *Belle Epoque* style of the 1890s when he first began to etch. But as early as 1907, about six years before the height of the Cubist period, he was already analyzing the structure and

mathematical perception of objects. In the monumental drypoint portrait of his seventeen-year-old sister, *Yvonne D. de Face*, 1913, he shaped the faceted surfaces as though they were pyramidal chips of wood. (Fig. 195) In spite of its obvious preoccupation with formal elements, the print did not ignore the mood of pensive reverie; it is an evocation of shimmering light. The range of shading, from white through endless modulations of grey, reveals his firm command of the medium. His style differed from the fluency of Picasso as well as from the more discordant approaches of other Cubists; the human figure took on an unusual richness and amplitude in his prints.

Villon followed up this period with a more classical style. The last word in meticulous line is his etching based on a 1911 sculpture by his brother Raymond, which was exhibited along with Marcel's *Nude* at the Armory Show, *Baudelaire avec Socle* (*Baudelaire with Pedestal*), 1920. (Fig. 196; see Fig. 185) The head is covered with a fine web of lines and placed against a simple linear background, which adds balance and distinction to the plate. The sober portrait, with each plane carefully modeled and clearly lit, suggests something of the morbid nature of Baudelaire, who was paralyzed and insane in his last years. Villon produced a large number of prints, although in the 1930s he turned exclusively to painting when he was financially able to do so.

Like Villon, Louis Marcoussis is considered by many to rank higher as a printmaker than as a painter. He also began as an illustrator, broadening his technique and ideas as he became acquainted with leading artists and writers, developing a bridge between art and literature. He was born in Poland, but in his style he was French to his fingertips. In his drypoint *Guillaume Apollinaire*, 1919, the poet appears very much in command, as though accustomed to authority and respect. (Fig. 197; see Fig. 192) The calligraphy was partly derived from Picasso's *Mademoiselle Léonie*, although it clearly differs in its avoidance of flat spatial elements and its straightforward, looser, and immediately intelligible form. (See Fig. 190) In this graphically complex plate, Marcoussis created a visual model of Cézanne's volumetric cylinders, spheres, and cones to suggest receding planes, and at the same time borrowed Picasso's playful scattering of words to represent Apollinaire's writings. Such arbitrary use of lettering originated with Picasso and Braque, although portraits in earlier periods frequently had identifying names and titles engraved neatly around their frames.

During the war years Marcoussis rediscovered the long-absent medium of engraving and took it up because it was a portable hobby that required the least amount of printmaking equipment. In his burin study of the American expatriate author Gertrude Stein, he highlighted her profile with

Opposite, left: Fig. 194. Pablo Picasso. *Femme au Fauteuil* (*Woman in an Armchair*). Courtesy Collection, Museum of Modern Art, New York, Curt Valentin Bequest. *Right*: Fig. 195. Jacques Villon. *Yvonne D. de Face*. Courtesy Brooklyn Museum.

Fig. 196. Jacques Villon. *Baudelaire avec Socle* (*Baudelaire with Pedestal*). Courtesy Philadelphia Museum of Art, Louise and Walter Arensberg Collection.

a few dark accents and placed a patient, almost mocking smile on her worn but still-optimistic features. (Fig. 198) Stein was a generous hostess and patron, opening her home to gifted artists and friends by the dozen. Her eccentric poetry has since been eclipsed by other messages, but during the 1920s she was as close to being a Cubist as a writer can be.

Cubism's duration was relatively short considering its impact on the direction of art. Picasso all along had been concerned that it was a "blind alley" and likened it to a difficult language. Perhaps it ended because artists couldn't figure out any more permutations or combinations of rectangular planes sliding about in space; at any rate, World War I interrupted the movement and no one seemed in the mood anymore for highbrow riddles.

After the war, however, Cubist prints began to attract public favor and shared significantly in the selling boom that lasted for about ten years until the crash of the stock market. In spite of political and economic dislocation and serious war preparations in the 1930s, artists continuted to create and publishers continued to bring out deluxe books and illustrated suites that were well received. French art typically remained temperate, its tone and ideology worlds apart from the paroxysms of German Expressionism.

"When I held in my hand a lithographic stone or a copper plate," Marc Chagall wrote, "I believed I was touching a talisman." He had suffered much during the Russian Revolution, but finally escaped to Berlin in the early 1920s. There, in a bittersweet world of fantasy, he began to etch illustrations for a book of poignant reminiscences, *Mein Leben* (*My Life*). He portrayed himself with a child-like joy in an etching and drypoint from this series, *An der Staffeli* (*At the Easel*), 1922. (Fig. 199) Although he distorted its scale and shape, he arranged his body in a well-balanced but upside-down design, his head whimsically and irrationally right side up. Odd juxtapositions were common in Surrealist art, a term which Apollinaire is said to have coined after seeing a Chagall painting. The style was intended to encourage the free association of the subconscious, and, suspending time and space, to release the mind from its customary restraints.

Psychological notions were in the air. Freud, who said that nothing

Left: Fig. 197. Louis Marcoussis. *Guillaume Apollinaire*. Courtesy Philadelphia Museum of Art, Louise and Walter Arensberg Collection. *Right*: Fig. 198. Louis Marcoussis. *Gertrude Stein*. Courtesy Collection, Museum of Modern Art, New York, gift of Victor S. Riesenfeld.

is more interesting than the way one looks, paid great attention to the deceptive masks that serve most of us for a face. Surrealist artists, following his lead, attempted to create psychoanalytical portraits. Chagall concluded that "our inner world is more real, perhaps, than the visible one." He concealed his usual amiable appearance in order to focus on the wry, or perhaps suppressed, side of his personality in a lithograph closely related to German Expressionism, *Selbstbildnis mit Ziege* (*Self-Portrait with Goat*), 1922. (Fig. 200) Made soon after he arrived in Berlin, it is a rather ill-natured image, with the slanted eyes and mouth conveying untypical malevolence and just enough of the unexpected to appeal to modern tastes. The symbolism of the goat, which in Biblical tradition carried man's sins into the wilderness, may represent simple faith and a state of spiritual innocence.

In 1923 Chagall went to Paris, his "second birthplace," still the art center for hopefuls from all over the Western world. Much of what he drew reflected his memories of Jewish family life in Russia. His brilliantly colored canvases of people, animals, and objects floating in a dream-like space attracted the attention of the ever-observant and insightful Vollard,

Left: Fig. 199. Marc Chagall. *An der Staffeli (At the Easel).* Private collection. *Right:* Fig. 200. Marc Chagall. *Selbstbildnis mit Ziege (Self-Portrait with Goat).* Courtesy Collection, Museum of Modern Art, New York, Larry Aldrich Fund.

who commissioned him to illustrate albums of fables and Biblical subjects. When war in Europe became imminent, and his people and himself were in great jeopardy, Chagall emigrated to America, where he lived until he could return safely to Europe. He decorated synagogues and churches with stained-glass windows and painted the ceilings of opera houses in Paris and New York. Like Picasso, he worked well into old age, designing original ceramics and sculpture, and leaving an equally generous heritage to the twentieth century.

Alberto Giacometti was born in Switzerland, trained in Italy, and then made the inevitable move to Paris, taking up and dropping Cubism and Surrealism along the way. He made his name as a sculptor, probing the relationships of elongated, distorted figures in space. He had, perhaps, an even greater pleasure from his lithographs than from his bronzes, since he often seemed able to transmit stronger feelings to his prints. Yet in spite of the moving quality of his work, he was always afraid that he was incapable of reproducing the constant flow of ideas that registered in his mind's eye. "All that I will be able to make will be only a pale image of what I see," he wrote in frustration.

There is an element of detachment in much of his work, though less

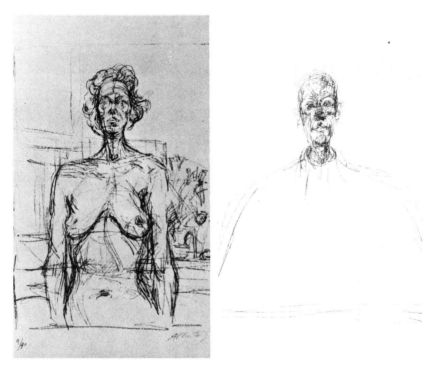

Left: Fig. 201. Alberto Giacometti. *Nu aux Fleurs* (*Nude with Flowers*). Private collection. *Right*: Fig. 202. Alberto Giacometti. *Diego*. Courtesy Collection, Museum of Modern Art, New York, gift of Mr. and Mrs. Eugene Victor Thaw.

so after the mid-1930s when he took up printmaking. In his portraits he strove towards an understanding of the inner nature of his sitters. He worked in a linear rather than a painterly style, hardly varying or differentiating the quality of the etched line itself. However, the interlaced meshwork creates its own emotional charge as he depicted himself, his family, and his friends with a sense of anxiety and isolation. His wife, Annette, who shared posing and other honors with his mistress, Caroline, was the model for the lithograph *Nu aux Fleurs* (*Nude with Flowers*), 1960. (Fig. 201) Her eyes gaze past the viewer and stare at the world with apprehension. They evoke the chief force of the portrait, although the dramatic frontal view also invites close examination of her broad shoulders and sagging breasts. The lacerating strokes that cut across her face complete the sense of poignant alienation.

Although Giacometti feared that he was "incapable of expressing any human feeling at all," the lithograph of his brother *Diego*, 1964, is full of sympathetic interest and less obsessive than his earlier pieces. (Fig. 202) The tiny head, almost lost on the very large sheet of paper, contributes to the sustained and moving intensity typical in his later works. Diego was a prominent furniture designer and sculptor himself. For forty years they worked

Fig. 203. Pablo Picasso. *Peintre et Modèle Tricotant* (*Painter and Model, Knitting*). Courtesy British Museum.

closely together, Diego not only posing for many of his brother's cast figures, but also taking charge of the technical production. It is unfortunate that Alberto's prints are not often seen, but he generally pulled very small editions, and they are, consequently, quite rare.

After World War II, although he and artists such as Picasso, Matisse, Rouault, and Chagall continued to work in France, the newest ideas in abstract design developed chiefly in the United States as the primary international art market moved across the Atlantic. French art was no longer in the vanguard. Many of the younger Frenchmen, such as Bernard Buffet, returned to the figurative tradition. Buffet's etched heads are dominated by black tones, similar to those of his paintings. Their drawn and haggard expressions speak more clearly of disillusion than of hope.

The last word must be reserved for Picasso. His pure line etching of 1931, *Peintre et Modèle Tricotant* (*Painter and Model, Knitting*), is an amusing self-parody showing the portraitist analyzing his subject as she sits knitting. (Fig. 203) The picture that develops under his hand has an energetic life of its own, passing through his eyes and the artistic circuits of his mind to unravel itself in an ambiguous form on the canvas. Picasso's ultimate message is that in twentieth century art the creative decision belongs to the artist alone.

II. Germany

In 1871 Prince Otto von Bismarck pulled together a group of Germanic states and turned them into a nation. While he instituted socialized medicine, sickness, accident, and old age insurance some thirty years before England, he gave Germany an imperfect constitution which allowed undue influence of the army in the operations of all the branches of government. The country's political weaknesses and activities were not limited to its own soil; like other European powers, it exploited its African colonies with forced labor and the destruction of their tribal societies and natural resources.

In the early years of the twentieth century Germany entered into a naval race with England, claiming that parity would be a deterrent to future wars. But neither a great navy buildup nor an alliance with Austria-Hungary and Italy was sufficient to give Germany a feeling of safety against the combined strength of Britain, France, and Russia. When the Archduke Francis Ferdinand was assassinated at Sarajevo and Austria-Hungary used that tragedy as an excuse to move on Serbia, Germany was ready to support its ally and expand into southeastern Europe. World War I began. Germany introduced submarine warfare in an effort to force England into submission, but the plan backfired and drew the United States into the contest. After incalculable suffering by all the involved countries, the war ended with humiliating results for Germany and the loss of its African colonies.

The general anxiety to return to normalcy, and the reluctance of the American government to participate fully in the League of Nations, permitted an unfortunate peace settlement, creating a situation that virtually guaranteed another global conflict; confiscation of territory, in addition to unrealistic economic reparations, was laid on the fledgling democracy of the Weimar Republic. It was a penalty that was beyond her power to cope with or repay. As foreign trade declined, the country ran out of cash and began to print paper, falling into debt and one of the deepest inflations ever known—the cost of a loaf of bread was billions of worthless marks. The pre-1914 mark corresponded to approximately four per U.S. dollar. By November 1923 it had fallen to over four trillion per dollar. Those who owed debts or mortgages made a killing; almost everyone else lost their savings and security.

In spite of the great contributions of Freud, Einstein, Thomas Mann and others, the shock of defeat, together with political disturbances following the disastrous inflation, created such a loss of self-esteem that extremist right-wing parties were able to make substantial inroads in the elections during that decade. The world depression of the 1930s brought Hitler to power when the constitutional government was no longer able to function competently. He came into office by legal, if strong-armed, methods, with over 88 percent of the electorate approving his regime. He persuaded them that salvation lay in a fatherland that would redress their suffering and chasten their conquerers. They listened willingly, since of all nations, Germany had experienced the greatest hardship from the depression, with almost half of its population out of work or needy. Although the nation appeared to adopt democratic ideals in the 1920s, the facade of well-structured government was superficial, and its basic instability was soon revealed.

By the mid-1930s Germany was a police state bent on world aggression and the extermination of the Jewish population of Europe; the fatherland was about to embrace the destruction of millions of their own people as well as their neighbors. In addition to hundreds of thousands of Catholics, Protestants, Communists, labor leaders, gypsies, and "misfits," six million out of about eight million Jews perished. The "inferior and impure" that were destroyed in concentration and death camps were among the pick of Europe's intellectual and artistic resources.

For five years Hitler challenged the European powers with *faits accomplis*, annexations, aggressions, and occupations without serious hindrance until 1939, when France and Great Britain declared war after the invasion of Poland. By 1943, the full force of American strength was added to the Allied forces, and the unyielding Russian winter checked German victories. Hitler no longer dominated the European continent. From 1944 to April of 1945, Germany confronted destruction, finally submitting to unconditional surrender and a partition into Eastern and Western blocs, both still troubled by problems of national identity.

West Germany's economic and political road back to respectability and responsibility in the post-war years has been one of the most spectacular accomplishments of the second half of the century. But the spirit of the people seems not to have made a comparable recovery, particularly in the sciences and arts, which reflect a greatly disturbed society attempting to deal with post-war problems. A recent article by a West German journalist, Gunter Hofmann, indicated the continuing legacy of the Nazi defeat: "Germans still live unhappily with the confident 'We're regaining face' — and the uncertain 'Who are we?'" It will perhaps take a generation not yet born to come to terms with its historical conscience.

The history of twentieth century German Expressionism, which flourished until Hitler came to power, does not begin in the year 1900, but rather in the previous decade in its immediate development, and long before in its early roots. As early as the sixteenth century Dürer, Cranach, and their contemporaries were already working with subjective, expressive, and spiritual raw materials, propagating the notion that portraiture must express the artist's feelings as well as the physiognomy of the subject. The influence of these early artists remained a latent source of capital for three hundred years in spite of the negative effects of political and economic troubles on subsequent German art. It paid off its accumulated dividends in the emotional art of the Expressionist movement.

To understand its more recent sources we must investigate the conglomeration of styles which were distilled into an artistic adventure based on externalized sensation. Romanticism, Art Nouveau, the Symbolist movement, Impressionism, and the work of the Post-Impressionists, mostly originating in England and France, were among the germinal influences of Expressionism. While German nineteenth century art contained lyrical works of high quality by such artists as Casper David Friedrich, Wilhelm Leibl, and Adolf von Menzel, much of that Romantic tradition leaned strongly towards nymphs, shepherds, coy maidens, and other excessively sentimental whimsies. By the end of the century reaction set in and most of these artificial subjects were discarded as embarrassments along with the rigid impositions of the Academy and conventional ideas of beauty and fashionable portraiture that had been inherited from generations of acclaimed artists. The Romantic touchstones of spontaneity, emotional excess, and freedom of choice in subject matter and design were retained and became part of the new art style.

Metaphysics and spiritualism were also derived from the Romantic idiom and attracted a coterie of young men calling themselves Symbolists. Symbolism was a literary and aesthetic philosophy or state of mind which was initiated in France from 1880 to 1890 and was concerned with abstract ideas and mystical powers that represented otherworldly, evanescent, and intangible experiences. The theory was itself evanescent and mostly unintelligible to anyone not in the inner circle, but through its Romantic emphasis, Symbolism furthered an interest in primitive crafts which were on display in many ethnological museums. These recently discovered ritual artifacts from Africa and the South Pacific were executed in distorted and emotive forms that appealed to the senses; the bold carvings and bright colors of the masks, along with other design elements, were absorbed into Expressionist art and had a substantial influence on portraiture, especially in prints. Both in their direct approach and in their ability to spread new stylistic and philosophical ideas, the etchings, lithographs, and above all, woodcuts of this period were often of more significance than the paintings by the same artists.

Like Symbolism, Impressionism reached Germany from France in the 1880s, but developed an intense emotional quality of its own. In its French version it reflected the momentary enjoyment of atmospheric color and light, and was an objective or scientific response to the physical appearance of nature, only marginally affected by the artist's personal experiences; the French tended to concentrate on surface patterns, eliminating firm outlines and solid structure. The Germans restored a focus on line, and concentrated more on the enduring qualities of nature than on the transient effects of shimmering light. However, both groups shared the excitement of taking their paints outdoors and depicting scenes of everyday life.

Max Liebermann and Lovis Corinth were among the Neo-Impressionist painters and printmakers in Germany whose linear experiments and moralizing emotional outlook provided an early direction to the Expressionist movement. At the turn of the century Liebermann led

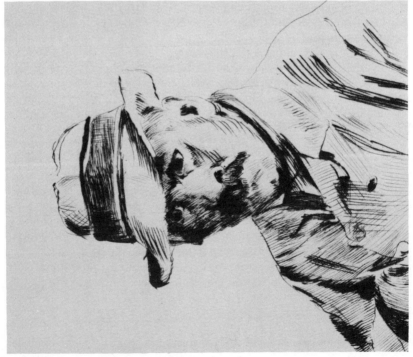

a young radical group of artists, Corinth among them, in the search for pictorial freedom, and they gratefully portrayed him in many of their prints. Liebermann and Corinth thoroughly explored the psychological role of design, whereas to Picasso and Braque in France, artistic means often were significant ends in themselves. Corinth's Impressionism had a gloomy Germanic undertone. French work by comparison appears naive in its insistent *fin de siècle* good humor and sociability, but both French and German Impressionists contorted reality with confidence and conviction. Corinth introduced a pervasive spirit of despair and loneliness, and, following his lead, German artists adopted decadent or bitter attitudes as they discovered that the problems of the world were intractable. Neither faith in the scientific theories of Darwin, Freud, Marx, or Einstein, nor hope for peaceful settlements of political differences, nor even charity for one another, would ameliorate the tragic symptoms that were already evident in Germany.

At first Corinth resisted Expressionism vehemently and likened it to savage art. But stress and anger following a stroke and partial paralysis in 1911, and his painful disillusion with nationalism following World War I, turned him inward and harsh, and his paintings and prints, reflecting those feelings, became less disciplined and more expressive in style. He was a competent artist and an exceptionally fine portraitist, particularly in the many introspective and penetrating studies he made during his last ten or twelve years. In his drypoint *Selbstbildnes im Strohhut* (*Self-Portrait in Straw Hat*), 1917, he appears in a melancholy mood, his eyes expressing bleakness and regret. (Fig. 204) *Death and the Artist*, an etching and drypoint, shows an interest in chiaroscuro uncommon in most of his work. (Fig. 205) The presence of the skeleton, above which is inscribed the Greek word for death, indicates not only anxiety, but also contact with classical scholarship, yet another ingredient in the Expressionist movement. Corinth's linearity and symbolism later became important features in German art.

Other strands, too, wove themselves into the Expressionistic fabric, including the drawing techniques of the Post-Impressionists Vincent van Gogh, Paul Gauguin, and Edvard Munch, which embodied heavy forms and dramatic subjects reduced to their essentials, dynamic color, unusually sensitive treatments, and the ornamental writing lines of Art Nouveau. Van Gogh's agitated paintings were first seen in Germany in 1901. His appeal lay in his extraordinary tonal arrangements and pulsating staccato strokes, which he seemed to use more for expressive than for technical or formal purposes. His admirers, and they were few, appreciated his great human sympathies and responded to his mystical relationship with color and shape. Gauguin's work, with its flat, simplified, decorative figures,

Opposite, left: Fig. 204. Lovis Corinth. *Selbstbildnes im Strohhut* (*Self-Portrait in Straw Hat*). Courtesy Brooklyn Museum. *Right*: Fig. 205. Lovis Corinth. *Death and the Artist*. Courtesy British Museum.

also had a material influence on Expressionism; like van Gogh's, his art was startlingly different from the canons of beauty that dated back to Classicism and the Renaissance. His romantic retreat to the South Pacific islands, for which he renounced the creature comforts of France, appealed to artists' utopian fantasies, though only occasionally to their life-styles. His experimental paintings and woodcuts symbolized enigmatic revelations to men from their environments, reflecting the naturalism of Jean Jacques Rousseau. His "primitive" line heralded an emancipation from Realism that German artists understood and would soon echo.

The last of the important connecting links between the nineteenth and twentieth centuries was Edvard Munch, who created most of his prints in Paris and Berlin. Like the other early Expressionists, he contributed an original observation and a uniquely emotive style to its vocabulary, with every idiosyncracy mandated by a distraught mind. An unhappy childhood and youth in Norway produced obsessive behavior. Severe sexual neuroses crippled his relations with women, and fears, stemming from mental and physical illness in his family and the premature deaths of his mother and sister, ultimately led to nervous breakdowns. In his prints he created a model of male-female torment and struggle which was adopted by later Expressionists.

Over-sensitivity and discontent seemed to induce a spiritual malaise among the young Bohemians in his circle. Not only did they repudiate Germany's encroaching militarism and mechanistic values, but in the process they automatically rejected every middle class standard of taste and manners. Freudian psychological notions were pervasive; self-destructive acts and open displays of exaggerated emotion became not only respectable but thoroughly irresistible. Depression lent a charm all its own, and young artists exploited their nervous disorders in the name of freedom and catharsis. In an epidemic of frustration they put their bleeding guts into a body of work that bewildered and shocked much of their audience.

Munch visited Paris in 1889 where a chance meeting with van Gogh stimulated his imagination and affected his style. But to Munch, at the age of twenty-two, Paris, the city which was filled with the lighthearted scenes and bright colors of the Impressionist palette, was a place of blight and forboding. He believed that the cheerful abandon and high spirits of the *Belle Epoque* were a distortion of truth and judgment, and that the brutality of pain was a more appropriate concern for art.

From 1892 to 1898 he was active in Paris and later in Berlin, doing some of his best work in those years. His erotic lithograph, the *Madonna* of 1895, is clearly influenced by the Symbolist motifs of birth, love, and death. (Fig. 206) It is a portrait of his mistress, Eva Mudocci, in which the

Opposite, left: Fig. 206. Edvard Munch. *Madonna*. Courtesy Museum of Modern Art, New York, William B. Jaffe and Evelyn A. J. Hall Collection. *Right*: Fig. 207. Edvard Munch. *Self-Portrait*. Courtesy Collection, Museum of Modern Art, New York, Purchase Fund.

swooning figure awaits the life-bearing spermatozoa, swimming upstream in troubled waters. The menacing embryo of that union visits in a lower corner, portending who knows what. His *Self-Portrait*, a somber lithograph from 1912, is a study of a man who has lost his bearings — his disembodied head mysteriously hangs like a dark unseeing specter in a white void. (Fig. 207) Munch's intensely mystical images, hovering on the surface of the psyche as well as on the surface of the paper, carried perplexing and disturbing messages that would haunt the Expressionist artists.

Together with van Gogh and Gauguin, Munch anticipated Expressionism by more than ten years, introducing garish and vivid color schemes that induced feelings of nervous anxiety and tension, yet he steered clear of the coarseness that many of the Expressionists adopted. Partly as a reaction against the overly graceful Romantic art of the nineteenth century, he and Gauguin revived the woodcut technique as it had been employed by both Japanese printmakers and sixteenth century German masters. Many Expressionist artists soon adopted the angularity that was inherent in the medium. Munch's woodcuts, which are among his greatest and most influential works, were the first by a western artist to allow the crude knife gouges and the accidental markings of the natural grain to appear in many of his impressions, thus revealing the expressive woodcut process itself. Printmaking was widely taken up by a number of Austrian and German artists, their work often disclosing a firmer structure and greater compression of power than their paintings. In many ways, prints actually determined painting styles. Woodcuts finally achieved artistic recognition on their own merits, putting an end to the taint that their chief value lay in their commercial and reproductive uses.

The term Expressionism was first used in its art historical meaning in 1911 in the magazine *Der Sturm* (*The Storm*) to describe the works of Cézanne, van Gogh, and Matisse. In its wider sense it connotes German art from about 1905 until shortly before World War II. It began with the work of a number of young art and architectural students representing various German and Austrian schools, who formed an organization in Dresden called *Die Brücke* (*The Bridge*). Intentionally avoiding the Impressionist influences of Liebermann and Corinth in Berlin, they saw themselves as a bridge or transition from the animal to the divine in nature, a concept drawn from the philosophic writings of Nietzsche. The group lasted, with additions and subtractions, from 1905 until about 1913, the same period during which the Fauves and Cubists were running riot in Paris. While the French were busy investigating universal artistic principles, the Germans were far more personal and excessively emotional in their outlook, searching for hidden meanings beyond everyday appearances. As their art became a subjective and symbolic communication between creative specialists and the public, it grew increasingly difficult to understand. Their aims were to depict life as a cruel experience, and to do it with whatever artistic means were considered appropriate; to convey cynicism as well as hopes and fears through distortion and violence; to find new truths in prosaic images; and to record a society that they believed was morally corrupt and betraying its own humanity. Much of the story of these extraordinarily sensitive artists would be told through portraiture in prints. The rough power of black and white and the great potential for a wide audience made printmaking an ideal medium to the Brücke members.

One of their founders was a twenty-five-year-old artist named Ernst Ludwig Kirchner. He attended an arts and crafts school in Munich where a cogent sense of design and a sure knowledge of printmaking, particularly woodcuts, were developed. He and his fellow students and friends, Erich Heckel, Karl Schmidt-Rottluff, and Emil Nolde changed the character of German art and helped establish the Expressionist movement. As a youthful and idealistic group, the Brücke artists put together their own exhibits based on theories which were quickly recognized as rejections of naturalistic traditional art, at the same time associating the woodcut with expressive feelings, the crafts of the middle ages, and the renaissance of humanistic German culture.

They focused on what the image meant to them alone, regardless of what it might look like to others. As the editors of the *Praeger Picture Encyclopedia of Art* put it, the very act of seeing was a subjective experience: "The way I *see* it became the way *I* see it." And what they saw were unorthodox images that bordered on caricature, that addressed the passions rather than the intellect, that warped perspective and exaggerated shapes, and that symbolized for them not only a chaotic, materialistic outer reality, but their inner life as well. Kirchner spoke of "proportions in art that take their cues from the emotions." Their portraits, mostly of themselves or their close friends, were as much projections of their own sensibilities as of real people; bruised, jagged lines and acute angles carried overpowering charges that harmonious or decorative portraiture could not hope to rival.

Kirchner's psychological references were marked by elongated forms with thrusting diagonals and other discordant elements. In his 1917 woodcut portrait of Ludwig Schames, an art dealer who helped popularize his work, Kirchner used an irregularly shaped plank of wood that forced his image into an oblique, compressed space. (Fig. 208) The great black holes that serve for Schames' eyes give the face its introspective, despondent appearance. Wedged tightly against the head is the flat angular shape of a nude, possibly one of Kirchner's own wood carvings; he used similar sexual motifs in self-portraits as a symbol of sensual and artistic involvement. Estrangement is the controlling factor in the print, with male and female avoiding confrontation.

Kirchner was sickly much of his life and his physical-emotional condition was exacerbated by army service. After World War I he continued to work at fever pitch in spite of contracting tuberculosis and experiencing a nervous breakdown. He moved to Switzerland in hopes of a cure, but

Left: Fig. 208. Ernst Ludwig Kirchner. *Ludwig Schames*. Courtesy Brooklyn Museum. *Right*: Fig. 209. Erich Heckel. *Der Mann* (*The Man*). Courtesy Fogg Art Museum, Harvard University.

mental problems, some stemming from the Nazi purge in which much of his work was destroyed, led to his suicide at the age of fifty-eight. Nevertheless he left behind an enormous output—over two thousand prints, most of them woodcuts, in addition to paintings and sculpture. In 1921 he outlined his credo that "intensification and simplification were much more important than shading and shadows." He believed that through the print medium, woodcuts in particular, he could best define character and personality, the "inner idea" of spiritual life.

One of Kirchner's co-organizers of Die Brücke was Erich Heckel, who gave up his architectural studies to help establish the group. His self-portrait woodcut of 1913, *Der Mann* (*The Man*), merciless in its judgment, reveals the uneasiness and doubt that was a part of German art immediately before World War I, when expressive feelings so often prevailed over intellectual acuity. (Fig. 209) There is a furtive, suspicious look in the sidelong glance; the sensitive face is gaunt; the glowing whites spotlight the ascetic features. The recurrent V shapes lend a powerful quality to the print, their angularity responding to the Cubist vocabulary. Heckel, like Max Beckmann, served in the medical corps, where he was exposed to the sick and wounded whom he depicted subdued and withdrawn, perhaps deadened to sensation. During the Second World War he sought refuge in Switzerland, where his work eventually lost much of its aggressive force, becoming more lyrical than that of most of the other Expressionists. He was very prolific, executing almost a thousand prints, many based on primitive sculptures.

Schmidt-Rottluff, who thought up the name Die Brücke hoping that the group might bridge personal artistic styles, encouraged them to study together and to share exhibitions and publications relating to the new Expressionist themes. He also introduced lithography to the other members, some of whom had little or no academic training. There was a monumentality to his heavy, dramatic work, in which stark black and white parallel stripes suggest shading; they resemble, in their staccato striations, a parade of black and white piano keys. *Man in Pain*, a woodcut self-portrait of 1916, is a jarring image with its grossly distorted, enlarged, and monstrous features adding a sinister aspect to the print. (Fig. 210) Dehumanized heads such as this were based on African masks and made a powerful impact with their strong emphasis on outline and characteristic sense of menace, the effect of the daily war-time presence of death. Later in his career, Schmidt-Rottluff took up religious art, his *Passion* series being an equally powerful, but more spiritual, example of his work. The constant inner search for personal meaning was the metaphysical thread common to both Expressionist art and the German Christian experience.

Religion also inspired Emil Nolde. It was a powerful theme in his prints and paintings, which were mystical in spirit and garishly brilliant in color. But he was hardly a Christian. He scorned his own church and erupted in fanaticism and intolerance against various Jewish artists and dealers on whom he placed the blame for his hard times. Ironically, he was the most persecuted of his colleagues, although he had joined the Nazi party in the early 1920s and repeatedly wrote letters to Joseph Goebbels, the Nazi propaganda chief, protesting his devotion to the cause and assuring him of his own racial purity. Among the group of fascinating and neurotic personalities, he was perhaps the most disturbed, as well as the most inventive. He joined Die Brücke in 1906, but withdrew by mutual agreement after a year and a half, not caring for cliques. He was frequently ill-tempered and over-sensitive and believed he was being singled out for insults. Although at first he was not as knowledgeable about woodcut technique as some of the other Brücke members, before they parted company both Kirchner and Heckel were greatly influenced by his compelling emotional fervor and imaginative etchings and lithographs.

Many of Nolde's prints have a nightmarish quality, powerful and

Top left: Fig. 210. Karl Schmidt-Rottluff. *Man in Pain*. Courtesy Brooklyn Museum. *Top right*: Fig. 211. Emil Nolde. *Head of a Man in Darkness*. Private collection. *Bottom left*: Fig. 212. Emil Nolde. *Hugo del Caril*. Courtesy Collection, Museum of Modern Art, New York, Purchase Fund. *Bottom right*: Fig. 213. Paul Klee. *Versunkenheit-Selbstportrait — Bildnis eines Expressionisten-Portrait (Self-Absorption-Self-Portrait — Picture of an Expressionist Portrait)*. Private collection.

frightening in their dynamism, impossible to ignore or forget. Among his many self-portraits is the *Düsterer Männerkopf (Head of a Man in Darkness)*, a color lithograph of 1907 with a severe broken quality more often seen in woodcuts. (Fig. 211) The head consists of massive dark and light areas with the white paper serving to convey its intense human quality. In 1908 he executed an aquatint and etching of Hugo del Caril, less violent and more painterly, but the white pincer shape around the eye gives the impression that Nolde feared light and could express himself only through the dark side of his soul. (Fig. 212)

As the city of Berlin matured from a regional to a national capital after the unification of Germany in 1871, it became a great commercial and cultural center. The Brücke artists regrouped there in 1911 and held exhibits and prepared woodcuts for magazine and book publications. Although the organization dissolved shortly thereafter, each member going his own way, another group of artists, based in Munich, came together in loose association in 1911 under the name *Der Blaue Reiter* (*The Blue Rider*). Wassily Kandinsky, of Russian birth, admired riders; Franz Marc, thoroughly disenchanted with mankind, singled out the horse as a metaphor of redemption; together they shared the opinion that blue was a spiritual symbol of inner well-being and truth. After seeing exhibitions by Picasso and Braque in Paris, they rejected the Art Nouveau formulas which they had favored, for a more formal or abstract style; ultimately they achieved a greater influence in the art world than the Expressionists.

Unlike the Brücke artists, many of the Blaue Reiter group were involved with non-figurative designs, which essentially excluded portraiture as a major factor from their interests. Nevertheless, Paul Klee, a Swiss-born artist associated with Walter Gropius' Bauhaus architecture and crafts school, who did some of his work with the Blaue Reiters, took the face to new lengths in his mask-like *Versunkenheit-Selbstportrait (Self-Absorption-Self-Portrait)*, a lithograph of 1919. (Fig. 213) The lines appear simple enough, but the print is far from simple-minded. Klee believed that no photograph or objective likeness could give as true an awareness of personality as an image that showed essential nature rather than descriptive appearance. The portrait met the criterion of "mystical inner construction" that defined the Blaue Reiter model.

These groups were not the only outlets for portraiture. Käthe Kollwitz, one of the greatest Realists of the century, worked independently and followed her own bent, always stressing the true or objective representation of nature. She was brought up in a Socialist family where she was taught to value and practice humanitarian principles. After her marriage she and her doctor husband lived for fifty years in a slum neighborhood where he had a clinic for the poor and sick. She suffered through two world wars, losing her eighteen-year-old son in the first and her grandson in the second, in addition to having her home and many of her prints and drawings destroyed by Allied bombs. From a firebrand revolutionary, she became a pacifist, horrified by war and the famine it brought to Germany.

She had learned printmaking as a young woman and was particularly attracted to the etchings of Rembrandt. Her prints were full of compassion for exploited working people and the mothers of boy soldiers who died in wars they never understood. She drew her life story in more than fifty introspective self-portraits without a suggestion of vanity or affectation. Resignation, but not defeat, is imprinted on her rounded shoulders and on her face in the profile *Self-Portrait* lithograph of 1938 (Fig. 214) Her stolid features tell something about stubborn courage. She had been forced to resign from the Prussian Academy of Art for anti–Nazi activities and was threatened with imprisonment in a concentration camp. Dozens of her prints, symbolizing the struggles and griefs of German laborers, were burned, and museums and galleries were systematically stripped of her moving works. A series of lithographs shows her wrestling with the Great Avenger for the bodies of young children. In the lithograph self-portrait *Ruf des Todes* (*The Call of Death*), 1935–36, a skillful interaction between diagonal and vertical strokes is present, as well as a full knowledge of tone, line, and sculpturesque modeling. But she made her point clearly: Death, which was ever present in the agonizing days of the Third Reich, would come not as an enemy, but as a friend. (Fig. 215) She died just one week before Hitler, her work having accomplished both altruistic and artistic goals.

Most of the Expressionists believed they made an important contribution to art by freeing it from the insipidities of the eighteenth and nineteenth centuries, yet much of the public either ignored or despised their work and their Bohemian behaviour. Oskar Kokoschka, a playwright and poet as well as an artistic prodigy, more than any one else provoked exasperation with his wild conduct and rebellious art. He apparently enjoyed outraging middle class sensibilities by posing as a cannibal, criminal, or inciter of riots. He left Vienna at the age of twenty-three to avoid a scandal because of the highly morbid and sexual material in one of his plays. He was born in Austria-Hungary and quickly imbibed the local Baroque art tradition of restless, shifting movement. He found the Brücke style somewhat to his taste, but he never formally joined the group. A great deal of his early work consisted of overwrought portraits in which he attempted, by emphasizing eyes, gestures, and mannerisms, to catch and record the essence or nature of intelligence.

One of the absorbing dramas in his life was his love affair with Alma Mahler, the widow of Gustav Mahler. At the time she married the composer she had been a young Viennese belle and a minor musician in her own right, but at his request she gave up whatever career she might have had. Years later Mahler, perhaps with due guilt, resurrected the songs of her girlhood and had them published, and although Kokoschka urged her

Opposite, left: Fig. 214. Käthe Kollwitz. *Self-Portrait. Right*: Fig. 215. Käthe Kollwitz. *Ruf des Todes* (*The Call of Death*). Both figures courtesy Collection, Museum of Modern Art, New York, Purchase Fund.

Left: Fig. 216. Oskar Kokoschka. *Das Gesicht des Weiber (Woman's Head).*
Courtesy Collection, Museum of Modern Art, New York, Purchase Fund. *Right:*
Fig. 217. Oskar Kokoschka. *Self-Portrait.* Private collection.

to consolidate them into a symphonic work, they lay forgotten until 1983,
when they were discovered and recorded. Kokoschka's 1913 lithograph
portrait *Das Gesicht des Weiber* (*Woman's Head*) shows her in a grim
mood, but without the barbarous ferocity of which Kokoschka was
capable. (Fig. 216) It is a portrait of psychological tension as much as a
likeness. Her unhappy features were perhaps a clue to their difficult relationship; he wrote that he was seeking to "recognize the woman who binds
him in chains. At the end she appears to him as a love-ghost, moon-
woman." A year later, she abandoned him for marriage to the architect
Walter Gropius. He brooded over her for years.

Kokoschka enlisted in the army in 1915 and was badly wounded in the
head and lungs. After his recovery his earlier emotionalism deteriorated
into periods of eccentric behavior. He moved a life-size, anatomically correct doll of Alma Mahler into his home and his bed; it accompanied him
on his daily rounds until he destroyed it in a drunken frenzy. Although he,
along with Kirchner and Nolde, was the most successful of the graphic
artists, his troubles overshadowed his naturally optimistic nature. His
work gradually mellowed into a less angular and disturbed style, although
his lithograph *Self-Portrait* in 1923 still registers a disjunction of spirit that
owes some of its conception, but none of its anguish, to Picasso. (Fig. 217)
His face has become an intense, though impersonal façade. A series of

portrait lithographs made during and after his convalescence from his war injuries were highly sensitive and caught the basic elements of his sitters' states of mind, but by 1945 portraiture was becoming increasingly difficult for him, he said, because men no longer had within themselves the nobility or passion indispensable for great images. Man was returning to the wilderness, he feared, and, in his great hurry, had sealed off his inner nature from the probing eye of the artist as well as from his own consciousness; decay and mankind's untimely end would logically follow. Logic, fortunately, was listening elsewhere; the world has rolled on.

Germany's collapse after World War I marked a change in the Expressionist movement; its disillusioned artists, who had been staunchly patriotic, no longer believed that social and political conditions would improve. They recognized that self-expressive art was an inadequate response to the post-war climate of corrupt militarism, nationalism, defeated Socialism, and industrialism; a reaction set in that became known as *Die Neue Sachlichkeit* (the New Objectivity). It was an attempt at clarity and an awareness of public policy, representing a style that was thought to reflect the true situation of Germany in the 1920s. Cynicism and political rhetoric took over; daydreams of perfectibility yielded to leftist revolutionary ideas and social planning. Some of the New Objectivity artists moved away from the mystical and religious elements of Expressionism, to a "truer" representation, less idealistic, often with bitter overtones. Distortion and sensationalism rather than inner feelings were increasingly explored as vehicles to depict political realities and attract the working class during post-war tensions.

Max Beckmann had been a successful conservative artist before the war, but during his army days he experienced a nervous breakdown brought on by war atrocities and temporarily gave up painting. However, after he met Heckel in the medical corps, they evolved a printmaking style in which coarseness and hostility were forcefully expressed. After the war Heckel adopted a milder, less troubled manner, but Beckmann remained uncompromising and inflexible. He made about fifteen woodcuts—in his *Self-Portrait*, 1922, the blacked-out eyes and impassive face shield his most intimate feelings behind a mask of assurance and determination. (Fig. 218) He used outline more than shading, and simplified the bold cutting so that only the most significant lines remained. The face appears like a sculpture, and was indeed based on a bronze.

Earlier self-portraits, many in drypoint, were gentler, with more tonal work, but after World War I he became pessimistic and disillusioned because of his physical and emotional problems, and his later portraits developed greater angularity and distortion as well as intellectual power. He accented them with a striking surface play of lights and darks.

In 1937 his works were removed from exhibition halls by the Nazis. He fled to Amsterdam and finally to America, where he lived and taught until his death in 1950. From 1901 to 1946 he turned out scores of prints. There was no finer or more prolific self-portraitist in the twentieth century.

Fig. 218. Max Beckmann. *Self-Portrait*. Courtesy Brooklyn Museum.

An even greater sense of alienation controlled another of the "newly objective" artists, Otto Dix, but too often his work was so overcharged that in the end it simply became incoherent. Perhaps only Callot, Bosch, or Goya has ever wished on the world such ferocity as Dix's 1923 color lithograph, *Madam*. (Fig. 219) In this portrait of the prostitute Léonie, whom he saw as a victim of Capitalism, the savagery is so unmitigated that its force is dissipated, yet the contrast between the modish hat and the cadaverous face whose features are open wounds remains a compelling symbol of pitiless degradation. Moral bankruptcy appears again in his *Self-Portrait* drypoint of 1922 — the face and heart of a spiritually exhausted Germany between the wars. (Fig. 220) Dry-point, whose line so often lends a softness, here has a corrosive quality, brutalizing the head. The cigarette that dangles from his mouth, the fierce scowl, the obdurate jaw line indicating insolence and swagger, are the personification of malevolence. Such human estrangement was the other side of the New Objectivity: the inability to communicate, to make concessions to reality, and a rejection of social conventions. Dix perceived Europe as a debauched civilization, and his feelings found their way into a series of anti-war etchings in the 1920s that rival Goya's, but were equally disregarded during his lifetime.

In 1933 Hitler came to power. Four years later he ordered the confiscation of thousands of Expressionistic or what he called "degenerate" works of art from museums and private collections, placing over seven hundred of them on public exhibit in the hope of generating public revulsion for "Bolshevik-Jewish" art. By war's end, about sixteen thousand works had been systematically destroyed. The Nazi government believed that the compassion and the political and social reforms urged by the Expressionists posed a grave threat to its program. It was a grim reminder of the words of Kaiser Wilhelm in 1902: "Art which presumes to overstep the limits and rules I have indicated, is no longer art.... If it does nothing more than present misery in an even more hideous form than it already possesses, then it sins against the German people." Fortunately the Kaiser had not been as extreme or tyrannical as Hitler, and the Expressionists had been able to continue their work under his reign. For the Nazis, however, art was to be exclusively at the service of state policy as it was in Soviet Russia. Most artists required written permission to show their works no matter what their political ideology. Adverse commentary was forbidden since Hitler took any criticism as a personal affront. Totalitarianism cannot tolerate independent art, certainly not a revolutionary style such as Expressionism, which defied the "traditional values" that Hitler prided himself were the strength of Germany. Since he considered himself something of an artist, he probably felt that his opinions were aesthetically valid.

The destruction or dispersion of their output was crushing, and those artists who could, left Germany. Others, with honors revoked, waited it out, often harassed or forbidden to work. Politics had never before had such a disastrous effect on art; perhaps no other group of artists had been so naive as to believe that they could make an impact on politicians. After World War II, middle-aged and less restive, they eventually harvested the rewards of study, experience, and resurrected tributes, but the freshness and passion of their youth was lost, leaving a void that has yet to be filled. However, there are portraitists in Germany today who still wield an unblunted pen. Vexation of temper and depression of spirit remain their legacy and their portion.

Horst Janssen's Surrealist etching and drypoint portrait *Edward*, 1958, still conveys blight, disillusion, and irrationality. (Fig. 221) The modeling and definition of the features, even the textures of skin and clothes, have lost all reality and significance; all that is left are the burned-out eyes, weird insect forms, and an obscene zipper of alligator teeth representing a nose. Janssen was born in 1929 and grew up during the Nazi regime. He has attempted to resolve the atrocities of his time and to relate those experiences to his own conscience. His more recent portraits are as withering as ever.

It is true that some of what the Expressionists produced was hardly more than adolescent exhibitionism, narcissism, and rebellion, but many of their portraits were sensitive responses to extreme emotional stress. Some were so violent as not to be taken seriously, but at its best German Expressionist art was a profound movement. It shared the nineteenth century Romantic philosophy of what Byron had called the "great object of life, sensation — to feel that we exist, even in pain."

When Byron died, Matthew Arnold offered a tribute that may apply equally well to the Expressionist artist: "He taught us little; but our soul had *felt* him like the thunder's roll."

III. England

The Victorian reign ended in 1901 with the death of the Queen. She had ruled for sixty-three years, a period that had seen unparalleled economic and social changes in England. The direction of national policies now increasingly turned towards democratization. A reform government

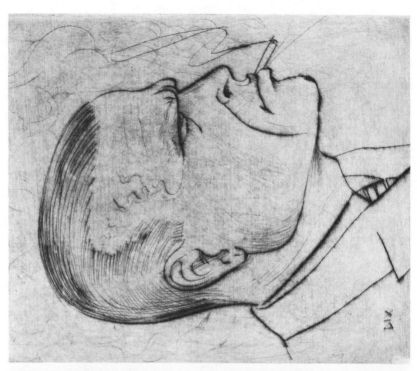

was elected which improved working conditions, initiated women's suffrage, and notably restricted the perquisites and power of the House of Lords. However, liberal and conservative forces were soon opposed on other issues, with colonialism and questions of disarmament the major battlegrounds of contention.

White control over vast native populations was still an acceptable policy, but its days were numbered. Formidable local resistance raged against the colonial system and many well-meaning citizens demanded justice and self-rule for the distant territories on which England depended for food and other supplies, as well as an outlet for her own exports. On the other hand, still louder voices warned that a lessened grip on the empire would mean a lessening of world influence for Britain, and they successfully argued that self-preservation and international leadership required a show of force in the colonies and a build-up of weaponry at home. However, Germany was an even bigger problem. She began a naval arms race with England, hoping to establish herself as a world sea power. But before reaching that goal, she invaded Belgium in 1914, placing France in immediate peril; Britain not only recognized her own danger, but her responsibility for a free Europe, and entered the war.

Since England's standing army was relatively small, it required almost two years of training to prepare enough soldiers for slaughter. She suffered losses so great that older men had to be recruited. Food shortages made rationing necessary, prices rose precipitously for rapidly disappearing goods, and labor strikes demoralized what little there was left of hope. The American entry supplied the final ingredient for civilization's first war that involved all the continents of the world. When it was over, England began a closer relationship with other countries than her geographic isolation had ever before warranted. She mingled her culture with French art, Russian ballet, Freud's celebration of the subconscious, and American know-how.

But more problems were in the offing. The Catholic majority in Ireland was campaigning for home rule, a struggle that has persisted and deteriorated and whose final outcome is still uncertain. In Europe disarmament movements were born and collapsed. With the rise of Hitler, international cooperation and negotiation turned into a cynical and hollow exercise. Troubled and fearful because she had fallen seriously behind in arms build-up, and desperately playing for time, England arranged a naval agreement with Germany in 1935 and then dissuaded France from retaliating when Hitler moved into the Rhineland. Prime Minister Neville Chamberlain acted on the naive assumption that Hitler's objectives were satisfied, and that his military operation was partly defensible in the light of the ill-devised Peace Treaty of 1919.

Opposite, left: Fig. 219. Otto Dix. *Madam*. Courtesy Grunwald Center for the Graphic Arts, UCLA, gift of Mr. and Mrs. Stanley I. Talpis. *Right*: Fig. 220. Otto Dix. *Self-Portrait*. Courtesy Collection, Museum of Modern Art, New York, gift of Samuel A. Berger.

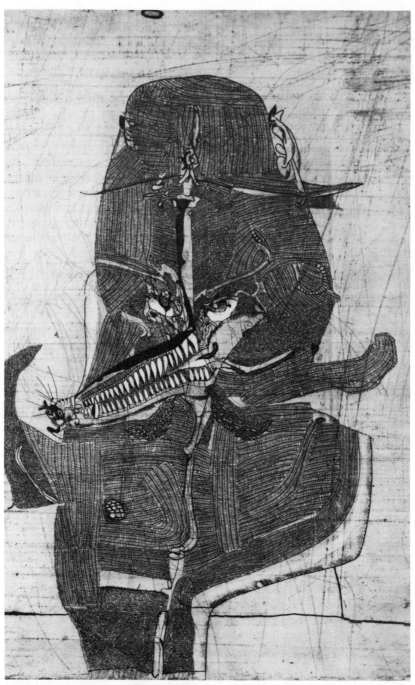

Fig. 221. Horst Janssen. *Edward*. Courtesy Grunwald Center for the Graphic Arts, UCLA, gift of Mr. and Mrs. Stanley I. Talpis.

Even during the most critical times, now and then a human interest story will claim the public's almost undivided attention. Edward VIII's decision to abdicate and marry the woman he loved rocked the throne and launched the greatest romance of the century. But while the love affair diverted her subjects, England's onerous preparations for war went on. In 1938, still hoping for a miracle, she continued to placate Germany; on Hitler's side there was as much good faith as in Judas' kiss. It was soon painfully clear that appeasement would not work and that there would be no peace in our time, although Chamberlain persisted in the belief that Hitler was a man "who could be relied upon when he had given his word." When Germany annexed Austria in 1938 and invaded Czechoslovakia and Poland in 1939, Britain went to war again.

No decisive battles were fought for almost a year. Then Hitler suddenly attacked Scandinavia and captured air bases that could be used against England's civilian population. The Chamberlain government had not prepared for such a contingency and was forced to resign in humiliation. Winston Churchill was recalled from a political wilderness to rescue the nation. When Belgium and then France fell to the Germans in a matter of days, Britain faced a seemingly invincible enemy disheartened and alone. Yet Churchill called it England's finest hour and roused the country to an incredible resistance and ultimate victory.

England moved into the second half of the twentieth century radically different from what it had been at the end of the Victorian era. Economically strapped by the rebuilding of its bombed-out cities, reduced in international prestige, dispossessed of its overseas empire, it was immeasurably hard-hit. Public ownership of many of its industries and services was inaugurated in 1948. The second Elizabeth came to the royal throne in 1952, the Beatles to the musical throne in the 1960s. But perhaps the major event of the century was the discrediting and destruction of Fascism in Europe. As Churchill reminded the world, "England always wins one battle – the last."

English printmaking in the twentieth century did not achieve the same degree of excellence or importance as German or French, generally lacking their strength, dynamism and innovation. Delicacy of finish, subtlety and penetration of expression, and extraordinary technical skill in etching and drypoint account for the best English work, much of which was still in the tradition of the nineteenth century etching revival. There were no breakthroughs such as Expressionism or Cubism that imposed a unique style or led in unexpected directions, with the possible exception of Pop Art, where likenesses were meant to be examined, not in terms of character or personality, but as a commentary on popular culture and mass media technology. However, on their own terms, most English artists turned in a good account, and now and then, a real triumph.

Particularly in portraiture, which has always been England's forte, there are many examples which can hold their own in almost any company. Certainly there was no deficiency in eliciting individuality or mood; the

Fig. 222. Muirhead Bone. *Self-Portrait of the Artist in a Hat, No. 2.* Private collection.

representation of the human face was actually better realized by printmakers in England than in Germany, where features were largely distorted, or in France, where clever manipulation of line was emphasized. If sensibility and interest in physical resemblances are preferred, then English work offers the best choice. The exploitation of small facial irregularities, the use or nonuse of symmetry to bring out or underscore a distinctive aspect or character trait, the ability to get beneath the skin—these were the special skills of England's printmakers.

Muirhead Bone straddled two centuries. Born in 1876, he was familiar with Haden's and Whistler's sketchy line work, but in his own portraits he went back to the seventeenth century's taste for fuller tonalities. He was trained as an architect, but as he leaned toward printmaking, he combined both disciplines in his etched views of scaffolded buildings. Before a stint as a war artist in 1916, he began a series of etchings and drypoints of which the *Self-Portrait of the Artist in a Hat, No. 2*, 1908–09, is obviously modeled on one of Rembrandt's plates. (Fig. 222; see Fig. 80) The print has an exceptional richness, not surprising since Bone was a great master of the drypoint technique. It is one of the few plates on which he permitted steel-facing, since it was to be used as the frontispiece for Campbell Dodgson's second catalogue of his works in 1916. Otherwise, his prints appeared in very small editions.

Augustus John was twenty-one years old when the century began. Welsh by birth, English by training, he developed into a very fine portrait painter and draftsman. He chose a gypsy life style over a conventional one, settling down long enough to become, along with several other painters, a war-time artist. The skills honed in the realistic drawings these army correspondents did for newspapers proved very useful when they returned to civilian life. Their training may have attracted them to portraiture, inasmuch as the harrowing events they experienced deepened their curiosity about human behavior and emotions; those who had been spared that suffering perhaps were sooner drawn to abstract art and the imaginary world of the mind.

John painted and etched in a free and spontaneous style, anti-academic and seemingly unconcerned with technical details; he said that nearly all his plates suffered from hasty and inaccurate biting. His refined and intense portraits were lively and moving, and he counted many celebrated sitters among his clients. When Thomas Hardy was asked whether he thought John's portrait of him was a good likeness, he answered, "I don't know whether that is how I look or not – but that is how I feel." In an etching and drypoint of 1902 John depicted his sister *Gwendolyn*, a very fine portrait painter herself. Her solitary and reflective life elicited portraits of sensitivity and richness that became widely known only after her death. (Fig. 223) John turned her face and hat into appealing ovals perched at right angles to each other. There is something a bit unsettling about her excessively long neck and homely features, but her quiet dignity was carefully observed and treated with affection. In 1906 he etched his own Rembrandtesque *Self-Portrait*, convincing in its sketchy linearity and ability to illuminate troubling emotions. (Fig. 224) As a technician and innovator he was constantly looking for unconventional, even heretical, methods, particularly in his earlier years.

The attention to the sitter's frame of mind was welcome after the profusion of stately public images commonly depicted in earlier periods. The natural partiality of English patrons for descriptive portraiture attracted them not only to the works of prominent artists such as Bone and John, but to many lesser-known etchers as well. Joseph Simpson was another of the war artists, serving in France with the Royal Air Force. Since both he and John were primarily painters, their etched works can only be considered as sidelines in their careers, but Simpson hit the mark in 1930 with his very striking, brightly lit portrait of an eccentric fellow artist and poster designer: *James Pryde (in Tall Hat)*. (Fig. 225) The strong cross-hatching and the rakish slant of the hat contribute to the impact of the print, while the slight air of disdain conveys the immediacy of a flesh and blood resemblance. Simpson's spare use of line and suggestive handling recalls Whistler's draftsmanship and Legros' manner.

A year younger than Simpson and a more consistently fine portrait etcher, Malcolm Osborne was also one of a group of artists influenced by Legros. He began his career by reproducing famous paintings, practicing until he commanded an exquisite control of the etching needle. Among his best portraits is a sensitive and shrewd evocation of age, *Mrs. Heberden*, 1913. (Fig. 226) She is a model of spirit, life, and mellow wisdom. Rembrandt would not have been ashamed of the compassionate rendering of her worn features and heavy body. (See Fig. 75) But Osborne's etching of Nathaniel Sparks, Esquire, 1921, an etcher and printer who occasionally worked for Whistler, presented an even greater challenge to his skills than the comforting maternal image. (Fig. 227) To portray an unprepossessing subject with sympathy and gentleness, yet without a trace of condescension, and to give him at the same time a great personal and intellectual appeal, defies commonplace artistic talent. Sparks, who considered himself ugly and was very sensitive about his appearance, retreats into his coat as if to

Fig. 225. Joseph Simpson. *James Pryde (in Tall Hat).* Private Collection.

shrink from public exposure. His melancholy frame of mind seems to permeate his entire being.

   Leon Underwood was a sculptor, as might be guessed from his *Self-Portrait*, etched in 1918. (Fig. 228) The planes are well considered: the rim of his hat, the bowl of his pipe, the gripping hand, each moves forward in successive intervals. The lightly etched landscape and the sprinkling of wildflowers lend a pleasant bucolic atmosphere to the design. He confronts the mirror with a direct and open gaze, only the tight knuckles indicating

Opposite, Left: Fig. 223. Augustus John. *Gwendolen.* Courtesy Collection, Museum of Modern Art, New York, gift of Abby Aldrich Rockefeller (by exchange). *Right*: Fig. 224. Augustus John. *Self-Portrait.* Courtesy Metropolitan Museum of Art, Harris Brisbane Dick Fund, 1932 [32.84.3].

Left: Fig. 226. Malcolm Osborne. *Mrs. Heberden*. Courtesy British Museum.
Right: Fig. 227. Malcolm Osborne. *Nathaniel Sparks, Esquire*. Private collection.

a latent tension. Other of his works also reflect this interest in the expressive quality of hands. Underwood's prints are hard to find. Many of his plates were stolen and melted for scrap.

Another of the war artists who took to portrait etching was Christopher Richard Wynne Nevinson. When hostilities began in 1914, like many young idealists he could hardly wait for his chance to be "dauntless in war." His service as an ambulance driver, however, rapidly disabused him of any romantic notions, and, appalled at the sight of wounded soldiers and the stench of the makeshift hospitals, he put his feelings about those terrible experiences into a series of powerful paintings and etchings. His acute reaction to the suffering caused a creative slump in his painting for a time, although not in his printmaking. In 1927 he etched an unusual portrait, *Edith Sitwell*, reflecting his interest in abstract and stylized, almost Cubist, patterns. (Fig. 229) Sitwell was a capricious member of a capricious literary family, writing poetry that was somewhat in the sly tradition of Lewis Carroll, yet often serious and moving. She was about six feet tall, of great dignity, and affected medieval clothing, a bobbed haircut and a glacial demeanor, all of which are formally recorded with strong black and white contrasts in Nevinson's offbeat design.

Of the many etchers in the early years of the century, Gerald Brockhurst alone devoted himself almost exclusively to portraiture, going back to early classical Italian models. His range was narrow—nubile women—but within those limits no one in his generation rivaled him. As a youngster he had difficulty with learning and suffered from a curious

Left: Fig. 228. Leon Underwood. *Self-Portrait*. Private collection. *Right*: Fig. 229. Christopher Richard Wynne Nevinson. *Edith Sitwell*. Private collection.

inability to write normally; his childhood letters to his family are a series of hieroglyphic scratchings. Nevertheless, he was an artistic prodigy and won a large number of awards for his drawings. In the 1920s he began a group of portrait etchings that are among the most imaginative of the period. He was influenced by Augustus John's use of short, scratchy lines, but he went much further back into printmaking history and revived facial stippling to achieve delicately graduated modeling. Although some of his prints were quick and free, the meticulous detail of most of his work was about as far away from Whistler's spontaneity as it is possible to get. Yet both artists defined the temperament of young womanhood with equal insight; in each case their portraits, though specific in their resemblances, are more idealized than psychologically oriented.

In the decade of the 1920s Brockhurst's wife frequently posed for him — the *Melisande* of 1920 and the *Dancer* of 1925 — and he spotlighted and shaded her figure with his usual superb control. But in the 1930s he fell in love with a young woman named Dorette Woodward and abandoned his family for her. She posed for two of his most famous etchings, *Adolescence* and *Dorette*, in 1932, when she was eighteen. (Figs. 230, 231) Both portraits are candidly seductive, yet suggest the awkward reticence of a young girl on the brink of womanhood. *Adolescence* has always had a special appeal for collectors and commands far higher prices than any of his other plates; there is a nakedness about this nude that fascinates viewers. The depiction of the glass surface itself, as well as the subtle differences between the reflection in the mirror and the "real" figure, were expertly done in terms of light and the organization of planes.

Fig. 230. Gerald Brockhurst. *Adolescence*. Courtesy Grunwald Center for the Graphic Arts, UCLA.

Fig. 231. Gerald Brockhurst. *Dorette*. Private collection.

Although the great outpouring of etchings was over by 1929, some traditional or derivative works continued to be produced until the 1940s. But Brockhurst's elaborate manner, minute dotting, and exquisite polish found no echo in younger printmakers, and his close style was left behind by those who could not or would not follow his laborious methods.

Everyone collected, driving some prices to levels that have never since been equaled. After the crash there was a considerable falling off in print-making that lasted until after World War II; public interest picked up dramatically in the 1960s. By that time art had become international in scope, with teachers and patrons such as Tatyana Grosman in New York, June Wayne in California, and the Englishman Stanley William Hayter at Atelier 17 in Paris. They developed experimental and creative workshops and prodded their colleagues and students to stretch their imaginations and talents.

The results were clever technical innovations, including combinations of various photographic and hand-drawn methods. In England as elsewhere, artists were desperately looking for something new. Their desperation, unfortunately, was all too often reflected in their work.

Although in every generation artists react to their own environments, the extraordinary events of the twentieth century demanded radically fresh ideas and sophisticated technical know-how in order to relate to the shapes, symbols and experiences of a popular commercial culture. Photography, rather than ringing the knell on hand portraiture, became its ally, an integral part of the printmaking process itself.

The most widely adopted medium was serigraphy (silkscreen), which had originally been used for printing labels and other commercial items. It caught on in the 1960s as an artistic tool, since it didn't require expensive equipment, could be readily taught, was the simplest method of color printing, and could produce an almost unlimited number of consistently good impressions. A stencil pattern is varnished on or fixed to a tightly stretched screen of silk, synthetic fabric, or metal mesh, so that when colored ink is scraped across the porous frame with a squeegee, it is forced through the interstices of the unmasked portions of the mesh, depositing a heavily inked image onto a sheet of paper below. The masked or impervious areas, corresponding to the empty places in the design, block the inks from penetrating the fabric. As with colored woodcuts or lithographs, which require different blocks of wood or stone, in this process a separate screen must be prepared for each color.

Richard Hamilton attracted the interest of the avant garde with his slick, sharp-witted projects that combined silkscreen with photo-mechanical techniques. Examining ordinary negatives or film clips of celebrities, such as Bing Crosby, for possible artistic content, and adapting them in prints through technical manipulation, stencil work, and drawing, was a new and exciting approach, although whatever personal qualities these images might once have had was essentially lost; the likenesses created were only symbolic. They were Hamilton's reminder that in spite of the redundance of information and gossip that superstars generate, their portraits, when interpreted through the viewpoint of Pop Art, remain impenetrable, and in the end, ambiguous substitutes for living beings.

His *Portrait of the Artist by Francis Bacon*, 1971, was taken from a Polaroid picture, using silkscreen for the background color and collotype for the image. (Fig. 232) The collotype photographic process, which produces high-quality impressions, originated in the nineteenth century and involves a gelatin coating over a glass or zinc plate, the picture becoming visible when the plate is exposed to light. Hamilton's print was actually a blow-up of the photograph of himself taken by Francis Bacon, one of the most notable contemporary artists, whose lineage goes back to the Elizabethan philosopher for whom he was named. The ghost-like apparition was later rejected by Bacon for his book *Polaroid Portraits*. It is typical of Bacon's terrifyingly uncouth probings, which explored the isolation and depravity of the human spirit. Hamilton was a brave man to give it to the world.

Hamilton became a prime mover in the growth of Pop Art, acquiring

Fig. 232. Richard Hamilton. *Portrait of the Artist by Francis Bacon*. Courtesy Collection, Museum of Modern Art, New York, Leo Castelli Fund.

some of his ideas of "found images" from the Surrealist experiments of his friend Marcel Duchamp. The style took root in England in the late 1950s as a reaction to the automatic or subconscious paintings of artists such as Jackson Pollock and William de Kooning, who dribbled or laid on paints by intuition rather than according to a plan. Pop artists like Hamilton took commonplace and clearly defined images, sometimes from art history, often from the world of advertising and cartoons, and turned them into a vogue of the trite, seen from an unfamiliar point of view. They made a great splash with their gaudy, hard-edged patterns. Pop portraits were neither traditionally interpretive nor translations of paintings, but rather a new genre of impersonal icons, where likenesses were meant to be examined as commentaries on popular culture and mass media technology. Pop artists pretty much ignored character delineation, expressive qualities, or refined techniques. Instead, they produced designs that reflected the realities of their times. True, they frequently were affected and pretentious and suffered from excessive virtuosity, but the same can be said of conventional work. At its best, Pop Art was clever, gaily colored, and occasionally provocative.

Hamilton himself saw Pop as a "modern printmaker's medium which has a certain appeal because it is less autographic than etching or litho — it hasn't their dependence on the hand of the artist." He described it as "designed for a mass audience, transient (short-term solution), expendable (easily forgotten), low cost, mass produced, young (aimed at youth), witty, sexy, gimmicky, glamourous, big business."

Serious questions have been raised as to whether such cynical attitudes pose a danger to aesthetic ideals, whether these technically clever and imaginative prints, assembled through various photomechanical and hand-made operations, are indeed original artistic achievements or simply whimsical craftwork in which the medium has become the message. Former definitions of originality, wherein the artist envisioned the concept and fabricated the image, have changed as art forms have changed; the definition of art itself has had to accommodate itself to twentieth century innovations.

The recurring need to discover something new, to constantly offer works that are unprecedented or unique, has become a dilemma for many artists who find themselves running creative risks or taking precarious, and possibly false, positions. It is also a dilemma for the public, since Pop Art, like much contemporary work, is often impossible to understand without some explanation by the artist. Interest in personal qualities, where a connection between artist and sitter was encouraged, gave way to interest in generalities, to mechanical treatments and new techniques. Pop artists seem to be deliberately impersonal in their attitudes, portraying subjects whose individualities were closed off to them and to the viewer. What remained was physical confrontation stripped of the human factor, its chief aim to draw a round of applause. Yet popularity as a goal in itself remains shortsighted and naive. Victor Hugo called it "glory's small change." Hamilton's appeal, however, now appears broad enough to suggest that his experiments may have some durability.

English-born David Hockney, whose work will be taken up in greater detail in the next section, followed Hamilton's direction, but has transplanted Pop and other modern art styles to America. There they have led a charmed life amid the blessings of California sunshine and the fleshpots of Hollywood.

With the rejection of many traditional guidelines, much of what had been romantic and stately in English life, or lofty and grand in English art, has already disappeared, and with it, a deeply felt interest in human relationships; without that, and an awareness of soul and spirit, the exacting and distinctive character of English portraiture cannot survive. Yet it is entirely possible that David Hockney may revive that spirit and be its heir.

IV. America

Enormous social and economic changes took place in the world after 1900, but nowhere were they as extravagant or vigorous as in America. Large corporations came into existence, frequently greedy and oppressive, but instrumental in increasing the country's wealth and providing jobs for millions. Until their mutual needs could begin to be balanced, there were great struggles between newly formed labor unions and monolithic businesses. Department stores began to replace smaller establishments, inaugurating a new system of family shopping. Communication and transportation miracles, inventions and new technologies, all spurred by scientific advances, continued to make a tremendous impact. Powerful medical procedures prolonged life or at least made it less painful. Agricultural production responded to chemically advanced fertilizers and changed the way farmers harvested and people ate. When the internal combustion engine was perfected, new industries were born — automobiles, airplanes, and submarines, among others. The women's suffrage movement came and stayed; Prohibition came and went. Psychotherapy was the newest middle class panacea. Jazz grew up in New Orleans and developed into an indigenous American musical tradition. Entertainment became big business and Hollywood was to become the new Mecca. There could no longer be any doubt: The United States was now a world leader, flexing its might and enjoying its prosperity.

In the spring of 1915, when a German submarine sank the British ship *Lusitania* and one hundred and eighteen Americans aboard were drowned, a cry went up that it was America's destiny to make the world safe for democracy and her obligation to insure the rights of peace-seeking nations. "Right is more precious than peace," President Woodrow Wilson declared, and the public agreed with him. The entire country geared up for war and sent its allies millions of tons of material and millions of dollars in loans. Its sacrifice of over one hundred thousand lives finally helped to bring an end to the fighting. All told, many millions died or were wounded, but the world had merely been made safe for another twenty years. American leadership was not sufficient to solve the fundamental problems of nationalism, industrialization, and the lack of international trust. As usual, the victorious powers imposed a peace treaty that promised another war, and, in the years following, did nothing that might have given it a living chance.

From the post-war period until 1929 America went on a binge: Skyscrapers, bootleg whiskey, bobbed hair and the Charleston symbolized the pre-depression years. When the stock market crash came, it brought about the worst economic catastrophe in American history, and with it, a sense of lost innocence. Banks failed, the market system faltered, factories closed for want of customers. Franklin Roosevelt inaugurated his New Deal, and the country slowly came back from economic collapse by instituting broad legislative programs designed to benefit the jobless, to build new projects, and to help the farmers feed a demoralized nation. The Works Progress Administration (WPA) underwrote job opportunities for writers and artists and salvaged a generation of creative talent. Social Security benefits were established to meet unemployment and aging problems, labor unions organized to protect workers from exploitation in a country whose president declared that one-third of its people were "ill-nourished, ill-clad, and ill-housed."

Not everyone was happy with Roosevelt's formulas for national recovery. He was charged with producing a vast, unmanageable administration, a government that meddled intrusively in the lives of its citizens — a superstructure that has never stopped growing. But when Americans stood at the brink of hopelessness, Roosevelt told them that they had "nothing to fear but fear itself" — and they took heart.

The threats and oppression that were menacing Europe were answered in some quarters by pacifism and isolationism, but when on December 7, 1941, Japan attacked the American navy at Pearl Harbor, killing twenty-five hundred servicemen, the United States became partners with the Allies and fought another world war; perhaps never before were liberty and freedom so close to extinction. Many tens of millions of military and civilian dead and wounded were recorded worldwide, in addition to the largest genocide in history. America's share in these casualties numbered over a million, with a cost six times as much as that of World War I.

On May 8, 1945, Europe was freed. Atomic bombs on August 6 and 9 ended the war with Japan. Two cities, Hiroshima and Nagasaki, whose names alone will forever define their place in the history of destruction, almost perished. America now turned its strength and will towards helping to rebuild Europe through the generosity of the Marshall Plan, and imposed an ungrudging and humane treaty on Japan. But the philosophy that generated hopes of amicable coexistence in the United Nations was soon shattered in the acrimonious cold war between East and West. By 1950 control of Eastern Europe and China passed to Marxist systems of government. America's involvement in no-win wars in Korea and Vietnam resulted from fear of monolithic Communism.

When John Kennedy was elected president in 1961, finally breaching a century of anti–Catholicism, an aura of goodwill seemed to infuse the country. His assassination in 1963 coincided with a series of violent changes in the moral attitudes of the country. The civil rights movement forced Americans to deal with the inequitable treatment of its minority citizens. The scandal that precipitated President Richard Nixon's resignation in 1974, the women's movement, the sexual revolution, the breakdown of many traditional family structures, the widespread appeal of drugs at all social levels, and ecological questions, all have been felt deeply in the final third of the twentieth century, Threats of nuclear annihilation haunt a world that wonders if it will make it to the twenty-first.

We are all dancing on the same volcano.

When the artist Robert Henri returned to New York in 1900 from his studies in Europe he was determined to break with its Grand Manner tradition and usher in a modern American art style. He announced that "the big fight is on" against established ideas, and gathered around him a group of students and colleagues who made a reality of his vision. He was the most influential teacher in the first half of the century and promoted the exhibition of art representing daily life among the not-very-beautiful people: blue-collar workers and newly arrived immigrants typically seen on the streets, alongside grubby garbage cans, in the corner saloon, or at the elevated train stations. American Realists now began to depict individuals as they typically appeared. Their work was neither charged with the heavy emotional content of German Expressionism, drawn in the playful calligraphic French tradition, nor imbued with the elegance and refinement of romantic models in the Whistlerian mold.

Henri had studied painting in the 1890s in Philadelphia and Paris, where he was influenced both by the rugged naturalism of Gustave Courbet and the spontaneity of Frans Hals. (See Fig. 135) When his own works and those of several of his friends were rejected for exhibition in the prestigious National Academy of Design, they banded together as "the Eight" and turned their interests away from idealized formal decoration and their talents towards painting the New York urban scene, particularly in its more sordid aspects. In 1908, refusing to perpetuate the axiom that only the tasteful merited translation into art, these "Ashcan artists," as they were known, showed their work independently of the Academy, which had nothing but contempt for their squalid subject matter and crude force. As artistic reporters of the life style of the city, they chose a realistic point of view over fashionable splash and glitter. Their plain-speaking likenesses, presented without composed backgrounds or theatrical lighting, possessed great vitality and directness, replacing conventional society portraiture with an honest and open expressiveness that became the hallmark of big city art; outside of the metropolitan centers almost everyone was still quite provincial in both knowledge and taste.

The only serious printmaker among the Eight was John Sloan. As a founder of the Ashcan school and a follower of Robert Henri, he helped to develop the theme of Realism in printmaking, giving it characteristic intensity and energy. It was he who thought up the name Ashcan because it suggested the drabness of Greenwich Village slums. In his early years he was a newspaper and poster illustrator, and he trained himself to look at his subjects with objectivity. His attempts to capture ordinary daily experiences in his etching series *New York City Life* occasionally produced an awkward appearance, but straightforward drawing and the lack of affectation were more important to him than refined treatments, and gave his work a directness and validity that is very appealing. His best prints were highly original and unconventional — commonplace scenes in tenements, on roof tops, or in meeting places where he and his friends often gathered.

Fig. 233. John Sloan. *Copyist at the Metropolitan Museum*. Courtesy Whitney
Museum of American Art, New York.

He frequently incorporated portraits of himself, his family, and his
fellow artists taking advantage of the city's amusements, although he said
that the difficulty he had depicting those close to him made it necessary to
rework their faces innumerable times. However, he included himself and
his wife, Dolly, as wry observers in the etching *Copyist at the Metropolitan
Museum*, 1908, a mildly satirical but good-humored depiction of a sheep-
like crowd watching an artist reproduce a crowd of sheep. (Fig. 233) It is
worth noting that the painter is a woman. Degas had earlier portrayed the
artist Mary Cassatt in a museum setting; women, such as Peggy Bacon and
Isabel Bishop, were just beginning to find a place in the art world. (See Fig.
143) Sloan's quick, loose strokes caught a variety of facial expressions,
reflecting Henri's teaching that the impulsive, undeliberated line produces
the greatest immediacy. At the time critics considered such low-life scenes
uncouth and not fit subjects for art; for years Sloan hardly sold any work,
but claimed that he "regarded contemporary success as artistic failure." In
any case, his more.than three hundred unsentimental etchings, made over
many years, greatly influenced printmaking until World War II.

Sloan chose the Armory Regimental Building in New York for a
famous exhibition in 1913 because he felt it had a specifically American
identity. That event not only changed cultural patterns in the United

States, but eventually drew American and European art into a modern international school. For the first time American audiences were introduced to Gauguin, Cézanne, Picasso, van Gogh, and Munch, as well as to native-born artists such as Sloan, Whistler, Cassatt, George Bellows, and Edward Hopper. The organizers were well aware that the unfamiliar and often startling designs would require time and an open mind to be absorbed and accepted. The exhibition catalogue tried to ease the shock: "Art is a sign of life. There can be no life without change, as there can be no development without change. To be afraid of what is different or unfamiliar is to be afraid of life."

Nevertheless, most of the three hundred thousand spectators who jammed the shows in New York, and later in Chicago and Boston, could not swallow such a radical break with the past, and in what is by now a familiar scenario, charges of barbarism, quackery and immorality were hurled at many of the fifteen hundred or so items on display. Critics as well as the public were aghast. The featured attraction was Marcel Duchamp's outrageous *Nude Descending a Staircase*, a futuristic painting owing much of its inception to the camera's ability to freeze motion and represent movement through a rapid sequence of images. Those who came expecting to be titillated by the nude couldn't find her in this Cubistic rendering and went away disappointed or exasperated. A reporter remarked that the picture looked like an explosion in a slat factory. Like it or not, however, Modernism was here to stay. World War I interrupted its development, but once normalcy returned, the novelties of the Armory Show were gradually assimilated and incorporated into architecture, literature, the theater, and other aspects of cultural life.

At this point the movement split into two directions. One offshoot, in revolt against Impressionism and Post-Impressionism, adopted abstract elements which stressed balance, form, and color, irrespective of content, thus almost eliminating portraiture. The other, by far the more pervasive branch, maintained close ties with the recognizable image for another three decades. The majority of artists stayed with Realism because aesthetic principles associated with "truth to nature" and an enormous interest in psychology motivated them to probe and interpret the hidden and forbidden as they were mirrored in the human face. Realism persisted because it responded to what most people expected of art, in spite of the fact that the avant garde considered it more and more of an anachronism. Some critics thought Realism looked too far back to outmoded Roman ideals; others believed it was simply a lag or lack of understanding, a fear of the unknown, or a too-rigid commitment to old-fashioned values. For the average person in the leftist political climate of the 1930s, Abstract art seemed irrelevant to grim social problems, while Realism, ripening into Expressionism, appeared to have a connection with the class struggle through its sympathetic imagery of ordinary working people.

For whatever their reasons, many artists chose Realism, often resorting to unpolished or slashing lines, quickly sketched to capture and hold their initial inspiration. The style was compatible with their training in newspaper illustration and was based on the reporter's matter-of-fact observation. Through the wide dissemination of their prints, far more than their paintings, many of these artists provided access to a new spirit of authenticity, and educated the general population in current art trends as well. They had the field pretty much to themselves since most of the Abstract artists, particularly before 1960, felt that printmaking was not direct or spontaneous enough for them.

George Bellows was a pupil of Robert Henri, and although associated with the Eight, was not one of its members. His uninhibited and virile prints of sporting scenes were very much admired for their forcefulness, his frank and open portraits for their solid strength and intense emotional rapport with his sitters. The high quality of his experiments with lithography in 1916 helped to reinstate much of the medium's artistic credibility, lost through associations with commercial hack work. He recognized its unusual ability to imitate textures, but it was not until after 1920 that he made the most of its suitability for the factual, unaffected portrait style he favored. In 1923 to 1924, not very long before Bellows died from a ruptured appendix, his young daughter posed for the appealing lithograph *Jean*. (Fig. 234) The sincerity and earnestness in this composition make an interesting companion piece to Cassatt's equally sensitive *Sara Wearing her Bonnet and Coat*, and point up the striking differences between the more robust modern American and the gentler older European styles. (See Fig. 146)

When the depression struck, Ashcan Realism was superseded by Social Realism. Artists such as Thomas Hart Benton, Grant Wood, and John Steuart Curry began to depict small-town scenes far from the great population centers. (It was Benton's pupil Jackson Pollock, a Regionalist in the 1930s, who pioneered Abstract painting in the following decade.) Another branch of Social Realism depicted sorrow and loss of hope; rather than being portrayed in terms of its colorful tenement life, the city was now seen as an adversary. Poverty and loneliness were described with compassion, and occasionally with cynicism. The shock of severe unemployment and economic crises affected the viability as well as the whole spirit and focus of printmaking, as it did all the arts.

Fortunately, the United States government initiated a series of projects which remained in effect from 1933 to 1943, alleviating some of the hardships. The Works Progress Administration and other public and private organizations provided millions of dollars for studios all over the country; an estimated four thousand prints were made in that decade. WPA artists worked for ninety-five dollars a month with experienced printers, but since no real market existed for their output, few expectations were raised. Nevertheless, many lively experiments were made in lithography and wood cuts. Silkscreen especially was used to advantage; many WPA artists gave it a higher status than might have been predicted from its humble mercantile origins, where it was commonly used for posters and advertising. WPA programs also helped create an interest in print collecting. Membership societies and galleries such as the Associated American Artists were formed, which sold inexpensive prints by mail and in department stores, and foreshadowed the establishment of printmaking studios in the 1950s.

Thousands of artists took advantage of various support programs, through which the printmaking tradition was kept alive, although only a handful ever made much noise in the world. Ben Shahn, the WPA's most outstanding beneficiary, was a major success. He decorated numerous public and federal buildings with socially conscious murals, and turned out patriotic posters for the war effort. His family had emi-

Fig. 234. George Bellows. *Jean.* Courtesy Collection, Museum of Modern Art, New York, gift of Abby Aldrich Rockefeller.

grated to the United States when he was a child and already a junior scholar in Biblical studies. His love of Hebrew calligraphy became explicit in his later compositions. When asked why he became an artist, he speculated that a quotation from Ecclesiastes had a great impact on his choice of a career: "Wherefore I perceive that there is nothing better, than that a man should rejoice in his own works, for that is his portion."

Like many other Realists he was committed to leftist polemics at an early age and helped to kindle the American conscience by boldly confronting moral issues in his art. While growing up in New York's poorest neighborhoods, Shahn was stirred by the wretched troubles he saw around him and dedicated much of his talent to awakening a still, small voice in his generation. He was only twenty-two when the most sensational murder trial of the century began. Two Italian immigrants, one a shoemaker, the other a fish peddler, were accused of a payroll murder, their admitted radical politics inflaming the Massachusetts community where the killing took place. Their trial lasted from 1920 to 1927; many people believed they were found guilty of Socialism and anarchy rather than of murder, since the legal evidence against them was inconclusive. Shahn was among the thousands who raised an angry protest against their execution; his own passion was still burning thirty years after the fact in his serigraph *The Passion of Sacco and Vanzetti* in 1958. (Fig. 235) He presented the two men handcuffed but triumphant above a touching statement by Vanzetti that has established them as martyrs in the American liberal pantheon. With

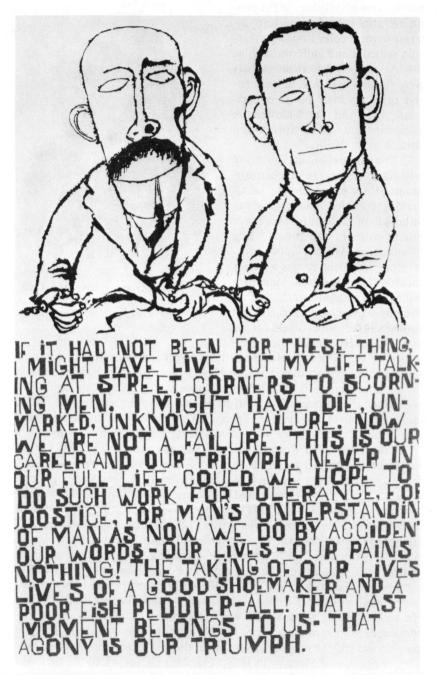

Fig. 235. Ben Shahn. *The Passion of Sacco and Vanzetti.* Courtesy Philadelphia Museum of Art, purchased from funds given by Dr. and Mrs. William Wolgin.

Fig. 236. Raphael Soyer. *Self-Portrait*. Courtesy Brooklyn Museum, gift of Mr. Samuel Goldberg in memory of his parents, Sophie and Jacob Goldberg, and his brother, Hyman Goldberg.

a stringy, almost child-like outline, he reinforced their message by drawing their simplified bodies small and flat and their heads oversized, suggesting that their deep-rooted principles were of greater significance than their physical attributes.

Another artist who expressed a great sympathy for the poor was Raphael Soyer, also employed by the WPA. He was a year younger than Shahn, likewise nurtured in the Ashcan school, and, as a mature artist, similarly concerned with the catastrophic effect that the economic upheaval was having on American culture; it left him with a pessimism and fear that were embodied in his prints. He was born and spent his childhood in Russia and then settled with his family in the Lower East Side of New York where he and his brothers, Moses and Isaac, took to sketching the local attractions, particularly as they were affected by the encompassing poverty. His deeply introspective vision exemplified one of the psychological tenets of the 1930s — the cult of the lonely and alienated man in the midst of a crowd. By 1933, when he lithographed an unidealized *Self-Portrait*, the full impact of the depression mentality was vividly and movingly rendered with a Rembrandtesque sensitivity. (Fig. 236) Like the German Expressionists, he was able to communicate estrangement; but his mood, revealed in the half-lidded eyes and slack jaw, was quietly sober rather than vehement or brutal. He didn't break new ground in his technical means — his tones and line quality are reminiscent of Degas and other Impressionists, and he followed the Realist tradition in his later work — but his very personal prints have a trenchant appeal as well as social and political interest.

Once the depression ended, the propaganda value of Social Realism became less relevant and other themes took precedence. The progressive spirit of native American artists such as Jackson Pollock and Mark Tobey contributed a welcome lift, with their vivid dribbles and splashes, to fatigued and weary emotions barely recovering from the depression. Their accidental or random styles of applying paints, resulting in works of art supposedly controlled by the unconscious mind, emphasized the physical and psychological moment of creativity — the moment of artistic impulse.

When it became clear that war was imminent, a group of European artists, including Hans Hofmann, Josef Albers, and Piet Mondrian, established themselves in the United States, chiefly in New York. As much as was consciously possible, subject matter was eliminated in favor of design elements. They developed different formulae in art, particularly the hard-edged, bright colors and new structural ideas of Abstract Expressionism. The influx and competition of European painters, writers, and musicians challenged the level of competence of Americans, diversified and broadened their creative skills, and motivated them to explore revolutionary new visual and technical effects. Europe was no longer the hub of artistic life; the most dynamic work was being done in the United States, where an international style evolved. By the late 1950s, government, industry, and museum support, together with serious public patronage, made New York the new cultural capital of the world.

Many artists found a professional haven after 1940 at S. W. Hayter's Atelier 17 workshop in New York, which he maintained until his return to France in 1950. Hayter resurrected engraving from long years of oblivion, integrated it with other media, and gave it a new lease on life. He was an inspired conduit for the Surrealist sources of Abstract Expressionism, although he attracted criticism for stressing technical means and haphazard lines at the expense of composition and ideas.

One member of Hayter's group, Mauricio Lasansky, an émigré from Argentina, later became a highly charismatic teacher and artist at the University of Iowa. He required scrupulously candid self-portraits from his students in order to train their eyes to "see reality without fear." He depended heavily on his family and himself for subject matter in his own prints, which were not literal images by any means, but they possessed an intensity which gave them great force. Like Picasso and Goya, with whom he shared an Hispanic birthright, he was very attracted to portraiture.

When Abstract Expressionists began to produce huge paintings, Lasansky competed for the available wall space with very large prints. He remained highly committed to figurative work, although Abstraction was making the greatest

Fig. 237. Mauricio Lasansky. *Self-Portrait*. Courtesy Brooklyn Museum.

impact on American art. His melancholy *Self-Portrait* in profile, 1957, a combination of engraving, drypoint, and etching, is almost a yard high. (Fig. 237) The nervous grip and the set of the jaw provide an indication of his obsessive personality. The print is about head and hands, and about shapes — the sinuous curve from the back of his neck to his waist and the rotundity of his belly. While graceful in their linearity, in the context of the deliberately unlovely silhouette of bowed shoulder and bloated paunch, their significance and rhythm undergo subtle changes as we watch the magic sleight-of-hand of the artist playing fast and loose with our perceptions: Is that an elegant line or simply a humped back? Is beauty absolute regardless of the setting?

While most of the printmakers in the second half of the twentieth century were primarily painters, Leonard Baskin's favored medium has been sculpture, though his prints are equally well done and he has produced important humanistic works in other categories, including literature. His early education was rabbinical, after which he trained in New York, at Yale, and at the obligatory art centers in Europe, where the works of Goya, Rouault, and Kollwitz stimulated his imagination. His artistic themes range from Talmudic questions on the meaning of man's role in the universe to the lamentations of the Biblical prophets, to whom he appears not too distantly related. There is a fundamental correlation between his creations and the great questions of life and death. The tensions and

Fig. 238. Leonard Baskin. *Self-Portrait*. Courtesy Library of Congress, Washington, D.C.

vexations of his personality emerge in his woodcut *Self-Portrait*, 1952, an indomitable character study very much in the spirit of German Expressionism, made when he was twenty-nine. (Fig. 238) The vulnerability of the interior man explodes like forks of lightning on the face; the thunderbolts are repeated on his coat. His reproving look is boldly expressed, with the linear severity and heavy blacks of the head depicting veins and nervous system rather than muscle and flesh. The contrast to the dead-white background creates a stark and dramatic image.

Lasansky's and Baskin's interest in portraiture ran counter to the post–World War II affinity for Abstract Expressionism and to some extent, Surrealism, which appealed to the artistically ecumenic generation of the 1940s and 1950s. Figurative art was still alive and well in the hands of Picasso, Chagall, Matisse, and other senior artists, but Abstract art was increasingly sought after by sophisticated connoisseurs on both sides of the Atlantic, possibly because non-organic shapes were less threatening to the human mind than was the human form. Two world wars, atomic bombs, and the real possibility of self-annihilation were fears that might easily have turned the public away from portraiture and the flawed human spirit.

When World War II was over, the American G.I. Bill provided educational opportunities for millions of returning servicemen and -women, many of whom had seen great art for the first time. Art appreciation courses in universities and museums catered to their interests, and soon many began to buy art works. During that period, fine paintings became increasingly prohibitive in price, and as a result many of these new collectors were forced to turn to prints. In addition, travel for pleasure, exposure to television, an eagerness to become more international in outlook, turned many neophytes into instant cosmopolites, at least to the extent that increased means and leisure command worldliness. Unfortunately, with the enormous renewed interest in the arts and the availability of large amounts of public and private money for collecting, the art community became vulnerable to the merchandising market, with all the clap-trap and skills of promotional advertising. Printmaking became more successful as an unabashed commercial speculation than it had ever been as a fine art.

Madison Avenue was one of the arbiters of what was art and who was chic. The over-confident novice, with a smattering of knowledge, was beguiled and too often misled by an army of managers, press-agents, self-styled and frequently unqualified "experts," or plainly dishonest print publishers who dominated the business. The combined exuberance of printmakers and tastemakers led to a boom in print buying in the 1960s that was unprecedented, as modern marketing techniques began to exploit a legitimate pent-up demand for art. A somewhat similar boom had occurred earlier in the century, particularly in England, when etchings were subscribed for even before artists finished their plates or had a chance to calculate their profits. It had been a heady experience for all concerned, lasting until 1929 when the Wall Street crash scattered the etching market to the winds. Unfortunately, then as well as in the 1960s, a large amount of indiscriminate work appeared for sale, valued mostly because of its high prices or name recognition. Some artists didn't know or didn't care, in their eagerness to produce merchandise, that each of the various printmaking methods had its optimal use—that perhaps a particular medium might be mismatched with the style or subject matter of the proposed work.

Very few buyers knew much about how prints are made or what constitutes good style. The fact that signed photomechanical reproductions of drawings or paintings were being offered as original works and priced accordingly was unsuspected by many collectors. Such prints were actually replicas or facsimiles and posed significant ethical and artistic problems that have yet to be fully resolved. Hosts of imitative printmakers were touted as the next Picassos, but when investors attempted to place their prints on the market they discovered that there was no market for them; while prints are periodically put up for auction, items by artists without established sales records are usually not accepted. Some fine work did emerge, but as soon as a significant innovative artist was discovered, along came the followers, technically capable of mimicry and mockery.

Many of these modern prints, with relatively low prices and relatively large sizes, were well suited to office buildings and homes; they became the darlings of interior decorators and were chosen, like wallpaper, according to how well they matched upholstery patterns. The momentum of print buying was also fueled by museum and university administrators who were initiating popular exhibits and print courses that required study collections. This again drove up prices, since art that disappears into institutions seldom comes back onto the market. When the boom ended in the late 1970s with the worldwide economic recession, demand for a great deal of contemporary material collapsed.

On the brighter side, it must be recognized that printmaking for a time was almost the only refuge for those who believed in content and the figure. Some vital and important contributions emerged from university departments. With greater maturity, there was a shake-out of the absurd, renewed interest in fine craftsmanship began to replace stunts, and there was a return to line, form, and integrity in both Abstract and Representational art. Criteria for connoisseurship were tightened and made more accessible to the public, as for example in Paul J. Sachs' book *Modern Prints and Drawings*, in which information basic to the understanding and appreciation of contemporary art was offered. We should keep an "open attitude" about work of the twentieth century, he says, and test each example with these questions: "Is there structural clarity of form? Is there clear distinction of planes? Is there flexibility and sensitiveness of touch? Is there expressiveness? Is there artistic economy? Is there originality of concept?"

Only future scholars, having the luxury of hindsight, will be able to sort through the profusion and publicity and determine how much was hype, how much was quality, and who among the younger printmakers will have followed Sachs' clues, becoming, perhaps, the leaders of their generation. Therefore, in discussing contemporary artists, it is reasonable to cite not only those who have real excellence or a current vogue and saleability, but also a few who may have lesser reputations, but are nevertheless producing sensitive and interesting prints.

The great upsurge in recent printmaking was largely initiated by June Wayne's Tamarind Lithography Workshop, funded by the Ford Foundation, and by Tatyana Grosman's Universal Limited Art Editions (ULAE) in New York. In the 1960s these studios provided a place where artists could find distinguished teachers and enthusiastic patronage, as well as the tools and equipment to execute intricate, high-quality prints. Students and established artists, encouraged to produce works of art at their own pace, turned out excellent prints at these and similar facilities.

While much of this output was non-representative, the trend in the Post-Abstract period slowly began to change as artists became less concerned that figurative work restricted or narrowed their options. Most portrait artists are indebted to Jean Dubuffet and others in Europe who, in the 1940s, once again created meaningful art, celebrating or submitting to the human predicament. Much European work, charged with psychological implications, had to do with anti-rational and Surrealist concepts, while the post-war American school generally avoided mystical elements. America was the most logical place for a renewed interest in portraiture. Neither the Ashcan nor the Pop Art schools, both of which valued skill and verisimilitude, had rebelled against traditional art forms. America seemed to have the chief element necessary for portraiture to flourish — a healthy societal egotism which presumes that man is worthy of remembrance, or, at least, that he is sufficiently attractive to hand his features down to posterity. In 1962 Congress recognized the public's attraction to portraiture and authorized the creation of the National Portrait Gallery in Washington, D.C.

Yet, apart from celebrities, this interest appears to be rather limited, perhaps owing to the increasing impersonalization of modern life. Self-portraits are probably the most prevalent type of likenesses, but even most of those hardly represent a search for deep meaning or psychological insights; often they are simply repetitive and self-aggrandizing. Nevertheless, there still are artists whose appreciation of humanistic values draws them to the investigation of their own species. They continue to work within self-imposed constraints, always seeking originality, though not at the expense of honesty, and knowing that novelty by itself is a threat to true creativity.

Robert Rauschenberg was one of the first mid-century artists to commit himself to figurative work, abandoning Abstract Expressionism because he may have perceived it as too elitist. He is a native Texan who was trained as a painter, and later pioneered in electronic recording as an adjunct to art, as well as performing occasionally in dance companies. In the 1950s he began to create paintings and assemblages out of commonplace elements, altering their content until they no longer appeared familiar or obvious. He incorporated apparently meaningless objects and trash in order to affect their visceral appeal and to train the eye to respond to unorthodox textures. These three-dimensional "combines," he believed, established a functional continuity between art and life experiences.

In 1962 he worked on lithographs and silkscreen prints at Grosman's ULAE. Some of his images, taken directly from the media, were of sports figures or contemporary newsmakers such as Robert and John Kennedy; in this context he was a forerunner of Pop Art. The use of easily recognizable commercial material which he combined in his prints helped to revive public interest in art after a bewildering experience with Abstraction, which most people never quite accepted or understood. However, Rauschenberg himself was also difficult to interpret because, like much

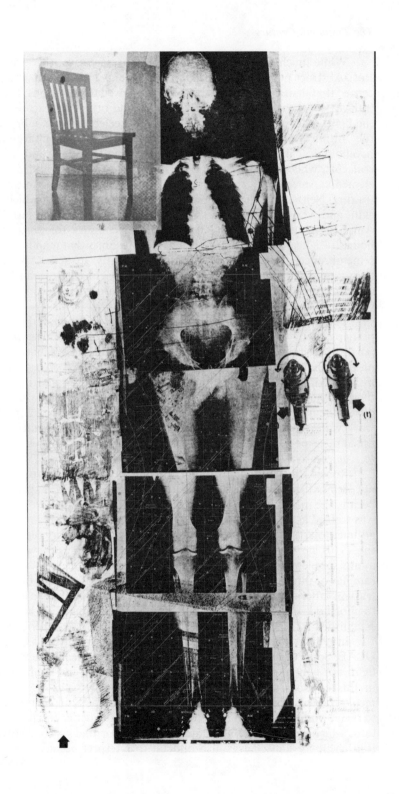

unprecedented art, his work was cast in an incongruous mold. Merging arbitrarily chosen images and forcing photography and various printing processes into unaccustomed partnerships were his ways of acknowledging the inconsistencies of twentieth century values.

His interest in special hand-made papers, unconventional materials, and photomechanical processes which gave radical camera techniques a legitimacy in the making of prints, focused attention on formal rather than human qualities. *Booster*, a color lithograph and silkscreen of 1967, is made up of X-ray negatives of his own body, which he linked with seemingly irrelevant items such as a photograph of a chair and an astrological chart, reflecting discontinuity both in his life and in his art style. (Fig. 239) This print has become a symbol of external stimuli impinging on the internal man. It is six feet tall and the last word in objective composition. While it is more of an impersonal self-document than a self-portrait, like some of his other works it marked another step in the growing figurative approach to art.

Alex Katz was born in Brooklyn and received his education in New York and Maine. He is basically a figural painter who derived some of his flat, linear and unmodeled style from Matisse and Gauguin. His large prints, readily understood and requiring no high-brow knowledge or insight, were a relief to those who were anxious to relate to an easily comprehensible art. Like the Pop prints of the 1960s, his works were rejections of Abstraction. As curator Richard Marshall of New York City's Whitney Museum put it, "he reconciled abstraction and realism in post–World War II America." He frequently placed his well-groomed models against a nondescript background, their eyes averted from a meaningful confrontation with the viewer. In his lithograph of the poet Kenneth Koch, 1970, while the eyes do meet the spectator's, there remains in the cropped head, brought far forward, an unemotional self-imposed remoteness which denies two-way communication. (Fig. 240) "I'd like to have style take the place of content, or the style be the content," Katz says. "I prefer it to be emptied of meaning, emptied of content." This rejection of psychological relationship between artist and subject implies a disinterested art, which in turn risks translation into uninteresting art. However, Katz's work is rescued by its strong lighting, hard-edged shadows and other design elements. Its shallow billboard or comic strip unreality, lack of modeling, and sense of transience are expressed in an immaterial, almost disembodied manner. The isolation and anonymity of contemporary life are unmistakably suggested in his impenetrable stereotyped faces, from which he purposely withheld any natural appearance. His portraits were geared to immediate recognition, which was one reason why they, as well as all Pop Art, attracted such wide public interest. "I have a weakness for painting beautiful people," he wrote. "The portrait form is where the challenge is."

Opposite: Fig. 239. Robert Rauschenberg. *Booster*. Courtesy Gemini G.E.L., Los Angeles, Calif. (© 1967).

Fig. 240. Alex Katz. *Kenneth Koch*. Courtesy Brooke Alexander, Inc.

Pop was generally accepted as a legitimate art style even though the cheerful primary colors of its images were simply recreations of soup cans, newspaper clippings, comic strips, or photographs. Actually it was a clever example of reproductive printmaking, with precedents reaching back to the 1930s when a similar interest in commonplace images represented the American experience. As a cult devoted to celebrities, Pop lent itself to portraiture, although its treatments had more to do with surface pattern than with the human situation; faces were simply neat and impersonal arrangements. The case for individuality was fast becoming an endangered point of view. Method counted more than character or likeness, the system itself having priority over perception. Pop was a significant formula, however, because its intentions accurately reflected the conflicts and ambiguities of the times in which it developed. Its conventionalized linear designs, ritually flattened to destroy volume and mass, trivialized the mock-heroic leaders of contemporary society into aloof or superficial symbols, denying them an existence in the real world. Sharp-edged patterns and strongly defined boundaries give their figures a wooden appearance, an artistic perception that had long been known and was noted by Leonardo da Vinci among others.

Of all the popular cultural phenomena of the 1960s, Andy Warhol was the best known, and through his self-promotional hi-jinks, the most flashy of the lot. His parents emigrated to the United States from Czechoslovakia, after which he became an art student at the Carnegie Institute of Technology in Pittsburgh. Soon he was putting his ideas to work for the advertising departments of Lord and Taylor, I. Miller Shoe Company, and other prestigious stores. In the 1960s, he replicated Campbell soup cans, Brillo boxes, and other ready-made items from newspaper and magazine ads, transforming banal illustrations into a type of objective art. His images were silkscreened in a flat, two-dimensional format, intended to be carefully examined and reappraised outside of their obvious utilitarian contexts. As part of the mass cultural environment, he wanted the items, as they existed, to become instant experiences.

Many of his subjects were movie stars or members of the glamour world. Neither their mystique nor their celebrity fazed him; he, too, was a high-powered member of the upper ten thousand. The impact of his personality was so strong that in 1968 a woman acquaintance shot and nearly killed him because she feared that he controlled her. However, in spite of an extravagant life-style, he maintained a steady, though possibly misunderstood, interest in portraiture, one of the first contemporary artists to do so. His *10 Marilyns*, 1967, which represent the actress simply as articles of commerce, were derived from greatly enlarged photographs. (Fig. 241) He then intensified their brash coloring and stenciled them in the silkscreen process, purposely mis-registering their outlines to express scorn of the shoddy techniques that passed for artistry. They were produced as a series, varying only in their colors and lighting. Miss Monroe appears in gaudy repetition, each print a yard square, each the same and yet more unnatural and morbid than the last until they are all monotonous and inanimate perversions of reality. "The single, stable portrait of an individual has little significance," the Irish painter Louis le Brocquoy has commented, "conditioned as we are by photography, the cinema, and the insights of psychology to view that individual as multi-faceted and kinetic." Warhol's preoccupation with multiple representations of banal images eventually resulted in diminished communication with the viewer, and led, not only to depersonalization, but to surfeit.

By reducing the individual to a blurred cliché, Warhol suppressed psychological interaction between himself and his subjects, cynically

Fig. 241. Andy Warhol. *Marilyn Monroe*. Courtesy Whitney Museum of American Art, New York.

expressing the artificial values of his generation and the tedium of mass culture. It was his intention to move printmaking in new directions. Although he would typically oversee the final arrangement of his work, he did not do the serigraphy himself, relying on craftspeople to do the hand work; actually this is a common procedure in printmaking history. However, for Warhol, rejecting the idea of original printmaking as developed and executed by the artist, and distancing himself from his creations, was basically part of his philosophy, not simply a conservation of time and effort. When his work was accused of appearing mechanically inspired and produced, he was the first to concede that he would like to be a machine.

He knew that public taste is drawn to novelty and shock and profitably manipulated that notion to his own ends. However, Barbara Rose, a perceptive art critic, has suggested a deeper meaning to his work: "Certainly Warhol's grotesque portraits of his patrons ... will stand as an indictment of American society in the sixties as scathing as Goya's merciless portraits of the Spanish court . . . this irony has escaped most of the nouveau-riche collectors who rejoiced in owning the art that mocked them." Warhol, who had a great sense of the ridiculous, denied any significance at all to his art or any importance to the limelight. He stated that someday soon, everyone will be famous for fifteen minutes. Perhaps he knew himself best of all.

Like Warhol's portraits, those of Chuck Close exist in a totally anonymous environment; whatever human interest or personal qualities they have are swallowed up by their monumental size and sacrificed to a formal system and technology. Close was born during World War II and received his art training at the University of Washington and at Yale. Among his early influences was Abstract painting; later he searched for a realistic style that he could call his own. In his prints, he found it in greatly blown-up portraits, photographed head-on like an I.D. card, then reproduced onto a metal plate over which he superimposed a grid-like pattern. They have been described as meticulous computer printouts or graph-paper designs, and could serve very well as giant paint-it-yourself kits, their little boxes subtly filled in with colors or tones ranging from white to black. He said he was "trying to nail down that frozen moment in time. I wanted the thrust to come from the way all the incremental bits stack to build something powerful and aggressive."

Originally conceived as paintings up to nine feet tall, they are among the largest prints ever made: The mezzotint of his friend Keith, 1972, is about three by four feet, its grid network not as clearly indicated as in some of his other works, although the squares are still visible. (Fig. 242) Because of its size, the traditional mezzotint technique could not be used; rather than scraping up a burr, minute dots had to be photographed and etched on the plate, after which Close proceeded to burnish the surface in the time-honored manner.

He strengthened the anti-expressive elements of Pop Art further than ever, disintegrating human character and manipulating structural elements to an extreme degree. However, he did not find his subjects in the popular arena, but rather among his acquaintances and in the mirror; also unlike Pop, his prints are not silkscreened, but etched or mezzotinted. His aim was not to satirize celebrity worship, but to suggest that in the post–Vietnam period, complacency had deteriorated into insensibility and apathy. His self-portraits are the antithesis of vitality, rejecting energy, mood, temperament, and even self-awareness. They confront the viewer with a trance-like torpor, their huge dimensions paralyzing emotional response. Though these images may appear to be mindless perfunctory statements, they are in fact an internalized cry against twentieth century impersonality, fear of namelessness, and the inability to communicate in a modernist age.

Jim Dine was born in the midst of the depression. He grew up and completed his formal education in Ohio, after which he lived in New York and London before settling in Vermont. Both Abstract Expressionism and

Fig. 242. Chuck Close. *Keith II*. Courtesy Pace Editions, Inc.

Pop Art contributed to his interest in "assemblages," which he wrought from wood, metal, painted canvases, and other ordinary objects. Although he started working as early as 1960 in Grosman's ULAE, it wasn't until 1970 that he began to concentrate seriously on printmaking. His most characteristic image, first introduced in his prints in 1965 and repeated in successive paintings and prints, is an empty dressing-gown, neatly belted, drawn with arms akimbo. The idea of entirely withdrawing his person came to him in 1964 from a magazine advertisement, after which it became his logo and a symbol of lost presence and individuality. One of these self-portraits, *Yellow Robe*, 1980, a lithograph printed in three colors, typically was a commentary about non-attendance at his own life, a Surrealist approach in which the man himself is concealed inside an otherwise straightforward object. (Fig. 243)

Among Dine's other trademarks were sets of hardware tools and paint brushes, used as references to his family's business, but also treated as phallic images. Like the untenanted bathrobes, they were dehumanized substitutes or private disguises for himself, somewhat in the Pop tradition, though more painterly and introspective. He has continued to invest his robes with human personalities, but as he entered his prime they lost much of their vicarious and Pop qualities and became simply dressing gowns. He said that much of his earlier avant garde work was born of immaturity, and that he had been caught up by fame and notoriety at too young an age.

By 1972 he decided it was time to promote a real existence for himself—to expose his face and divulge its vulnerability, although he continued to alternate the bathrobe with more recognizable likenesses. At first he could barely allow himself any public revelation: a drypoint *Self-Portrait Head* slides off the bottom of the picture, leaving the top two-thirds empty of any image. By placing the head below the center of the composition, Dine was immediately successful in creating a depressive or hopeless mood. However, in the etching and drypoint *Self-Portrait with Glasses in Sepia*, 1978, the head fills the entire plate, now almost pushing itself out of its cramped confinement. (Fig. 244) The intensely drawn features, softened by the etching process, exist in a shallow depth in

Fig. 243. Jim Dine. *Yellow Robe*. Courtesy Pace Editions, Inc.

contrast to the flat-looking sharp edges of the '60s. When Dine was asked what his most important concern was as a printmaker, he answered, "Subject matter. The depiction of the human face is at the top of the hierarchy of subject matter—because it is the depiction of ourselves." His work in the 1970s helped to mark an important artistic transition, the reinstatement of human qualities as well as formal ones. Although he began his career with symbolic portraiture, his later images are no longer totally artificial constructs or caricatures on which a set of mannerisms have been imposed.

This more personalized approach to portraiture was reinforced by David Hockney, an Englishman who found a niche for himself in the

Fig. 244. Jim Dine. *Self-Portrait with Glasses in Sepia*. Courtesy Pace Editions, Inc.

laid-back ambiance of Southern California. He said he loved the socially permissive, glamorous lifestyle which encouraged art forms that could easily be grasped by a trendy public. His early Pop designs were epitomized by the palm trees and swimming pools of Hollywood, but he developed into a dexterous portrait specialist, concentrating on erotic male nudes; later he etched famous artist and writer friends in a return to a more academic manner. His lithograph *Henry Reading Newspaper*, 1976–1977, somewhat reminiscent of Whistler's sparing and subtle use of line, depicts Henry Geldzahler, a former curator and commissioner of cultural affairs in New York. (Fig. 245) The use of the sitter's first name in the title is an indication of Hockney's informal approach to art.

Hockney's interest lay not only in the modeling of the cheek, but in the self-contained quality of Henry's personality; the hands, legs, and newspaper are merely suggested. The narrow color chart at the right edge, which casts the only shadow, adds an extra dimension to the print, as does the cut-off leg which moves the figure to the foreground and adds the illusion of volume and perspective. Here Hockney repudiates Pop Art's remoteness and hard-edged technique and shares with Dine a renewed accent on the psychological image. "Portraits aren't just made up of drawing," he said, "they are made up of other insights as well." Yet the simplicity and quiet isolation of the figure, set in an unspecified background and ignoring the viewer, still retains impersonal Pop associations. While Hockney sometimes avoids decisiveness and conviction in his portraits, his contour lines are sensitively differentiated with reference to heavy or light strokes, indicating a greater concentration on calligraphy and direct observation than on technical wizardry. Although occasionally too facile, he is an extraordinarily talented draftsman and innovative artist. Since the early '80s, he has applied something of Picasso's broken focus to a group of photocollages, piecing together snippets of his own camera work. "There are a hundred separate looks across time," he observed, "from which I synthesize my living impression of you."

Beginning in the 1960s, pluralism in art, as well as in society, effected sweeping changes. An unexpected emergence of nostalgia began to revive

Fig. 245. David Hockney. *Henry Reading Newspaper*. Courtesy Brooke Alexander, Inc.

an almost vanished romantic interest in portraiture; outmoded notions seem to pop up again sooner or later as the avant-garde. Artists were readier to accept a wider variety of styles and techniques. Different media were explored. Three-dimensional compositions, made up of molded plastics and conventional lithography, were included in the definition of prints; painterly and linear, abstract and representational, intellectual and intuitive approaches, all were pursued. Life-style choices, particularly for women, were influenced by the growing feminist movement. Women were constantly re-examining their roles and seeking new opportunities for themselves. June Wayne and Tatyana Grosman had already moved into the mainstream of the art world. Without their determination and will, the lithographic revival could never have occurred. Their studios altered the

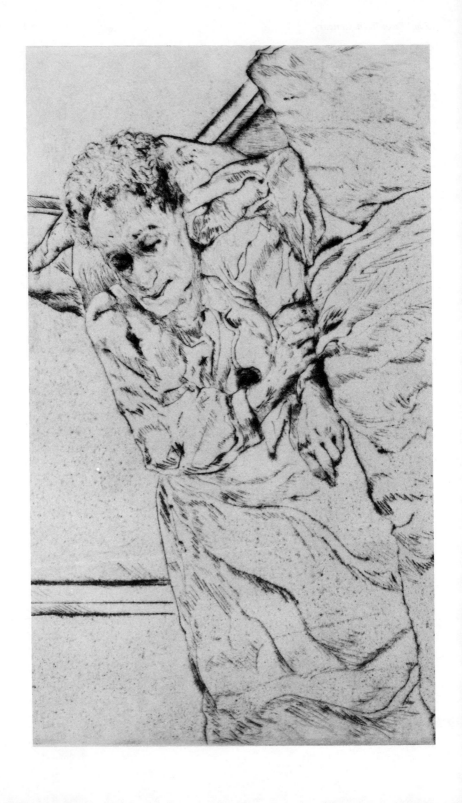

course of printmaking in America and helped to establish the United States as front-runner in modern art. It is hard to believe that only a little over a hundred years ago, because she wished to become an artist, Mary Cassatt had found it necessary to leave her home in Pennsylvania to avoid tarnishing the reputation of her family.

In the 1970s and 1980s many women achieved recognition in the art world, often specializing in a humanistic approach to the figure. Joyce Treiman, primarily a painter, is also a sculptor and printmaker. Originally from Chicago, she now lives in the Los Angeles area. She acquired a sense of social consciousness from her mother, Rose Wahl, with whom her life was in a great measure intertwined. Her early work included the currently favored styles of Abstraction and romantic Expressionism; when she turned to figure painting in the 1960s, it was with some trepidation because that was "frowned upon and very bad news." Her graphic work, which spans four decades, was influenced by nineteenth century French and early twentieth century American artists. Most of her prints were made in very small editions and are therefore not widely known, but they exhibit a sureness of hand and an ability to measure character and personality. The 1974 drypoint *Portrait of Rose* was made two years before her mother's death. (Fig. 246) In spite of an obvious deep emotional component, Treiman carefully observed academic and structural design elements, balancing the diagonal composition with the vertical uprights behind the bed. The meager body appears wasted, but the sense of control, as well as of affection, is fully affirmed in the large and powerful head.

Ruth Weisberg grew up in Chicago and received her training at the University of Michigan. After a year at S. W. Hayter's Atelier 17 in Paris, she moved to the University of Southern California, where she has taught figure drawing and printmaking, stressing draftsmanship as well as technique. Since the late 1960s when she joined the feminist movement, she has adopted autobiographical material, portraits of her family and friends, and depictions of her own body as expressive statements. Her prints reflect a type of Surrealism that has not appeared in many art works of the 1980s. The complex lithograph *Tableau*, 1983, is linked to a series of her paintings in which the metaphysical aspect of the sacred and profane images is emphasized. (Fig. 247) At left, in a self-portrait, Weisberg suggests the sheltering repository of traditional knowledge and hard-won experience. On the right sits the embodiment of the unregenerate worldling of the postmodern era, a portrait of Linda Burnham, theatrical artist and editor of *High Performance* magazine. The two symbols fuse in the fantasies of Weisberg's central figure — Ms. Burnham again — emerging from an ambiguous backdrop, endowed with transcendent visions that must be resolved before they can come into existence.

The synthesis of traditional and contemporary values suggests a new attitude in art and perhaps in life as well. More and more works are being

Opposite: Fig. 246. Joyce Treiman. *Portrait of Rose.* Collection of the artist.

produced in the 1980s that foster and encourage emotions. Following the period of the 1960s and 1970s, which often suppressed personal content, the latter years of the twentieth century appear to reaffirm the impulse to strong and meaningful responses. If artists continue to explore and rediscover the human spirit, portraiture, as an attempt to understand and investigate human nature, may yet undergo a dramatic rehabilitation.

For over five hundred years man's essence has been made explicit in the printed portrait. Character and personality have probably not changed much, but the perception of how people appear to each other has been remarkably diverse. Given the almost infinite possibilities in the facial map, can we expect even further creative permutations and combinations in coming generations? After Dürer, Rembrandt, Nanteuil, Whistler, Matisse, Picasso, Heckel, and the best printmakers of the post–World War II era, will there be anything left for the artists of the next five centuries?

We might as well ask if there are any more new tunes in the octave or any more new shapes in the fashion world. Just when we think that artists have exhausted their inventive potential, undreamed-of geniuses will surely emerge to find something different, promising, and fascinating—perhaps even ennobling—in the continuing search for expressive meaning as one human being looks at another.

Opposite: Fig. 247. Ruth Weisberg. *Tableau*. Collection of the artist.

Appendix

Collecting Portraiture in Prints

There are many considerations that influence print collectors. Connoisseurs look for the quality of the printed surface, whether the lines or tones are pristine or faded and worn, evenly or defectively printed; the physical condition of the paper is also taken into account, particularly since the mid-nineteenth century, when destructive wood fibers were added to its manufacture; whether the margins have been trimmed and if so, by how much; whether there are stains, creases, abrasions, folds, tears, or worm holes; whether there is a seal of a famous collector (usually stamped on the back); and whether the paper bears a watermark (not always present). The quality of the particular impression as it compares with other examples of the same image must be evaluated, and its historical significance assessed. The rarity of an important print, as well as its state or sequence in the printing process, dramatically affects its value.

Photoprinted copies for book illustrations in no way give an adequate idea of the quality of the actual prints. All the nuances of the slightly raised lines that are intrinsic to intaglio or incised plates are destroyed, the strength and depth of the impressions from relief cuts are eliminated, and the tonal qualities of the lithographic stone or silkscreen are distorted. Particularly in older prints, the texture and color of the paper itself, which contribute greatly to the appearance of the original works, are also lost in the photoprint process.

The practice of pencil signing and numbering below the image dates only from the time of Seymour Haden and James Whistler in the latter nineteenth century. Numbers are indicated as a fraction, i.e., 5/30, meaning that a total of thirty impressions were taken in that particular edition and this is the fifth copy annotated. These numbers do *not* guarantee that there are no further editions, that the impression is the fifth actually taken from the plate or stone, or that its quality is necessarily finer than the one which is numbered 30/30, since in the interval between printing and signing, the sheets are usually disarranged as they are handled.

Reading, and looking at as many originals as possible, are the best ways to learn; there are scores of books to be had, although many are out of print and must be searched for. Most curators, teachers, dealers, or fellow collectors are happy to answer questions. These experts have an extensive knowledge of paper, restoration, ways of detecting fraud, histories of sales, how to read catalogues, and the sources of information on particular artists.

Prints for sale may be found at dealers' shops and at auction houses or through their mailed catalogues. Subscriptions are available to periodicals such as the *Print Collectors' Newsletter*, 72 Spring St., New York, New York 10012, or the *Journal of the Print World*, 1000 Winona Road, Meredith, New Hampshire 03253. Reasonably current lists of museums, print clubs, and print dealers can be found in *Fine Prints: Collecting, Buying, and Selling* by Cecile Shapiro and Lauris Mason, Harper & Row, Publishers, 1976.

Prices do not always reflect or determine quality. The most desirable examples are indeed beyond the aspirations of most collectors, but fine portraits, as well as other subjects, are still available for less than one hundred dollars; superb pieces can be bought for considerably less than a thousand. Not only artistic merit, but also condition, rarity, and fashion dictate the cost as in anything else. The value of most prints increased spectacularly during the 1960s and 1970s, and more moderately since then; portraits, in many cases, are still undervalued. Recent prices for a random selection of the illustrations in this book are given below, but they are only very general indications. The price for two impressions of the same image can easily vary by 50 percent or more according to the criteria discussed above.

Max Beckmann: *Self-Portrait* (Fig. 218) $4000.
Barthel Beham: *Ferdinand I* (Fig. 33) $500.
George Bellows: *Jean* (Fig. 234) $1600.
Gerald Brockhurst: *Adolescence* (Fig. 230) $10,000.
Leonard Gaultier: *Jeanne d'Albret* (Fig. 54) $35.
Richard Hamilton: *Portrait of the Artist by Francis Bacon* (Fig. 232) $600.
Erich Heckel: *Der Mann* (Fig. 209) $13,000.
Charles Jacque: *M. Luquet* (Fig. 136) $150.
Kathe Kollwitz: *Ruf des Todes* (Fig. 215) $2800.
Lucas van Leyden: *Maximilian* (Fig. 43) $100,000.
Jan Lievens: *Ephraim Bonus* (Fig. 81) $1200.
Edouard Manet: *Lola de Valence* (Fig. 137) $1100.
Berthe Morisot: *Leçon de Dessin* (Fig. 147) $450.
Edvard Munch: *Madonna* (Fig. 206) $115,000.
Georg Pencz: *John Frederick the Magnanimous* (Fig. 35) $6500.
Pablo Picasso: *Le Repas Frugal* (Fig. 189) $100,000 (one of about a dozen printed before the plate was steel-faced; another impression, one of about two hundred fifty after steel-facing, $40,000).
Camille Pissarro: *Self-Portrait* (Fig. 141) $40,000.
Rembrandt van Rijn: *Self-Portrait Leaning on a Stone Sill* (Fig. 77) $42,000.
Pierre Renoir: *La Dance à la Campagne* (Fig. 148) $6800.
William Strang: *Thomas Hardy* (Fig. 176) $75.
Henri Toulouse-Lautrec: *Mlle. Marcel Lender* (Fig. 164) $16,000.

Jacques Villon: *Yvonne D. de Face* (Fig. 195) $35,000.
James Whistler: *Drouet* (Fig. 171) $700.
Anders Zorn: *Ernest Renan* (Fig. 155) $800.

The care of prints should always be of major concern since the owner of any work of art is merely a custodian for the next generation. Food, soiled fingers, or the presence of a pen can be sources of permanent damage. Prints should be held by their mats and not touched at all. They should be hinged carefully, covered with acid-free material, matted with rag paper, and kept out of direct sunlight.

Glossary

aquatint A powdered material, often resin, is dusted onto a plate, which is then heated so that the porous ground melts. The plate is then placed in acid, which etches minute specks around each particle. This intaglio method creates tonal, rather than linear, passages.

burin Engraving tool used to plow or dig out the design on a metal or wood surface.

burr An irregular wall of metal thrown up by the drypoint needle. It retains enough ink to create a rich woolly or fuzzy imprint.

chiaroscuro A woodcut technique which imitates wash drawings. Tonal blocks, each cut for separate shades, are superimposed one over the other to create graduated lights and shadows.

color printing A method of side-by-side or overprinting reds, blues and yellows to obtain a variety of different tones. Wood blocks, metal plates, lithographic stones, or screens, separately colored, are typically used.

crayon manner An etching and engraving method that mimics the line of chalk or crayon. Toothed roulette wheels are used to create dotted lines in imitation of drawings.

drypoint An engraving method using a tapered needle to create a burr or metal ridge that prints as a soft and rich velvety tone.

engraving A printmaking technique that involves incising a metal plate or wood block with a burin. Typically employed on copper, a V-shaped section is removed, creating a line that prints with great sharpness and clarity.

etching A print technique that depends on a mordant to incise a design into metal. The image is drawn through an acid-resistant ground. This exposes the bare metal, which can then be bitten one or more times to produce a range of faint to dark lines. When the plate is sufficiently bitten, it is passed through a printing press like an engraving.

309

intaglio   A type of printmaking in which the lines to be printed lie below the surface of the plate. The great pressure of the press forces the ink out of the incised lines onto the paper.

lithography   A printmaking technique that retrieves a drawing from a stone or zinc plate. Greasy inks create the image, after which the matrix is dampened. Grease and water being chemically antipathetic, the wet areas reject the oil-based inks that are rolled over the surface, while the original greasy design adheres to the rolled ink. It is a planographic printing method, since the image lies neither above nor below the surface. The design is often drawn first on paper and then transferred to the stone.

mezzotint   An intaglio method which first requires a roughening of the plate by means of a spiked tool called a rocker. This creates a surface that, if inked, would print as solid black. The image emerges as the surface is scraped away with a burnishing tool to develop increasingly lighter areas. It is a tonal, rather than a linear, process.

planographic   A printing method that creates impressions from a level surface, neither incised nor in relief.

relief   A printmaking method in which the design is printed by inking the raised surface.

serigraphy or silkscreening   A stencil process in which inks are forced through a mesh, the desired image first masked or painted with impervious varnish or film. The print is developed as the ink is scraped with a squeegee across the screen and through the unmasked areas, depositing the image onto the paper beneath. A separate screen is required for each color.

stipple   An intaglio printmaking technique utilizing dots and flicks that are incised on the plate with various types of curved burins. A soft tonal pattern is achieved.

woodcut   A relief technique in which the areas that are not meant to print are cut away with gouges and knives so that the remaining raised design can be inked and printed. Soft woods, cut on the plank sides, are used.

wood engraving   A relief technique in which the cutting is done on the end grain of a hard wood. The ink prints from the surface, the design appearing in fine white lines against a dark background. (The engraved lines lie below the surface.) The hardness of the wood permits very close work.

Selected Bibliography

Ackley, Clifford S. *Printed Portraits*. Boston: Museum of Fine Arts, 1979.
_____. *Printmaking in the Age of Rembrandt*. Boston: Museum of Fine Arts, and the New York Graphic Society, 1981.
Adhémar, Jean. *Graphic Art of the Eighteenth Century*. New York: McGraw-Hill, 1964.
_____. *Twentieth Century Graphics*. London: Elek Books, 1971.
American Portraiture in the Grand Manner: 1720–1920. Los Angeles: Los Angeles County Museum of Art, 1981.
Arms, John Taylor. *Handbook of Print Making and Print Makers*. New York: Macmillan, 1934.
Artists by Themselves. New York: National Academy of Design, 1983.
Austin, Stanley. *The History of Engraving*. London: T. Werner Laurie.
Averill, Esther. *Eyes on the World: The Story and Work of Jacques Callot*. New York: Funk and Wagnalls, 1969.
Baigell, Matthew. *Dictionary of American Art*. New York: Harper and Row, 1982.
Barkley, Harold. *Likeness in Line, An Anthology of Tudor and Stuart Engraved Portraits*. London: Victoria and Albert Museum, 1982.
Bechtel, Edwin De T. *Jacques Callot*. New York: Braziller, 1955.
Binyon, Lawrence. *Dutch Etchers of the Seventeenth Century*. London: Seely, 1895.
Blanc, Charles. *The Grammar of Painting and Engraving*. Hurd and Houghton, 1874.
Bliss, Douglas Percy. *A History of Wood Engraving*. London: Spring Books, 1964.
Bloch, E. Maurice. *The Golden Age of German Printmaking*. Los Angeles: University of California at Los Angeles, 1983–84.
Bradley, William Aspenwall. *French Etchers of the Second Empire*. Boston: Houghton Mifflin, 1916.
Breeskin, Adelyn Dohme. *Mary Cassatt: Graphic Art*. Washington, D.C.: Smithsonian Institution Press, 1981.
Bromley, H. *Catalogue of Engraved British Portraits*. London, 1793.
Brooks, Alfred Mansfield. *From Holbein to Whistler*. New Haven, Conn.: Yale University Press, 1920.
Buchsbaum, Ann. *Practical Guide to Print Collecting*. New York: Van Nostrand Reinhold, 1975.
Buckland-Wright, John. *Etching and Engraving*. New York: Dover, 1973.
Burgess, Fred. W. *Old Prints and Engravings*. London, 1924.
Calloway, Stephen. *English Prints for the Collector*. Guildford and London: Lutterworth, 1980.

Carey, Frances, and Griffiths, Antony. *From Manet to Toulouse-Lautrec, French Lithographs, 1860–1900*. London: British Museum Publications, 1978.
_____, and _____. *The Print in Germany, 1880–1933: The Age of Expressionism*. London: British Museum Publications, 1984.
Carlson, Victor, and Ittman, John W. *Regency to Empire: French Printmaking, 1715–1814*. Baltimore, Md., and Minneapolis, Minn.: Baltimore Museum of Art and the Minneapolis Institute of Arts, 1984.
Carrington, Fitzroy. *Prints and Their Makers*. New York: Century, 1912.
_____. *Engravers and Etchers*. Chicago: Art Institute of Chicago, 1917.
Castleman, Riva. *Prints of the Twentieth Century: A History*. New York: Museum of Modern Art, 1976.
Chaloner-Smith, John. *British Mezzotint Portraits*. Sotheran, 1878.
Chipp, Herchel B., and Breuer, Karin. *The Human Image in German Expressionist Graphic Art from the Robert Gore Rifkind Foundation*. Berkeley, Calif.: University Art Museum, 1981.
Cleaver, James. *A History of Graphic Art*. Westport, Conn.: Greenwood, 1969.
Cox, William D. *The Etching Hobby*. New York: William Farquhar Payson, 1932.
Dalke, Lady. *French Engravers and Draughtsmen of the Eighteenth Century*. George Bell and Sons, 1902.
Daniel, Howard. *Callot's Etchings*. New York: Dover, 1974.
Davenport, Cyril. *Mezzotints*. London: Methuen, 1904.
Davis, Bruce. "In Honor of Ebria Feinblatt, Curator of Prints and Drawings, 1947–1985." Essay and catalogue in *Los Angeles County Museum of Art Bulletin*. Los Angeles: Los Angeles County Museum of Art, 1985.
Delaborde, Henri. *Engraving: Its Origin, Processes, and History*. London, Paris, New York, and Melbourne: Cassell, 1886.
_____. *Gérard Edelinck*. Paris: Librairie de l'Art, 1886.
Donson, Theodore B. *Prints and the Print Market*. New York: Crowell, 1977.
Duplessis, Georges. *De la Gravure de Portrait en France*. Paris: Rapilly, Libraire et Marchand d'Estampes, 1875.
Eichenberg, Fritz. *The Art of the Print*. New York: Abrams, 1976.
Elliot, Brian. *Silk-Screen Printing*. London, 1971.
Elson, Albert E. *Purposes of Art*. New York: Holt, Rinehart and Winston, 1972.
Evans, Edward. *Catalogue of Thirty Thousand Engraved Portraits*. 1860.
Fine, Ruth E. *Drawing Near: Whistler Etchings from the Zelman Collection*. Los Angeles: Los Angeles County Museum of Art, 1985.
First Century of Printmaking: 1400–1500. Exhibition of the Art Institute of Chicago, 1941.
Fowler, Alfred. *The Romance of Fine Prints*. Kansas City: The Print Society, 1938.
Furst, Herbert. *Portrait Painting: Its Nature and Function*. London: Lane, 1927.
_____. *Original Engravings and Etchings: An Appreciation*. London: Nelson and Sons, 1931.
Getlein, Frank, and Getlein, Dorothy. *The Bite of the Print*. New York: Bramhall House, 1963.
Getscher, Robert H. *The Stamp of Whistler*. Oberlin, Ohio: Allen Memorial Art Museum, Oberlin College, 1977.
Gibson, Robin. *Twentieth Century Portraits*. London: National Portrait Gallery, 1978.
Godfrey, Richard T. *Printmaking in Britain*. New York: New York University Press, 1978.
Goldman, Judith. *American Prints: Process and Proofs*. New York: Whitney Museum of Art, 1982.
Gray, Basil. *The English Print*. London: Adam and Charles Black, 1937.

Griffiths, Antony. *Prints and Printmaking: An Introduction to the History and Techniques*. New York: Alfred A. Knopf, 1980.

Haas, Irvin. *A Treasury of Great Prints*. New York: Yoseloff, 1956.

Hamerton, Philip Gilbert. *Etching and Etchers*. Boston: Roberts Brothers, 1883.

_____. *Man in Art*. London: Macmillan, 1892.

_____. *Drawing and Engraving*. London and Edinburgh: Adam and Charles Black, 1892.

Hamilton, Sinclair. *Early American Book Illustrators and Wood Engravers, 1670–1870*. Princeton, N.J.: Princeton University Library, 1958.

Hayden, Arthur. *Chats on Old Prints*. London: T. Fisher Unwin, 1923.

Hennessey, William J. *The American Portrait: From the Death of Stuart to the Rise of Sargent*. Worcester, Mass.: Worcester Art Museum, 1973.

Hind, Arthur M. "Van Dyck: His Original Etchings and His Iconography." *Print Collector's Quarterly*, Vol. 5, No. 2, 1915.

_____. *A History of Engraving and Etching*. New York: Dover, 1963.

_____. *An Introduction to a History of Woodcut*. Vols. 1 and 2. New York: Dover, 1963.

Hollstein, F. W. H. *Dutch and Flemish Etchings, Engravings and Woodcuts*. Amsterdam, 1949.

_____. *German and English Etchings and Woodcuts*. 1954.

Horne, Henry Percy. *An Illustrated Catalogue of English Portraits and Fancy Subjects by Gainsborough and Romney*. 1891.

Hunnisett, Basil. *Steel-Engraved Book Illustration in England*. Boston: David R. Godine, 1980.

Inside Out: Self Beyond Likeness. Newport Beach, Calif., Portland, Ore., and Omaha, Neb.: Newport Harbor Art Museum, Portland Art Museum, and Joslyn Art Museum, 1981–1982.

Ives, Colta Feller. *The Great Wave: The Influence of Japanese Woodcuts on French Prints*. New York: Metropolitan Museum of Art, 1974.

Ivins, William M., Jr. *How Prints Look*. Boston: Beacon Press, 1958.

_____. *Prints and Books*. New York: Da Capo, 1969.

_____. *Prints and Visual Information*. New York: Da Capo, 1969.

Jacobowitz, Ellen S., and Marcus, George H. *American Graphics, 1860–1940*. Philadelphia: Philadelphia Museum of Art, 1982.

Jim Dine Prints: 1970–1977. Williamstown, Mass.: Williams College, 1977.

Johnson, Una E. *Ambroise Vollard*. New York: Museum of Modern Art, 1977.

_____. *American Prints and Printmakers*. New York: Doubleday, 1980.

Kaplan, Ellen. *Prints, A Collector's Guide*. New York: Coward-McCann, 1983.

Keppel, Frederick. *The Golden Age of Engraving*. New York: Baker and Taylor, 1910.

Kistler, Aline. *Understanding Prints*. New York: Associated American Artists, 1936.

Laver, James. *A History of British and American Etching*. New York: Dodd, Mead, 1929.

Leipnik, F. L. *A History of French Etching from the Sixteenth Century to the Present Day*. London: Dodd, Mead, 1924.

Levey, Michael. *Dürer*. New York: Norton, 1964.

Linderman, Gottfried. *Prints and Drawings*. New York: Praeger, 1970.

Lister, Raymond. *Great Images of British Printmaking*. London: Garton, 1978.

Lochnan, Katherine A. *The Etchings of James McNeill Whistler*. New Haven, Conn.: Yale University Press, New Haven, 1984.

Longstreet, Stephen. *A Treasury of the World's Great Prints*. New York: Simon and Schuster, 1961.

Lumsden, E. S. *The Art of Etching*. New York: Dover Publications, 1962.

Lynton, Norbert. *The Story of Modern Art*. Ithaca, N.Y.: Cornell University Press, 1980.

Maberly, Joseph. *The Print Collector*. London, 1844.

Madigan, Mary Jean, and Colgan, Susan. *Prints and Photographs*. New York: Billboard Publications, 1983.

Man Through His Art, The Human Face. Vol. 6. Greenwich, Conn.: New York Graphic Society Greenwich, 1968.

Mayor, A. Hyatt. *Prints and People*. New York: Metropolitan Museum of Art, 1972.

Melot, Michel; Griffiths, Antony; and Field, Richard S. *Prints*. New York: Skira/ Rizzoli, 1981.

Modern Portraits: The Self and Others. New York: Columbia University Press, 1976.

Murray, Peter, and Murray, Linda. *A Dictionary of Art and Artists*. New York: Penguin Books, 1975.

Myers, Bernard S. *The German Expressionists*. New York: Praeger, 1957.

Nevill, Ralph. *French Prints of the Eighteenth Century*. London: Macmillan, 1908.

Pennell, Joseph. *The Graphic Arts*. Chicago: University of Chicago Press, 1920.

Plowman, George T. *Etching*. New York: Dodd, Mead, 1929.

Pope-Hennessy, John. *The Portrait in the Renaissance*. Princeton, N.J.: Princeton University Press, 1979.

Prints: 1400–1800. Exhibition of The Minneapolis Institute of Arts, Cleveland Museum of Art, and Art Institute of Chicago, 1956–1957.

Prints: 1800–1945. Exhibition of The Minneapolis Institute of Arts, City Art Museum of St. Louis, Achenbach Foundation for Graphic Arts, and California Palace of the Legion of Honor, 1966.

Rawlinson, W. G. *English Mezzotint Portraits, 1750–1830*. London: Burlington Fine Arts Club, 1902.

Reaves, Wendy Wick. *American Portrait Prints*. Charlottesville: University Press of Virginia, 1984.

Reed, Orrel P., Jr. *German Expressionist Art: The Robert Gore Rifkind Collection*. Los Angeles: University of California at Los Angeles, 1977.

Richter, Emil H. *Prints*. Cambridge: Riverside, 1914.

Robins, W. P. *Etching Craft*. London: B. T. Batsford, 1924.

Roger-Marx, Claude. *French Original Engravings from Manet to the Present Time*. London: Hyperion, 1939.

_____. *Graphic Art of the Nineteenth Century*. New York: McGraw-Hill, 1962.

Rose, Barbara. *American Painting, Twentieth Century*. New York: Skira/Rizzoli, 1980.

Rose, James Anderson. *A Collection of Engraved Portraits*. London: Marcus Ward, 1874.

Sachs, Paul J. *Modern Prints and Drawings*. New York: Alfred A. Knopf, 1954.

Saisselin, Rémy G. *Style, Truth and the Portraits*. Cleveland, Oh.: Cleveland Museum of Art, 1963.

Salaman, Malcolm C. *The Old Engravers of England*. London: Cassell, 1906.

_____. *Old English Mezzotints*. London: The Studio, 1910.

_____. *The Great Painter-Etchers from Rembrandt to Whistler*. London: The Studio, 1914.

_____. *C. R. Nevinson: Modern Masters of Etching*. London: The Studio, 1932.

Salamon, Ferdinando. *The History of Prints and Printmaking from Dürer to Picasso*. New York: American Heritage, 1971.

Sandler, Irving. *Alex Katz.* New York: Abrams, 1979.

Schneider, Rona. "The American Etching Revival: Its French Sources and Early Years." *The American Art Journal,* Vol. 14, No. 4, 1982.

Selz, Peter. *German Expressionist Painting.* Berkeley, Calif.: University of California Press, 1957.

Shadwell, Wendy. *American Printing: The First One Hundred Fifty Years.* Washington, D.C.: Smithsonian Institution Press, 1969.

Shapiro, Cecile, and Mason, Lauris. *Fine Prints.* New York: Harper and Row, 1976.

Shapiro, Meyer. *Modern Art, Nineteenth and Twentieth Centuries.* New York: Braziller, 1982.

Sparrow, Walter Shaw. *A Book of British Etching.* London: Lane/The Bodley Head, 1926.

Stauffer, David McNeely. *American Engravers upon Copper and Steel.* New York: Grolier Club of the City of New York, 1907.

Steegmuller, Frances. *Apollinaire, Poet Among Painters.* New York: Farrar, Straus, 1963.

Sumner, Charles. *The Best Portraits in Engraving.* New York: Keppel.

Thomas, T. H. *French Portrait Engraving of the Seventeenth and Eighteenth Centuries.* London: G. Bell and Sons, 1910.

Tyler, Francine. *American Etchings of the Nineteenth Century.* New York: Dover, 1984.

Vogler, Richard. *The Hopfers of Augsburg.* Los Angeles: Grunwald Graphic Arts Foundation, University of California at Los Angeles, 1966.

Walker, John. *Portraits: Five Thousand Years.* New York: Abrams, 1983.

Wallen, Burr, and Stein, Donna. *The Cubist Print.* Santa Barbara: University of California at Santa Barbara, 1981.

Watrous, James. *American Printmaking, 1880–1980.* Madison: University of Wisconsin Press, 1984.

Wechsler, Herman J. *Great Prints and Printmakers.* Bentweld-Aerdenhout, Netherlands: Abrams.

Wedmore, Frederick. *Fine Prints.* Edinburgh: John Grant, 1905.

_____. *Etchings.* London: Methuen, 1911.

Weisberg, Gabriel P. *The Etching Renaissance in France: 1850–1880.* Utah Museum of Fine Arts, 1971.

_____. *Rediscovered Printmakers of the Nineteenth Century.* Merrill Chase Galleries, 1978.

_____, and Zakon, Ronnie L. *Between Past and Present: French, English and American Etching: 1850–1950.* Cleveland, Ohio: Cleveland Museum of Art, 1977.

Weitenkampf, Frank. *How to Appreciate Prints.* New York: Charles Scribner's Sons, 1921.

_____. *American Graphic Art.* New York: Macmillan, 1924.

_____. *Famous Prints.* New York: Charles Scribner's Sons, 1926.

_____. *The Quest of the Print.* New York: Charles Scribner's Sons, 1932.

Wentworth, Michael Justin. *James Tissot: Catalogue Raisonne of His Prints.* Minneapolis, Minn.: Minneapolis Institute of Arts, 1978.

Whitman, Alfred. *Print Collector's Handbook.* Revised and enlarged by Malcolm C. Salaman. London: G. Bell and Sons, 1921.

Wick, Wendy C. *George Washington: An American Icon.* Washington, D.C.: Smithsonian Institution Press, 1982.

Willshire, William Huges. *An Introduction to the Study and Collection of Ancient Prints.* London: Ellis and White, 1874.

Wolf, Alice. *The Edward B. Greene Collection of Engraved Portraits and Portrait Drawings at Yale University*. New Haven, Conn.: Yale University Press, 1942.

Wright, Harold. *Gerald Brockhurst*. London: The Studio, 1928.

Younger, Archibald. *French Engravers of the Eighteenth Century*. London: Simpkin, Marshall, Hamilton, Kent.

Zigrosser, Carl. *The Book of Fine Prints*. New York: Crown, 1956.

_____. *The Appeal of Prints*. Pennsylvania: KNA Press, 1970.

_____. *The Expressionists*. New York: Braziller, 1957.

_____. *Prints and Their Creators*. New York: Crown, 1974.

Index

Titles of prints appear in *italics* and are followed by the identity of the subject where known (life dates are given in parentheses). The name of the artist follows in brackets. **Boldface** page numbers indicate relevant illustrations.

A

Achillini, Philotheo, Italian author and musician [Raimondi] **52**

Adams, Samuel, American statesman (1722–1803) 142

Adolescence, Dorette Woodward (q.v.) [Brockhurst] 269, **270**

Adrian VI, Italian pope (1459–1523) 57

Albers, Josef, German artist (1888–1976) 284

Albert, co-ruler of the Netherlands, died 1621 [Muller] 76, 77, **78**

Albert, Prince Francis, consort to Queen Victoria (1819–1861) 199

Alberti, Leon Battista, Italian architect and author (1404–1472) 18, 28

Albrecht of Brandenberg, German cardinal (1490–1545) [Dürer] 25, **26**, 28, 37

Albret, Jeanne d', Queen of Navarre (1528–1572) [Gaultier] **56**, 57

Aldegraver, Heinrich, German artist (1502–1555/1561) 37, **38**

Altdorfer, Albrecht, German artist (about 1480–1538) 33, **35**

Amelia Elizabeth, Regent of Hesse-Cassel (1602–1651) [Von Siegen] **89**, 94

Amman, Jost, Swiss artist (1539–1591) 40, **42**, **43**

Anderson, Alexander, American artist (1775–1870) 211

Andrea, Zoan, Italian artist (flourished about 1475–1505) 15

Aphrodite, Greek goddess [anonymous] 2, **5**

Apollinaire, Guillaume, French poet (1880–1918) 230, 231, 232, 235, 236, **237**

Apollinaire, Guillaume (q.v.) [Picasso] **230**, 231; [Marcoussis] **237**

The Apostle Jean Journet see *Journet, (Apostle) Jean*

Aquatint, description 140 *see also* Glossary

Aretino, Pietro, Italian satirist (about 1480–about 1530) [Raimondi] 51, **53**

Ariosto, Lodovico, Italian poet (1474–1533) 23, 52

Aristotle, Greek philosopher (384–322 B.C.) 48

Arnold, Matthew, English poet (1822–1888) 259

Artist's Mother [Geddes] **198**

The Artist's Mother [Rembrandt] 85, **86**

Arundel, (Sir) Henry, English statesman (1511?–1580) 98

Astor, John Jacob, American financier (1763–1848) 209

At the Easel, Marc Chagall (q.v.) [Chagall] 236, **238**

317

328

Index

Master of 1446, Upper Rhine (?) artist 11
Master of the Amsterdam Cabinet, German artist (flourished about 1480) 11
Matham, Jacob, Dutch artist (1571–1631) 46, 76
Mather, Cotton, American clergyman (1663–1728) [Pelham] 105, 142, **143,** 144
Mather, Increase, American clergyman (1639–1723) [Emmes] **142**
Mather, Mr. Richard, American clergyman (1596–1669) [Foster] **104,** 105, 142
Matisse, Henri, French artist (1869–1954) 220, 223, **224, 225,** 229, 232, 240, 248, 287, 291, 303
Matthilda, friend of Mary Cassatt (q.v.) [Cassatt] 173, **174**
Mavourneen, Kathleen Newton (q.v.) [Tissot] 179, **182**
Maximilian, Maximilian I (q.v.) [Burgkmair, the Elder] 40, **45;** [Van Leyden] 43, **47**
Maximilian I, Holy Roman Emperor (1450–1519) 31, 33, **34,** 37, 39, 40, 41, 43, **45, 47**
Maximilian I (q.v.) [Dürer] 31, 33, **34**
Mayor, A. Hyatt, curator 1
Mazarin, Jules, Italian, French premier (1602–1661) 59
Meckenem, Israhel van, German artist 11, **12**
Melanchthon, Philip, German scholar (1497–1560) [Dürer] 28, **30;** [Master I.B.] 28, **30**
Mellan, Claude, French artist (1598–1688) 64, **65, 66,** 67, 95, 101
Menpes, Mortimer, Australian artist (1855–1938) 206, 207, **208**
Menzel, Adolf von, German artist (1815–1905) 243
Meryon, Charles, French artist (1821–1868) 162, 167, 178, 186, 200
Metternich, Klemens von, Austrian statesman (1773–1859) 151
Meurent, Victorine, French model 165
mezzotint, description 89, 101, 102, Glossary
Michelangelo, Buonarroti, Italian artist (1475–1564) 23, 48, 61, 178
Mignard, Nicolas, French artist (1606–1668) 72, **74**
Mignard, Pierre, French artist (1612–1695) 103, 104
Millet, Jean François, French artist

(1814–1875) 154, 205
Milton, John, English poet (1608–1674) 98
Minuet, Peter, first governor of New York (1580–1638) 84
Mohammed II, Sultan, Turkish ruler [anonymous] 9, **10**
Molière, Jean Baptiste, French dramatist (1622–1673) 70
Mondrian, Piet, Dutch artist (1872–1944) 284
Monet, Claude, French artist (1840–1926) 167–169
Monroe, James, American president (1758–1831) 208
Monroe, Marilyn, American actress (1926–1962) [Warhol] 293, **294**
Montefeltro, Federigo da, Italian duke [Piero della Francesca] **17,** 18
Montesquieu, Charles de, French philosopher (1689–1755) 106
Montesquieu, Count Robert de [Whistler] 203, **204**
Montgomery, Richard, American general (1736–1775) 149
Montmar, Henricus Ludovicus Habert de, French court secretary [Mellan] **65,** 66
More, (Sir) William de la, English artist 147
Morin, Jean, French artist (before 1590?–1650) 67, **68,** 105
Morisot, Berthe, French artist (1841–1985) 165, **166,** 174, **175,** 176, 306
Morisot, Berthe (q.v.) [Manet] 165, **166**
Morse, Samuel, American artist and inventor (1791–1872) 215
Mourlot, Fernand, French printer 232
Mozart, Wolfgang, Austrian composer (1756–1791) 115
Mucha, Alphonse, Czechoslovakian artist (1860–1939) 181
Mudocci, Eva, mistress of Edvard Munch **246,** 247, 248
Müller, Friedrich, German artist (1782–1816) 114
Muller, Jan, Dutch artist (1571?–after 1625) 76, **78**
Müller, Jean-Gotthard, German artist (1747–1830) 113, 114, **116**
Munch, Edvard, Norwegian artist (1863–1944) 245, **246,** 247, 248, 279, 306
Murillo, Bartolomé, Spanish artist (1617–1682) 125

Strange, (Sir) Robert, Scottish artist
(1721-1792) **136**
Stuart, Gilbert, American artist (1755-
1828) 208
Suyderhoef, Jonas, Dutch artist (about
1610-1686) 69, 89
Sylvius, Jan Cornelis, Mennonite
preacher [Rembrandt] **88**

T

Tableau, Ruth Weisberg (q.v.) and
Linda Burnham (q.v.) [Weisberg] 301,
302
Talleyrand, Charles, French statesman
(1754-1838) 157
Tardieu, Nicolas-Henri, French artist
(1674-1749) 116
Tennyson, Alfred (Lord), English poet
(1809-1892) 197
Tetzel, Johann, German monk (1465?-
1519) **25, 28**
Thessalonus II, Prince of Bavaria [Am-
man] 40, **43**
Thomas, T.H., author 115
Tiebout, Cornelius, American artist
(about 1777-1830) 149, 211, **212**
Tiepolo, Giovanni Battista, Italian artist
(1696-1770) 139
Tiepolo, Giovanni Domenico, Italian artist (1727-1804) 139
Tintoretto, Jacobo, Italian artist (1518-
1594) **51**
Tissot, James, French artist (1836-1902)
179, 181, **182**
Titian, Vecelli, Italian artist (1477?-
1576) 37, 51, 52, 85
Tobey, Mark, American artist (1890-
1976) 284
Tocqué, Jean Louis, French artist (1696-
1772) 114, 116
Tocqueville, Alexis de, French author
(1805-1859) 218
Toulouse-Lautrec, Henri Marie Raymond de, French artist (1864-1901)
158, 171, 184, 187-188, **189, 190, 191,**
192, 222, 227, 228, 306
Tourny, Joseph, French artist (1817-
1880) 171
Tredwell, Daniel M., American lawyer
and author (1791-1872) [Chase] 215,
217
Treiman, Joyce, American artist (1922-)

300, 301
Trumbull, John, American artist (1756-
1843) 211
Turner, Joseph Mallord William,
English artist (1775-1851) 101, 167,
197, 204
Twain, Mark *see* Clemens, Samuel
Langhorne

U

Ugo da Carpi, Italian artist (about 1450-
about 1524) 52
Underwood, Leon, English artist (1890-
1977) 267, 268, **269**

V

Vaillant, Wallerant, French artist (1623-
1677) 91
Valadon, Suzanne, French artist (1865-
1938) [Renoir] 176, **177**
Valck, Gérard, Dutch artist (1626-1720)
91, 101
Valence, Lola de, Spanish dancer
[Manet] **164**
Valentino, Rudolph, Italian actor (1895-
1926) 198
Van Buren, Martin, American president
(1782-1862) 213
Vanderbilt, Cornelius, American financier (1794-1877) 209
Van Dyck, (Sir) Anthony, Flemish artist
(1599-1641) xiii, 46, 62, 64, 70, 79, **80,**
81, 82, **83,** 84, 89, 91, 97, 99, 103, 110,
128, 129, 132, 136, 157, 163, 203, 205
van Gogh, Vincent, Dutch artist (1853-
1890) 169, 183, 184, 185, 186-187, **188,**
222, 247, 248, 279
Vanzetti, Bartolomeo, Italian anarchist
(1888-1927) [Shahn] 281, **282,** 283
Varnbüler, Ulrich, German statesman
[Dürer] 29, 31, **34**
Vasari, Giorgio, Italian artist and his-
torian (1511-1574) 22, 48, 51
Vauxelles, Louis, French art critic 223
Velazquez, Diego, Spanish artist (1599-
1660) 139, 203, 227
Verelst, John, Dutch artist (1648-1719)
144
Verlaine, Paul, French poet (1844-1896)
[Rouault] **226,** 227

W